Confronting History

Confronting History

A Memoir

George L. Mosse

With a Foreword by
Walter Laqueur

THE UNIVERSITY OF WISCONSIN PRESS

The University of Wisconsin Press
2537 Daniels Street
Madison, Wisconsin 53718

3 Henrietta Street
London WC2E 8LU, England

1   3   5   4   2

Printed in the United States of America

Illustrations for this book are reproduced courtesy of the following sources:
Leo Baeck Institute, New York: pp. 12, 15, 18, 21, 24, 25, 27, 29,
30, 34, 35, 45, 49, 51, 143
John Tortorice: pp. 8, 41, 89, 91, 138, 141, 201, 206, 208, 214, 215, 216, 218
University of Wisconsin–Madison Archives: p. 162
Hochschule der Kunst Archiv, Berlin: p. 10
The Capital Times: p. 167
Erwin Lachmann: p. 14
David Berkoff: p. 201

Library of Congress Cataloging-in-Publication Data
Mosse, George L. (George Lachmann), 1918–1999
Confronting history: a memoir /
George L. Mosse
236 pp.   cm.
ISBN 0–299–16580–9
1. Mosse, George L. (George Lachmann), 1918–1999
2. Historians—United States—Biography I. Title.
D15.M668 A3   1999   99–6425
940.5′092—dc21   CIP

Contents

Illustrations

Illustrations

Foreword

Of the American historians of his generation George Mosse was one of the greatest teachers, perhaps the best known abroad, and certainly one of the most beloved. There were many long and thoughtful reviews of his life and work in the German and French press, in Italy and Israel. They showed among other things that George had become a legend in his own lifetime, for they also included stories which almost certainly had not happened, or, to put it more accurately, had not happened the way they were described. In the United States, for better or worse, historians are considered of less public interest than entertainers or politicians, and there were with a few exceptions only short and perfunctory obituaries. The *New York Times* featured the picture of another person with the caption "G. L. Mosse." George would have been greatly amused.

He was born into a very prominent and wealthy German Jewish family. His great-grandfather Markus Mosse had been a physician in a small town in the province of Posen. Markus's son Rudolf moved to Berlin and founded in 1867 what was to become the greatest advertising agency in the country and later yet a media empire with the famous *Berliner Tageblatt* as its flagship. Shortly after George's death a huge volume was published presenting the history both of the German Jewish Mosse family in the nineteenth and twentieth centuries and of their business empire (Elisabeth Kraus, *Die Familie Mosse: Deutsch-jüdisches Bürgertum im 19. und 20. Jahrhundert* [C. H. Beck: Munich, 1999]).

George spent much of his youth on a manor south of Berlin. He had part of the mansion for himself, there were servants and governesses, usually from Britain and France, and on his birthday the local band would serenade him. It could well be that his background gave him the self-confidence, security, and generosity in later life which, alas, are not a universal phenomenon even in his profession. He would always appreciate the

ix

work of others; there was little aggression, no boasting, no urge to show his own brilliance. In brief, there was no meanness in him. The family lost most of its possessions in 1933 but regained some after the war. I have known no other person to whom money meant so little. I doubt whether George at any time of his life had more than two suits, and he lived more than modestly. The priceless family collections of china and musical instruments he regarded mainly as a nuisance.

He seems to have been a disruptive influence in primary school, and so his parents sent him to one of the most progressive schools, Schloss Salem, which was also attended by Prince Philip. From there by way of Switzerland and France he went to England. Bootham, the Friends' school near York, accepted him, and he later went on to Cambridge to read history. But there was little encouragement: the master of Emmanuel College told him, "You people become journalists, not historians." At the outbreak of the war he found himself a tourist in New York. With his last money he bought a ticket to Philadelphia, where, he had been told, there were many Quakers, asked for the nearest Quaker school, introduced himself to the president of Haverford, and, having made a good impression, heard the magic words: "We will take thee."

In his memoirs George writes that he never experienced the personal and mental deprivations of exile; on the contrary, exile energized him and challenged him as nothing had ever done before: "My existence had been secure, my future programmed, and I would eventually have entered the family firm and stayed there. As a result, I was a youth without direction, without much of a purpose in life . . . ." Purpose and direction came in England and even more so in America when he became interested in history and politics. He had the good fortune to discover that Harvard had a scholarship for students born in Berlin-Charlottenburg; he was the only one to qualify. But at Harvard his career almost came to an abrupt end since there were two eccentrics on his doctoral committee, one of whom had persuaded himself that since George came from a publishing family he must be an expert on printing, a subject on which he knew next to nothing. Having overcome this hurdle, he was on his way to the University of Iowa, where in 1944 he arrived for his first teaching job.

It soon appeared that he had a rare talent for public speaking. Diffident, almost withdrawn in personal life, his persona changed in the presence of five hundred students, and his voice became firmer; he had the rare gift of generating interest and even enthusiasm for his subject among young people. Over the years many thousands came to his lectures, and he became so popular among the students that unbeknownst to him they put his name forward as a candidate for county coroner. (He was defeated by a few votes.) In the late sixties and seventies with the move to the University of Wisconsin his fame spread. In addition to his duties in Madison he was appointed to a chair at the Hebrew University, in Jerusalem, where he was one of the few professors permitted to lecture in a language other than Hebrew. There were annual courses of lectures at Cornell, in Munich, Paris, and Cambridge, England.

George was generous to a fault with his time. He would seldom turn down invitations even in later life when it was difficult for him to attend. He was not impervious to honors bestowed (he received three honorary doctorates during the last month of his life), but he cared even more about his students, and of the many distinguished teachers who emerged from among his students almost all were helped by him in their first, difficult steps in the profession. It was a delight to work with him. He and I founded the *Journal of Contemporary History* in 1965 and were in almost daily contact editing it to the week he died; I do not remember a single quarrel during more than three decades, and not because we always agreed or found it easy to compromise. He was neither a saint nor a perfectionist. His spelling was uncertain in all languages (the stress in Schloss Salem had been on character building, not orthography), and he had the disdain of a grand seigneur vis-à-vis dates in history. In a memoir about his parents he had written that his father had invited Edith Piaf to perform in Berlin in 1919. I pointed out that this seemed unlikely since Piaf was five years old at the time. Did he mean perhaps Yvette Guilbert or Mistinguett? Yes, of course, he said, but did it really matter?

George was a radical by temperament, but this came with a spirit of tolerance, rare among rebels. He encouraged his students to read Marx at a time when this was distinctly unfashionable, but they also had to read the thinkers of the Right. The spirit of orthodoxy and sectarianism was alien to him, just as he had no sympathy for radical chic and political correctness. Among those who came out of his stable were people of the Left as well as the Right, and he cared about the ones as much as the others.

His interests ranged widely. He began his professional career as an expert on England during the Reformation with an abiding interest in religion. (He claimed to be able to celebrate a mass, and I have no reason to disbelieve him.) Later on he was attracted by the era of fascism, especially its ideological and cultural aspects—the highways and byways of the doctrine of extreme nationalism and racist thought in twentieth-century Europe. It was in this field that he made his most lasting contributions. But, restless spirit that he was, the study of fascism led him to yet other fields not considered by some at the time as proper subjects for traditional historians—the nationalization of the masses, political symbolism in our time, and, increasingly toward the end of his life, the study of masculinity and sexuality.

Why did he prefer in later years the study of fascism to pursuing his studies in the history of the Reformation in England? He probably reached the conclusion that so much work had been done in the field of sixteenth-century history that there was not much room for any significant contributions on his part. On the other hand the field of fascism was not yet systematically studied in the later 1950s and early 1960s. As George put it in the very first issue of the *Journal of Contemporary History,* "In our century two revolutionary movements have made their mark upon Europe: that originally springing from Marxism has occupied historians and political scientists for many decades but fascism has been a neglected movement." True, some of the standard works had already been published, but they dealt mainly with political and institutional history, or with the foreign policy of the Third Reich. George's interest was above all in the field of intellectual history, which he interpreted in a very liberal (and in my view realistic) way, including in his purview not only the great thinkers of the age but also popularizers and crackpots, some of them quite influential at the time; not only high literature but also *Trivial Literatur.* Today it is accepted that the extreme Right in Germany cannot be understood without paying attention to its sectarian forerunners: Thule and Liebenfels and the early racist thinkers as well as obscure novelists, forgotten long ago, whose influence was by no means insignificant at the time. There was a whole volkish subculture which few outside these circles had ever taken seriously, and it was George's merit that he was one of the first to do so and to give the whole field a major impetus.

There was, no doubt, also a psychological reason. George had lived, after all, through the period of Nazism and Italian fascism; this was not, as far as he was concerned, an abstract subject but one which had had an enormous impact on his own life, and that of many others, in the most fundamental way. George presumably thought, that he had an instinctive understanding of the spirit of the epoch, simply because he had been exposed to it.

For the same reasons George joined me in 1965 as coeditor of the *Journal of Contemporary History.* My interests at the time were close to his own. I had written a few years earlier on both the German youth movement and the Protocols of the Elders of Zion, and both topics were, so to speak, close to his heart. I had been appointed a year earlier head of the

Institute of Contemporary History and the Wiener Library in London, and the idea to establish a journal had been mine, but George had infinitely more contacts in the field than I had and a better general picture of what was done by others and what needed to be done. Without this our venture would probably never have gotten off the ground, let alone continued with reasonable success for so many years.

Why contemporary history and how to define it? The answer to this question was by no means as obvious in 1965 as it is now. In an editorial note in the first issue of the *Journal* we tried to make what seemed to us the essential points concerning the new publication. We briefly dealt with the issue of detachment and the availability of courses and announced that the field of study and discussion would be Europe in the twentieth century; that after centuries of Eurocentrism the pendulum had swung to the other extreme, and current fashions had led to a neglect of contemporary Europe. But we also said that the journal would have to be sufficiently elastic to accommodate contributions that at first sight seemed to transcend the *Journal*'s frame of reference; that it was difficult to view Europe in isolation from the rest of the world; and that, to give but one example, it was impossible to study the First World War without reference to trends that went back well into the nineteenth century. I think we have lived up to our statement of 1966, and as the years passed by and the documentation for a later period became gradually available, we began increasingly to publish contributions covering the period after the Second World War. I stress George's part in editing the *Journal of Contemporary History* because it does not appear in this autobiography. He had finished writing the draft of his memoirs but was not able, because of the suddenness of his last illness, to go over them carefully to fill in the major gaps and to make necessary changes.

Perhaps it was also modesty, because George was of course aware that through the *Journal* he had given an enormous impetus to the study of the field of contemporary history. He was coeditor for thirty-three years. In this time some fifteen hundred articles were published in the journal, many were translated into German, Italian, and other languages, a dozen books appeared based on contributions originally featured in the *Journal*. There are not many studies covering Europe in the twentieth century, except perhaps those of a most specialized character, which do not refer to articles originally published in the *Journal of Contemporary History*.

As for George's own interests, he always returned to the topic of fascism. Shortly after his death a greatly expanded version of an article originally written in 1979, "Towards a General Theory of Fascism," was published. The title is perhaps slightly misleading, because George would have been the first to admit that the differences between the various fascisms, between Germany and Italy, between the movements which seized power and those that remained in opposition, were so marked that a general theory covering all of them will forever remain a distant and indeed unattainable goal. He showed that the emphasis on economic and social factors which prevailed for a long time as an explanation of the fascist phenomenon made only a modest contribution. The most painstaking investigations have shown that Nazism had support in all classes, and that although it did better in the Protestant regions of the country than in the Catholic, even there the difference was not overwhelming. The Nazi electorate was amorphous: there was strong middle-class support, but the Nazis also scored higher than the parties of the Left among the working class. The industrialists and the bankers, with a few exceptions, did not support Hitler before the seizure of power in 1933 simply because the Nazis were too radical and unpredictable. The specifics of fascism were its revolutionary character, and its emphasis on youth, which symbolized vigor and action, and on national mystique. The Left in Germany and Italy had difficulties in coming to terms with the experience of the First World War, whereas Nazism and fascism thrived on it. Mosse believed that cultural rather than economic factors were preeminent in the rise and victory of fascism, and he argued that the contention that fascist culture diverged from the mainstream of European culture could not be upheld, for it absorbed what had the greatest mass appeal in the past: "in fact, it positioned itself much more in the mainstream than socialism which tried to educate and elevate the tastes of the worker. Fascism made no such attempt; it accepted the common man's preferences and went on to direct them to its own ends." This argument probably needs further refinement because there was not one mainstream of European culture but several, and while fascism certainly derived its ideas from one such tradition fashionable at the last turn of the century, it emphatically rejected others such as democracy, liberalism, and the tradition of the enlightenment.

Does fascism have a future? Are nationalist movements in our age bound to end up in something akin to an updated and streamlined version of the plague of the 1930s? Writing almost three decades ago, Mosse sounded optimistic: It did not seem likely that Europe would repeat the fascist or Nazi experience. He no doubt had Western and Central Europe in mind, but what of Eastern Europe, the Balkans, and the world outside Europe? He added a prophetic warning: Aggressive nationalism was still rampant, the basic force which had made fascism possible in the first place. It had not only remained but was growing in strength as the principal integrative force among peoples and nations. The danger of successful appeals to authoritarianism was always present, however changed from its earlier forms.

The dangers to freedom and civilization seem less than in the 1930s when young George Mosse discovered and embraced antifascism at Downing College, Cambridge, but they have certainly not disappeared. Just as the political experience of the thirties had a decisive impact on his academic pursuits in the postwar world, his students and the students of his students may opt for continuing this tradition, trying to understand and explain the sources of the discontents and threats in the present world.

WALTER LAQUEUR

Confronting History

1

Introduction
On Native Ground

WHY WRITE an autobiography? Is it because having spent a life-time in encounters with other people's histories, I finally want to encounter my own? The usual reasons for writing an auto-biography hardly apply. The most common reason is to pass one's own history on to one's descendants, and I have none. Then there are those who have lived a public life or who regard themselves—rightly or wrongly—as makers of history, and I cannot make such a claim. As an academic I deal with documents, ideas, and theories which could presumably influence the present-day conduct of affairs of state. But even here I do not qualify, ex-cept perhaps in the most indirect manner, for historical analysis is always relevant, especially that of recent history, and who knows what person at present active in public life has been influenced by one's lectures or read one's books? To be sure, someone who has actively contributed to the fund of ideas which determine how we look at the world would be justified in writing an autobiography: it would certainly have been helpful to read that of Karl Marx. It is much too early, however, to tell whether such ideas as I have expressed in the course of my historical writings or lectures will have consequences. I was never what is called a systematic political thinker.

Yet, some of the books I have written have had an impact on the way in which we see the past, and over many decades I have taught thousands of students in large classes at large state universities, as well as in seminars in Israel and Europe. I have always enjoyed teaching and lecturing, and proba-bly have given more lectures at academic institutions and community cen-ters than most in my profession. But though I have had many of my former students tell me that I touched and sometimes even changed their lives, the consequences of teaching are not easy to measure. They are more often than not hidden within individual lives.

Why then write this book? Because an encounter with my own history might be instructive to myself as well as to others, illuminating a very personal corner of recent times. If one believes, as I do, that what man is only history tells, then it is tempting to put one's own life in historical perspective—especially when that life contains discontinuities and experiences which were brought about by the course of history, and when what was experienced as a personal challenge, in reality mirrored events which swept over Europe. The phrase "Life and Times" has been overused in the biographies of the last century, but it must nevertheless be true of a life which encompasses the now-vanished lifestyle of the German Jewish wealthy and established middle class, a sudden exile, a rude political awakening, and an immersion in the life—and even to some extent in the politics—of the American Middle West.

My life has seen the ever more rapid passage of time, which seems to sum up my own sense of change. When I was a teenager, motor cars existed (I learned to drive on a Model T Ford), but only the rich could afford them; they were not yet a means of mass transport. Passenger airplanes were unknown, and so were television, computers, and the automatic telephone exchange. Stefan Zweig, in his autobiography, *The World of Yesterday,* tells us that before the First World War he never saw his father run, only walk. I did see my father run now and then, but rarely. It was considered undignified. Examples abound: I shifted from crossing to Europe by ship—an agony for one who was once shipwrecked (as I shall recount later)—to crossing the ocean by plane; from my trusty manual typewriter to my not quite so trusty computer. Distances shrank and time fled.

And yet the swift passage of time was marked in my memory, above all, by political crises and upheavals, even before Adolf Hitler's election to power. The increasing power of the nationalist, racist, and anti-Semitic political Right in the Weimar Republic, the growing insecurity of the Jews, and the economic dislocations, which have their place in the history books, certainly left their stamp on my surroundings. My life reflects the often cataclysmic events of our time, but it is still a personal life: these events are filtered through my own perceptions and experiences. Some of these were only to be expected, but others were contrary to the usual, normative reactions, especially in the case of my experience of exile. I cannot claim to be truly typical for anyone but myself.

Even so, a historically informed perception, one that has never been a stranger to politics, can serve to transmit a certain atmosphere, a sense of what it was like for someone so informed to live through the first half of our century. If all perceptions and experiences are personal, they do not have to be unique. The Spanish Civil War in the 1930s, for example, led not only to my own political awakening, but to that of a whole generation— just as the antifascist struggle was shared with most of my own friends and contemporaries. There are in every life private compartments which seem intensely personal, but even these are to a large extent dependent upon the context in which a life is lived.

The starting point is important in all of life, and my own beginning was hardly typical or widely shared. Starting with life in Germany—at home and at a rather famous boarding school—I do not merely recall a vanished world. What I remember is a way of life which had a direct impact upon all that came afterwards even if, in my own mind, there seems little connection between the spoiled child, the toughened-up and conformist schoolboy, and the politically aware young man and future unconventional historian. I have proceeded chronologically in this book, for only in this way can I myself make sense out of the continuities and discontinuities of my life.

As a trained historian, I have some practice in attempting to go back in time to see how people living then understood their world. I have always believed that empathy is the chief quality a historian needs to cultivate, and I hope this belief has stood me in good stead as I come to look back upon my own long life. Empathy means putting contemporary prejudice aside while looking at the past without fear or favor.

Any autobiography, apart from some general themes, must seem episodic because human memory is not a seamless web. I have had to rely almost exclusively upon my memory of the past, and as a result some episodes loom large while there are stretches which will be missing. This incompleteness serves a purpose, however: obviously I remember those events which left a lasting impression and which, in my own mind, helped to determine the future.

Nevertheless, some unifying themes have run throughout my life, and they should provide a focus for this book. My status as a real or potential outsider, as a Jew living in a decidedly hostile environment during my formative years, was bound to leave its mark, as was my existence as a sexual outsider, which, if known, could have blocked any chance of advancement. These themes, to be sure, have been important, but they were often muted, overshadowed by commitments to a political struggle or to the writing and understanding of history. I do not belong to a more recent generation where victimization is a badge of pride rather than a frustration or a test of character.

5

The themes which will dominate my narrative for long stretches of time derive from coping and trying to make a space for my own development. I had to confront nationalism as well as racism—both reached their climax in Europe when I was a very young man—and then there were the wars which disfigured the first half of the century, though I experienced these on the home front rather than in the field. Having lived for various lengths of time in the United States, Germany, France, Israel, and England, I was once asked in what country I like to live best. My answer was, in any nation where passports don't matter, where I will never need one, where I am appreciated for my own sake, without labels or stereotypes. Sometimes the United States comes closest to this ideal and then again, perhaps such a nation does not yet exist. And yet, nationalism with its sense of belonging did have a certain appeal, though paradoxically I have never been able to shake the refugee mentality and I remain from that day to this, in part of my mind, an eternal emigrant, still traveling.

But in the last resort the sense of belonging, so desirable for the up-rooted, won out, as the eternal emigrant became Americanized. I wanted to be considered a true American, naturalized on the western side of the Mississippi, instead of the effete eastern side, so close to Europe; nevertheless I continued to consider myself a European and a permanent outsider. If this seems confusing, so be it, but this confusion is explained by a life lived through times which allowed no rest.

The image of the "free-floating intellectual" appealed to me for the longest period of time, and I still think that in order to empathize a historian has to be the eternal traveler, the spectator, rather than being committed to a set worldview, least of all a nationalist belief-system. I have always been instinctively suspicious of historians who have held an overriding belief, including a faith in a traditional religion. Now I realize that this attitude, while still desirable as an ideal, was unfair. I myself shared strong commitments at various points of my life: involvement in the antifascist movement, for example, or, on a less intensive plane, in Zionism and in liberal causes. The temper of the times made a neutral stance impossible and perhaps even undesirable to maintain. Life's ambiguities will not be denied, just as in the end the settled citizen of the American Middle West was destined to win out, if uneasily, over the eternal emigrant.

This, then, is not the usual story of immigration and settlement, nor does it project the usual perception of exile. But then even the setting in which I grew up was itself highly unusual.

2

The Setting

N O SENSE of impending doom marred my childhood, lived in Berlin during the last years of the Weimar Republic. I witnessed those years as a spectator cushioned from the real world through an opulent lifestyle which served to block out the realities of life. What other child had a car and driver of his own when not yet ten years of age and was driven to primary school when other children walked? Moreover, a series of governesses took care of all my needs. I had my own living room as well as bedroom at my disposal both in Berlin and on the country estate just outside the city.

I took such a lifestyle for granted; it was all I knew. I never felt or saw myself as a small boy dwarfed by such vast spaces, nor did it astound me that I could command servants three or four times my age to do my bidding. And indeed there was nothing small or niggardly about our homes, except the broom closet which became my prison when I had been an unbearably naughty child. As I look back on these first years of my life, I realize that they did give me a certain self-confidence, or, better, the qualities of a sleepwalker, which have helped me transcend presumably dangerous situations by largely ignoring them, as, for example, when I had to run the gauntlet of a row of Brownshirts on leaving Germany. I have always been able to disinvolve myself when I seem to be up against a dead end.

And yet I was an angry child, an *enfant terrible*, when I should have been happy in my own kingdom. I was lonely, surrounded by grown-ups; when it was thought time for me to play with youngsters of my age, boys from the village of Schenkendorf, where our country estate was located, were summoned up to the house. No real friendship could arise this way. Perhaps just as important, the family as such did not provide much real

Portrait by Max Oppenheimer, 1927

support, because it was present so rarely. Breakfast and lunch were taken with the governess in my living room, and only occasionally was I allowed to join in the evening meal where all of the family were present. My parents came to say good night, but that was usually all I would see of them. I craved attention, no doubt seeking it in many disruptive ways.

But it was the opulence and the availability of space which characterized the setting of these early years. Although I was an infrequent visitor there, my grandfather's mansion in Berlin is the house which, more than any other, seems to symbolize the background against which my childhood was lived. My maternal grandfather, Rudolf Mosse, built his "palace," modeled on those of Renaissance Italy, on Berlin's Leipziger Platz in 1882 in order to demonstrate the solidity of his publishing empire founded two

8

decades earlier. As an additional sign of his status, he bought the rural estate of Schenkendorf in 1896, with its palatial country house, some forty minutes by car outside Berlin. The Berlin residence was a large stone building in the classical style; its courtyard enclosed a fountain by Walter Schott which, with its dancing maidens, was to be imitated by one at another estate in East Prussia and another in New York's Central Park, which still stands. But this was not all; the mansion, besides the lavish living quarters, also contained my grandfather's art gallery and extensive library.

The existence of such a gallery and library in a private house reflects the German middle-class ideal of *Bildung:* the acquisition of self-worth through continuous self-development in which education, culture, and the visual arts played an important part. The paintings and sculptures in a collection like that of Rudolf Mosse, with their historical, sacred, or national themes, could be absorbed without difficulty and given a spiritual dimension in which they exemplified truth and beauty and elevated the human spirit.

What must have been the most startling painting in the mansion decorated one large wall of the dining room. The artist, Anton von Werner, was famous for his 1877 painting of Bismarck's proclamation of the new German Reich; he was an expert in crafting paintings with historical themes. I remember his huge fresco in the dining room well; it was a source of endless fascination. *The Festival Dinner,* as it is called, was a portrait painting in brilliant colors completed in 1899. Rudolf Mosse, along with his wife and daughter—my mother—and some of his important political friends, are all clad in Renaissance costume, seated at a large banquet table in an Italian setting, talking and proposing toasts. This was a gathering of leading liberals such as the physician-politician Rudolf Virchow and the liberal parliamentarian Heinrich Rickert. Others of the middle-class elite had themselves painted in the same manner, and frescoes in their homes, also built at the end of the last century, often showed the family in Renaissance dress.

This vogue, which would not survive long into the new century, documented a new self-confidence on the part of a new middle-class elite, as well as their quest to attain legitimacy by appropriating a nonaristocratic past that had been one of the high points of Western taste and culture. Moreover, this was a past which in its republicanism suited the liberal elite, patrons of culture; thus it was especially appropriate for German Jews as a sign of their integration into European history and tradition. I knew nothing of all of this, just the fun of looking at such a costume party, and I was always struck by the beauty of my mother as a young girl.

9

The Festival Dinner: Grandfather Rudolf Mosse, his family, and friends, portrayed by Anton von Werner, 1899

10

After my grandfather and my grandmother died, the living quarters of the mansion stood empty until 1933, except for the custodians and the occasional meetings sponsored by our publishing house. There must have been servants, but, though I got to know those in our own Berlin house and in Schenkendorf, I have no memory of those living at the Leipziger Platz.

The villa which my grandfather Mosse had built for his daughter and her husband—my parents—in Berlin's west end was quite different, more modern and nondescript. Here is where I spent part of my early childhood. Upstairs every one of us three children had a bedroom and a playroom (or sitting room as my brother and sister grew older). Here too I lived in my own little world. The public rooms and the dining room were downstairs, together with my father's study. I remember the two large and ornate sitting rooms only as public rooms because of the many gatherings which took place there; after them came a large dining room decorated with Medici tapestries. A concert hall had been built behind the sitting rooms: there well-known musicians performed both as soloists or in quartets. The tradition of musical performances given in the home lived on in these circles. We, in turn, were invited to such concerts, and to this day I remember one given by a quartet in the house of the prominent banker Carl Melchior, perhaps because for once I was allowed to accompany my parents.

I was considered much too young to take part in the cultural life of Berlin at the time, and it is ironic when today students ask me what it must have been like to experience the excitement of cultural life in the Weimar Republic. To be sure, like other children, I was taken to the opera (usually those like Friedrich von Flotow's *Martha*—my own first opera—or Gustav Albert Lortzing's *Zar und Zimmermann*—my second), but never to the theater. My childhood was lived almost entirely in Schenkendorf or within my parents' villa on the Maassenstrasse, situated in one of Berlin's most elegant districts. There we were surrounded by the homes of other members of the Jewish elite, most of whom knew each other. A certain re-ghettoization, though far from complete, had taken place in the pattern of settlement. Even at Schenkendorf we were surrounded by estates which had been purchased by other acquaintances, bankers or industrialists for the most part. Most of this splendor even survived the Second World War. But then these villas were torn down in the 1960s to make room for urban renewal in the shape of ugly prefabricated apartment buildings.

In addition to the Berlin house, the second environment where I spent much time before I went to boarding school and later, on holidays, was the estate at Schenkendorf in the flat countryside surrounding Berlin, with its birch trees and sandy soil. Schenkendorf in its origin had been a feudal

Schloss Schenkendorf

The Maassenstrasse house

Rittergut, or knight's estate. The proprietor of such an estate could in Wilhelmian times carry the title of *Rittergutsbesitzer*—important in a world where title guaranteed status. The building itself dated only from the 1890s; it was surrounded by a large park, and beyond that by sizable farmlands. The actual farmyard which adjoined the park, with its stables and a disused sugar beet mill, always provided an attractive playground.

The village of Schenkendorf itself, by the 1890s, had lost the coal mines which had provided its livelihood. The mine workers' housing was left standing, however, and gave the village of a few hundred people its character. The drab houses built by the mine owners were called "Siemens houses" after the famous German company which had owned the mine. To this day the arms of the mine workers' union decorate the village's largest house, which had been their social center. But all of this was merely background as far as I was concerned. I do not remember mixing with the village children, although I was told recently that at times children were asked to the manor house for cakes and sweets in order to provide playmates for me. On my birthday the village band regularly serenaded me, beneath the manor's large terrace, a homage which, once more, I took for granted.

The village was extremely poor, and it was said that by 1933 one half of its inhabitants voted Nazi and the other half Communist. My parents, for all that, acted and were regarded as something like the lords of the manor. In 1928, for example, they donated the village church bells: one was inscribed with my sister's name and one with my own (I don't know why my brother was apparently omitted), and I vividly remember the ceremony of installment presided over by the Lutheran superintendent (Bishop) of the region. Today this bell is the only concrete link that still ties me to the village; for while my sister's was melted down during the Second World War, I myself continue to ring out over manor and village. The church itself had impressed me earlier only because it contained in the cellar the bodies of the children of the Count von Löben, who had owned the estate during the seventeenth century. The eighteen half-opened coffins which held their bones presented a fascinating, if gruesome, sight. (The interior of the simple church, after its restoration by the German Democratic Republic, turned out to be a seventeenth-century jewel well worth visiting.)

The Schenkendorf manor house itself I never found especially attractive, though it had a large hall at its center around which, on a gallery, some eight bedrooms intended for guests were grouped. My father had each of these rooms equipped with a private bathroom, an unheard-of luxury at the time. The two drawing rooms (red and green) were downstairs, as was the dining room, together with my mother's suite and a so-called winter garden off the great hall, leading to the large terrace with its view over a wide lawn toward a small lake.

The tower of the manor house was my own private domain, and the island in the midst of the lake, as well as the mysteriously abandoned stone tower next to it, were my playgrounds, sometimes shared with cousins on my father's side. But I also spent much time in the large kitchen in the basement with its huge stove in the center of the room (which still exists), sponging off the cook, my special friend.

This rather detailed description can perhaps provide a sense of the size of Schloss Schenkendorf with its twenty-four or more rooms, where every child also had a bedroom and a living room, just as in Berlin. Space is an important part of my memory of those times—the ease of movement, the grandeur of the environment. Having lived in such large spaces I was never to feel really comfortable in small, cramped surroundings. This love of spaciousness is no doubt related to the claustrophobia I experience when confined to smaller spaces (though they were never tiny, not even in exile). I

With cousins Ali and Erwin Lachmann on a sculpture outside the main entrance to Schenkendorf, 1929

The red car decorated for tenth birthday, September 1928

attribute this primarily, however, to the fact that in the Maassenstrasse house an often-used punishment for the unruly boy was to imprison him in a broom closet, a tiny black space in the midst of such spaciousness.

Schenkendorf held another and unique attraction for me. I think it must have been on my seventh or eighth birthday that our driver, Herr Barthmann, built a small red battery-driven car for me which I drove through the large park, usually proudly giving a ride to family and visitors. No wonder that I was the envy of my playmates, and in all probability was one of the youngest boys ever to drive a car.

The servants were a necessary and integral part of this opulent lifestyle. The house in Berlin and the one in Schenkendorf were maintained by some five or six servants each, including cook and butler, my mother's personal maid, various chambermaids, and a kitchen maid. The story is told that in Berlin my father once met on the stairway of our house a woman whom he had never seen before, and in answering his astonished question of who she was and what she was doing there, she said that she was the kitchen maid. Our relations with at least some of the servants must have been very close;

they were in any case far from hostile, as class-based theory would have had it. Whatever was saved of the contents of our houses was due to the actions of loyal servants, who rescued valuables, including tapestries and some furniture, from under the very eyes of the police who had confiscated our property after our flight into exile. Some of these possessions followed us halfway around the world; they eventually turned up when my father and stepmother lived in California. But as the pleasant was often mixed with the bizarre during the first years of exile, the loyal concierge of the Berlin house had packed among the Medici tapestries and Empire chairs a whole suitcase full of enema bags of the large old-fashioned kind. Perhaps she was afraid of what strange American food might do to our health.

While we were still in Germany, servants for a time took the place of close family members; they provided the layers between myself and my parents. The most important were the cooks in Berlin and Schenkendorf, my mother's personal maid, and the Schenkendorf butler, as well as the driver. I was not a forgotten child; on the contrary, I was spoiled by all and had a large territory to play or even drive in.

But still, those who spoiled me and looked after me were strangers, and I longed for more intimate bonds. My awareness of their concern and even love for my person was always laced with the suspicion that this could be a show put on for financial advantage. This unease I felt at home was strengthened in boarding school, at the Hermannsberg, when my parents repeatedly provided sweets as a treat for the whole school. I am sure their intentions were of the best, but I felt even then that this might be an effort to buy popularity for the ugly duckling. To be sure, I was short and rather ugly, where the others in my immediate family were handsome and tall, but appearance did not concern me much at the time; instead I wanted to make my own mark, to escape the shadow cast by my family.

Of the people who surrounded me at home, it was a governess who joined us when I was about eight years of age who held all my trust, and who seemed and indeed was beyond the suspicion of harboring ulterior motives.

She was not my first governess; I had been under the care of a series of French governesses earlier. I remember almost nothing about them, except the astonishing fact that all of them were confirmed royalists, so that I thought for a long time that France had best be ruled by a kindly king. Why this should have been so I do not know—perhaps they were "refined" gentlewomen who had come upon hard times and looked back to another age. Certainly, being my governess must have been hard, for none of them lasted any time before fleeing back home. That my first foreign language should have been French was only natural in a family which looked to France for inspiration, as did so many German Jews. Indeed, immediately after the First World War had ended, my father took the courageous step of inviting the famous French chanteuse Yvette Guilbert to sing in our private concert hall. Much later, it was the French ambassador to Germany, André François-Poncet, whose intercession with the Nazi authorities made it possible for my father's mother to visit us in exile in Paris.

Miss Squire from Belfast was hired so that we should learn English as well as French: foreign languages were not regarded as a luxury but, together with knowledge of other Western European cultures, as a necessary part of *Bildung*. But Miss Squire became much more than a teacher; in fact she was a true surrogate mother for me and, as I gather from my sister's diary, for her as well. Typically enough, despite this closeness and the role she was to play in helping to shape my future, I do not remember her first name. Governesses were "Miss" So-and-So, or if French simply "Madame." They shared our table and our time, and yet were still regarded as a superior kind of servant. Miss Squire exemplified some of the best Quaker traits as I was to know them both at my English boarding school, run by the Society of Friends, and at Haverford College in the United States. She was plainspoken, honest, and, above all, a good listener who seemed to possess an inner fortitude and security in contrast to my restless family and, especially, to my mother with her frequent scenes and hysterical outbursts.

The tension between Miss Squire and my mother was tangible; it disturbed me a great deal as a child and even today. Not only was I distressed because of my love for Miss Squire, but my basic sense of justice was violated by the accusations which my mother constantly leveled against her. Now I can see that my mother had reason to be jealous, but at the time I was totally on Miss Squire's side and lived in constant fear that she might be dismissed. As a matter of fact, Miss Squire stayed on even while I was in boarding school. In 1931 she married and my father established her as the proprietor of a Berlitz language school in her native Belfast. She had taken me there on a visit in 1928, and what I remember today was my astonishment and delight at the lifestyle of her near working-class family and the kind of family atmosphere that was usually missing from my own home.

This, then, was the setting in which I was brought up. The physical surroundings and the servants as well as the governesses were all part of an environment which determined the shape of my childhood. My immediate

With Miss Squire, Belfast, October 1928

family were, of course, crucial to this environment, but in many ways less real to me than the setting which I have described: my daily contacts at home were largely with servants, and then with Miss Squire, though my parents and elder brother and sister were always there on and off in the background.

3

Family Matters

THE SETTING in which I was reared, rather than the family itself, seems to have exercised the most direct influence on my life; nevertheless, it was my family's history which not only made the setting itself possible, but remained a constant if rather silent presence, even if I did not realize its full importance. The family's deeds which affected my life, and indeed defined my place in German society, seemed to have been accomplished before my time. No living family member, with the possible exception of my sister or my stepmother, was destined to play a decisive role in my life.

The decades before the First World War were an age in which, through the application of personal ingenuity and risk-taking, German fortunes were made and vast businesses founded—the Age of the Founders, as it is often called, after those who managed to establish economic empires which left their mark on coming generations. Here innovation and a love of action were rewarded in a Germany engaged in the process of rapid industrialization. Both sides of the family had such founders: Salomon Lachmann, my father's grandfather, more traditionally in the grain trade, and Rudolf Mosse, my mother's father, much more spectacularly as the initiator of modern advertising in Germany and as a newspaper founder and publisher.

Salomon Lachmann was a Prussian grain merchant who had gained great wealth in the 1860s when he began to supply the Prussian army with food during its wars against Austria and France. His service to the Prussian state was even greater, however. There was no well-established spy system at the time, and grain merchants were well placed to monitor the movement of enemy armies according to the amount of grain they confiscated in the countryside. Salomon Lachmann was able to inform the Prussian military of the movements of the Austrian army and later to provide a similar service during the Franco-Prussian War. High Prussian officers and gentlemen-in-waiting to the emperor attended his funeral. Apparently only one of his six children inherited his drive, directed no longer toward commerce but community service. Edmund Lachmann was president of the Berlin Jewish Community for forty years and was a leading figure in supporting and directing programs of social assistance. He was also one of the first Jewish officers in the Prussian army. The four other sons, including my grandfather, were rentiers who lived off the fortune their father had made and, as far as I can judge, never found adequate occupations.

The Lachmanns, for all that, were not like the characters in Thomas Mann's *Buddenbrooks,* a fictional family saga set in the same era, where the energy and virility of the founder were exhausted in later generations, leading to eventual decline and extinction. Some of the great-grandchildren of Salomon Lachmann were again to distinguish themselves. Whether this was due to the shock and consequences of exile will occupy us later. Meanwhile, my grandfather followed the course which many of the generation succeeding the founders had apparently taken.

Georg Lachmann was established by his family in several businesses, and he was a success at none of them (lamps from one of his failed ventures in manufacture were scattered all over our Berlin house until the end). He married into a distinguished family, however. My grandmother's father, Jacob Eltzbacher, had fled Germany after the revolution of 1848. He settled in Holland, where he made his fortune. He built a summer house on the coast near Amsterdam, which became the nucleus of the village of Sandfort, today Amsterdam's most popular and crowded bathing resort. At Sandfort my father spent some of the happiest hours of his youth. But when it came time to die, my great-grandfather asked that his body be buried in German soil. Nearly a century later a friend of mine in Bonn, then West Germany's capital, told me that he had discovered a small overgrown Jewish cemetery in the neighborhood where he lived. Soon I stood before Jacob Eltzbacher's grave.

The fact that Eltzbacher had apparently been a "48er," had taken part in the 1848 revolution, was to me a matter of considerable pride when, during the struggle against the Nazis, he became in my mind a premature antifascist. And yet, the family contained an even more spectacular revolutionary figure, though not in the service of Germany: my maternal great-grandfather Markus Mosse, a country medical practitioner in the Prussian province of Posen. Many of his patients belonged to the lesser Polish nobil-

Great-grandfather Markus Mosse

ity who were restless under enforced Prussian rule. What was more natural for Markus Mosse than to use his travels as a doctor, going from estate to estate, in order to help organize a revolt against Prussia? Markus Mosse was a German patriot, but just for that reason he may well have supported Polish independence. German patriotism in its formative stage often encompassed a love for Poland, also struggling for national unity. During the first great German national festival at Hambach in 1832, for example, some Polish flags were carried side by side with the flag symbolizing German unity. Markus Mosse was exemplary for patriotism without chauvinism and for commitment to liberalism and individualism as integral parts of national identity.

When the 1848 Polish revolt was suppressed by Prussian troops he was imprisoned for over a month in the Prussian fortress of Küstrin. (When, over a hundred years later, I was lecturing in Poland, someone asked me if I was related to this Polish patriot.) I discovered this tradition relatively late in life, not because my family banned talk about revolutions (after all, my father as a newspaper publisher was one of the first in Germany to send reporters to the new Soviet Union), but because the accomplishments of my grandfather, Rudolf Mosse, and his legacy, obscured all that went before and cast a long shadow, even up to 1995, when the Mosse Media Center (Mosse-Zentrum) opened its doors in reunited Berlin.

Rudolf Mosse had come to Berlin from Posen as a young man and made his fortune. He found work in journal publishing and soon realized that advertising, then in its infancy, could become a valuable link between the press and the public. He launched his advertising agency in 1867 and revolutionized the industry through his sustained publicity campaigns, which made advertising respectable in Germany. At the same time he foresaw that Berlin would rise to new importance as the capital of a united Germany, and in 1871 he founded the *Berliner Tageblatt,* which quickly became one of the most respected and widely read newspapers in Berlin, as well as one of the leading liberal newspapers in Germany. He added other newspapers to the *Berliner Tageblatt* over the years, one directed toward the less sophisticated bourgeoisie and another meant to appeal to the working class. At the time of his death in 1920 he owned a publishing empire and was one of the richest men in Germany. Rudolf Mosse was a true member of the generation of the founders, energetic and enterprising, not afraid to take risks.

He had been educated by his father in those virtues which the middle class cherished: hard work, modesty, and purposefulness. He never abandoned this way of life, and later, in 1892, when he founded the Rudolf and Emilie Mosse Home in Berlin for the children of impoverished parents of the "educated middle classes," its purpose echoed these principles: the children were to be educated to be both modest and industrious. But also, in accordance with their status as children of middle-class parents, they were to be introduced to cultural life: they were taken to museums, theaters, and concerts, as well as the Berlin zoo.

Rudolf Mosse himself enriched Berlin cultural life by encouraging some individual artists, but, most of all, he installed the library of Erich Schmidt, a famous nineteenth-century literary scholar, in his home, together with an art collection that was spread over twenty rooms of his mansion. Both were at times open to the public. The library had manuscripts relating to Wilhelm Grimm's encyclopedia which for some reason I remember to this day. It also contained many first editions, especially those of Goethe and Lessing. Goethe and Lessing were, of course, the patron saints of German Jewry, and my father himself later acquired an impressive collection of first editions of Goethe's works. My grandfather's art gallery typified the average taste of men of his standing and generation. Apart from a Rubens, most other paintings were by German artists of the second half of the nineteenth century, many of them, like Arnold Böcklin, Wilhelm Leibl, or Adolph von Menzel, famous at the time but today largely forgotten. The collection of sculptures, however, was a special feature of this gallery, reflecting an interest which was rare then. It was said later that only Emperor Wilhelm II did more than Rudolf Mosse to further this art form. But the sculptors themselves were, once more, typical of the fin de siècle; artists no longer familiar, such as Hugo Lederer, Fritz Klimsch, or August Gaul. Here, as among the painters, the avant-garde was not represented.

Rudolf Mosse's extensive philanthropic projects, such as the founding of the Mosse Home for children, again reflected his times and his status: they were at least partly a self-confirmation of his newly won position in society. Such activity was common among the generation of the founders in general, though Jews seem to have been proportionally over-represented among philanthropists, and few operated on such a large scale as my grandfather. Moreover, his belief in Berlin's economic success, which had caused him and his brothers to move to the capital in search of a living, was indicated in the fact that his charities were for the most part given or placed in that city, a tradition which my own father continued.

Rudolf Mosse's wife, Emilie Mosse, my grandmother, came from a modest background as well; her parents had been shopkeepers in the Rhineland city of Trier. A retail shop of that sort, where my great-grandmother stood behind the till, and which was open to all comers, had a shamefully

Grandfather Rudolf Mosse with his brothers, 1891. *From left:* Salomon, Theodor, Rudolf, Albert, Paul, Emil, and Maximus (Wolfgang had died before this photograph was taken)

Grandfather Rudolf Mosse's sisters, 1891. *From left:* Margarete Bloch, Anna Wetzlar, Clara Alexander, Elise Hartog, Leonore Cohn, Therese Litthauer

24

low status among those who had moved up (at least to where they did not have to confront the public directly). This ancestral shop was never mentioned in the family, and I do not even know what it sold. Emilie Mosse must have been an extraordinary woman. Not having children of her own, she adopted her husband's illegitimate daughter Felicia—my mother—surely a most unusual step at that time.

I do not myself remember Rudolf Mosse, who died when I was two years of age, but I recall my grandmother, who survived him by four years, as a decisive, strong-willed, rather tyrannical woman, who spent a great deal of time with me. Emilie Mosse had made her own mark on Berlin by founding the Mädchenhort, a collection of hostels which provided shelter and food as well as summer vacations for thousands of poor girls and single mothers. For her social involvement, she received a prestigious award, the Wilhelmsorden, founded in honor of the proclamation of the German Empire. Anton von Werner, the celebrated Wilhelmian painter, portrayed her proudly wearing the decoration and its sash. Rudolf Mosse, by contrast, in keeping with his democratic convictions, had refused all imperial decorations or titles.

When Hans Lachmann, my father, married Felicia Mosse, Rudolf Mosse's daughter, in 1910, he became the heir to the Mosse publishing

Felicia Mosse

empire, and from then on he hyphenated his name to Lachmann-Mosse, which became the family name. This was not an unusual practice then.

This business link was not the only common heritage which united the two families. Both sides of the family, however different their histories, were conscious and proud Jews. Here there was no either/or—either German or Jew. That dichotomy has too often been read back into history from later events. Jewishness was not merely a religion but was primarily linked to pride of family, from which it could not be divorced. When later I asked why we had to stay Jews in the face of rising anti-Semitism, my father answered that it was a matter of devotion to our family traditions. A business like ours could only last, as he once wrote, under the shadow of National Socialism if it was passed down from generation to generation in a spirit of honesty and conscientiousness. This ideal led to considerable tension with my older brother who, although the presumptive heir, had no interest in running a business. To be sure, such families as ours shared some of the self-criticisms of Jews and had a lively consciousness of anti-Semitism, but in the last resort, German, Jew, and family were interchangeable concepts.

Salomon Lachmann himself had been a pious Orthodox Jew, while my other great-grandfather, Markus Mosse, by contrast had been a man of the Enlightenment. Still, in a family crisis even he turned to his ancestral religion. When his wife, the mother of four children (eventually their number would increase to fourteen), entered into an affair with another man, he decided to take her back only after drawing up a draconian new marriage contract written in Hebrew and blessed by a rabbi: for example, she was to speak only when spoken to, and not to go out without supervision. This contract still exists as a mute witness to a different, though recent, age. Small wonder that, as my mother told me (without, of course, referring to her "sinful" conduct), her grandmother had always been such a silent woman.

Salomon Lachmann's Orthodoxy was soon discarded by his children, and, like Rudolf Mosse, they joined the Berlin Jewish Reform Congregation. Here they mirrored the rapid assimilation of German Jewry during the nineteenth century. Jewish Reform saw Judaism in moral terms, as an ethical system whose difference from Christianity consisted in doctrine, not in spirit. Worship was to be orderly and dignified. The service was conducted by the rabbi instead of, as in Jewish Orthodoxy, everyone praying in his own fashion; the Hebrew language was all but eliminated; women were no longer relegated to a separate gallery; and the prayer shawl was discarded. Judaism and its liturgy were adjusted to the spirit of the times, and they furthered, rather than hindered, the feeling of belonging to the German nation. One day when at the age of twelve or thirteen I was walking with my father in Berlin, he suddenly pointed at a building which must have been a synagogue and said, in a voice full of wonder, that he could still remember seeing his father standing there wearing a prayer shawl—as if this experience took us back to the Middle Ages. And just as significant, I had no idea what a prayer shawl was or looked like.

Being Jewish, then, played an important part in family life within the setting into which I was born, just as being Christian did for many Christian families of equal status. Traditional religion was the guardian of respectability, but it also provided counsel and a steadying influence in coping with daily life. Religion was a matter of lifestyle rather than faith.

The German Jewish world was characterized not just by the accomplishments and the religion of my family but also by the insistence on respectability which, for example, held the marriage of my parents together even while my father possessed a woman friend, and—as my sister confided to her diary—the rows between my parents had become general knowledge. Appearances had to be kept up because of the social prominence of the family; my parents were divorced only three years after they had left Germany. The society which I knew was an upper-middle-class

Hans and Felicia Lachmann-Mosse

society; "upper" because of its wealth and the lifestyle which the generation of the founders had adopted and which, again, approximated that of
the Christian economic elite.

Within this setting, my parents are shadowy figures. I am trying to
recall them as I saw them at the time: my mother was still beautiful and
very feminine, while my father had the figure of a Prussian officer, stately
and straight, nothing at all like the looks of his youngest son. That my
mother, who was born in 1888, was the illegitimate daughter of Rudolf
Mosse was apparently well known in Berlin, but not to me; I was told
about it by a cousin much later. It was shortly after the Second World War,
when I went to the former branch of the Mosse advertising agency in Basel,
that I discovered a chest with documents pertaining to her adoption and
her real mother. But I must have had an inkling earlier, for in 1934, when
he was living in exile in Paris as a hunted man, my father went across the
Swiss-German border in secret with a briefcase full of money. As my stepmother told me later, he performed this courageous but foolhardy act because he had promised Rudolf Mosse (on his deathbed, which added a
certain drama) that he would always support my real grandmother, who
was then married to a musician and lived in Cologne. I never penetrated
further into this family secret: was she a maidservant at a time when such
liaisons were quite common among the haute bourgeoisie? (I had at least
one German friend whose mother had such a history.)

My mother adored her father, but her adoptive mother seems to have
been overbearing and tyrannical—perhaps she was compensating for having taken in her husband's illegitimate child; but then, this may merely
have been a trait of her powerful personality. My mother was told about
her adoption shortly before her wedding night—at that presumably happiest moment of her life she was finally deemed fit to receive the distressing
news. I do not know if the problem of illegitimacy was addressed at that
time as well. The stuff from which novels are made sometimes intrudes into
real life. The shock to her psyche must have been very great, for when she
was in her eighties, living in New York, she asked me if I had minded that
she was an adopted child (nothing, of course, was said about the near
certainty that she was an illegitimate child as well).

But there may well have been additional stressful burdens imposed on
my mother. Like most upper-class women of the time, she was locked into
duties and obligations not of her own making. Though she was no intellectual or feminist, the constant need to act as a representative of the family
while in Germany isolated her from people with whom she might have felt
truly at home. She had hardly any close friends, and the few there seemed

With mother and grandfather Rudolf Mosse

With grandmother Emilie Mosse

to be tended to be the servants, such as her personal maid or those who had served her in childhood. There were some exceptions: Lunia Lachmann, a Russian, whom I adored, and Ida Nauth, a former Mosse retainer whom we all disliked, believing that she had wormed her way into my mother's favor. My mother was shy, and also had an inferiority complex, possibly due to her origins and the way in which she had been brought up at home, never going to school or meeting fellow classmates. Although she was maid of honor at the crown prince's wedding, I wondered if she had even enjoyed her role there; I could not ever bring her to talk about that.

The happiest I ever saw her was when she was surrounded by the beautiful Russian women who visited Schenkendorf together with the First World War flying ace Ernst Üdet (later recalled to the airforce by Goering and depicted in the film *The Devil's General*). I myself was impressed by his visit, one of the few I can remember. I am not sure if I should draw any conclusions from my mother's delight in the presence of these beautiful young women.

There was no question that she loved us children and tried to reach out to us, successfully only in the case of my brother. He really loved her and sided with her against Miss Squire, as well as later against my future stepmother during the divorce proceedings. I am not sure why he should have felt so differently from my sister or from myself—I was even more alienated from her than my sister was. Today I realize that she had great difficulty communicating her feelings, but I always felt nervous and restless in her presence.

The scenes my mother made with the servants were undoubtedly a major reason for my uneasiness while we were still in Germany. Some were public and embarrassing, and I felt all of them to be unjust. The servants were my friends and I was on their side. My mother was apt to have unexpected temper tantrums over even the smallest infractions, such as the driver's being a little late with the car or her personal maid's having done something not quite right. There were accusations of disloyalty. Indeed, some servants were dismissed for supposedly stealing pillow cases; why pillow cases always figured in such dismissals does not seem to make sense—I am at a loss to explain it.

And yet, most of the servants were devoted to her. They must not have felt such accusations as deeply as I did and were probably grateful for her frequent acts of generosity. For the rest of my life, however, I have not been able to stand scenes of any kind, and though I myself have a sharp temper I have been deeply disturbed whenever it showed itself, however justified the cause.

In the first months of exile my sister, then studying medicine in Basel in order to become a psychoanalyst, did try to help my mother overcome her temper and her anxieties. Together, we took her to Carl Gustav Jung, the famous psychoanalyst, in Zurich, for possible treatment. But, as my sister reported (I had to wait outside), Jung said that he could do nothing for her.

I do not mean to draw this portrait of family life in too stark colors; daily life proceeded normally, and my mother took part in all the many social functions which her position required. In addition she was the president of the Mädchenhort, which her mother had founded. Society ladies took over sponsorship of each of the organization's hostels, and they often met at our house. As a child out of control I sometimes tried to disrupt these meetings, once even by releasing some mice.

One of my very earliest memories is being taken by my mother to the nearby U-bahn station, at the Nollendorf Platz, under whose arches she helped maintain a soup kitchen. This must have been sometime in the early 1920s, during the repeated economic crises of the Republic. Moreover, during the same period, she also helped with an information booth at a railroad station through which Jews fleeing from Poland and Russia entered Berlin. During the Republic, at least, my mother must have taken her social responsibilities seriously.

My mother also was in charge of running the household, which must have been no mean task given its size. The episode I remember best in this regard is like a cameo in which I see my mother sitting at the desk in her own large sitting room, receiving the treasurer of the publishing house. He gave her the household money in cash, in what seemed to me even then a very large sum. The room itself was bright and airy, with all white furniture and with eighteenth-century prints of fashionable ladies on the wall.

Later, in exile, my mother withdrew more and more from life, spending long periods in bed. As I now realize, she tried ever more desperately to bind her children to herself, but the only way she knew to do this was through inducing guilt about supposed neglect; this, in turn, only served to increase my own unhappiness in her company.

Because my mother was so distant, as it seemed to me, there is not very much that I remember about her except her actual presence. We never had a really substantial, deep personal conversation, one which dealt with our feelings and which would have enabled me to get to know her better. The same is true for my father, and if there is more to tell about him it is not because we got to know each other better but because, unlike my mother, he had a public life which affected and dominated the family.

My father, roughly the same age as my mother, was quite different from her and, as a rationalist, must have had little or no understanding of his wife's anxieties. No doubt this helped alienate one from the other—each lived in a quite different world. At any rate, the night I was conceived, when my father was home on leave from the front less than a year before the end of the First World War, may have been the last attempt at a true reconciliation between my parents. My father also loved his children, but for him all emotions had to be kept strictly in check. He once told my sister, when she was considering living with a boyfriend, that undue passion must be overcome through application to work. There was something austere about him which my stepmother later managed to mitigate. His mother, my Lachmann grandmother, herself exemplified such an attitude toward life. Two brothers had married two sisters, and when one of the sisters died around 1912, the other one, my grandmother, largely took over her role in that family. But at the same time she was plagued by guilt feelings about this death. From that time on she wore nothing but black and showed a morbid interest in funerals; however, she also, much to the admiration of my sister, became the first woman anesthetist in Germany. When she died in 1937 she had worked for thirty-five years as a volunteer in Berlin's Jewish hospital.

My father had something of the coldness and self-restraint of his mother, but he could also be very warm, especially in later years, in exile, when he was surrounded by a loving family and no longer had the burden of being a rich man running a publishing empire. And for him it was a burden; he had married into the firm when his real passion was for music, architecture, and technology. Moreover, my father was not really interested in politics, a handicap in the position which he occupied during the Weimar Republic. When Heinrich Brüning was chancellor near the end of Weimar, for example, my father said only half in jest—and I remember it well—that we can dismiss our political editors and save money; all we need to do is to print every day that we support Brüning.

His approach to the times in which he lived is illustrated in the book *Russland, Europa, Amerika,* published in 1929, which he had commissioned for our publishing house. Here, Europe is shown struggling for world power against both America and Russia, not illustrated through conventional textual analysis but through photographs put together by the architect Erich Mendelsohn, who also wrote the captions. Both Soviet Russia and America are described as societies that understood that the traditional foundations of social life had undergone fundamental change and that reflected the change in their architecture. The book displays a fascination with the new; there is no prejudicial political judgment about Bolshevik Russia or America. However, in our home all nonliberal politics, whether communist, social democratic, far left- or right-wing, were summarily rejected.

My father was interested in Berlin real estate, but typically even here his aim went far beyond material considerations. In 1926, with short-term U.S. loans available during the economic boom, he developed prime building sites inherited from Rudolf Mosse. He hired Erich Mendelsohn to de-

With father, 1928

sign luxury apartments and a theater complex facing Berlin's famous Kurfürstendamm. The result is even today dramatic and stunningly beautiful, and what had at the time been regarded as a financial folly is properly now protected as a valuable part of Berlin's heritage. Earlier, in 1921, my father had given Mendelsohn his first big commission, the redesign of the façade of our publishing house; its soaring beauty became a landmark of Berlin, and after reunification it was fully restored. Hans Lachmann-Mosse left his impression on the Berlin landscape; he left it, too, upon the musical world.

Music was my father's chief passion; though he played no instrument, he was active in Berlin's musical life. He was a major supporter of the Berlin Philharmonic (among other things, donating the tuxedos for the

With Hilde and Rudolf, St. Moritz, 1931

orchestra), and we spent many a New Year's Eve at the Kulm Hotel in St. Moritz in the company of its conductor, Wilhelm Furtwängler, and his wife, Zitla. He also provided financial backing to the composer Paul Hindemith at the start of his career, and he gave Bronisław Huberman his first violin. But his chief enterprise was the liturgy for the Jewish Reform Congregation.

The new liturgy which my father financed and helped put together between 1928 and 1930 joined his interest in this congregation to his love of music. He believed that synagogue music was universally bad because congregations lacked either the money or the will to present an acceptable program. His interest in technology also came into play: why not use the newly invented gramophone to remedy this state of affairs? Together with Hermann Schildberger, the musical director of the Berlin Reform Congregation, he collected music to accompany the liturgy. His selection included many works by Louis Lewandowski, a Jewish composer (and pupil of Schumann) from the last century, along with German classics like Beethoven and Schubert.

The Berlin Philharmonic was enlisted, together with well-known singers, such as the baritone Frederick Lechner and Joseph Schmidt, who had been a synagogue cantor and was at the time a celebrated recording artist (he was too short—four feet ten inches—to sing in operas). This liturgy was then used by many German Reform congregations. My father himself, in his own congregation, sat high above the sanctuary, hidden by a curtain, cranking up the gramophone and changing the records. There, one day in the middle of a service, I drew aside the curtain which hid my father and his records from the congregation; here he was, visible to all, sitting next to the gramophone and reading the *Berliner Tageblatt*. I am afraid I cannot conclude that an event so long ago foreshadowed my preoccupation as a historian with looking behind events to discover what I think was their true nature and portent.

This music may well be one of my father's most enduring legacies: it was reissued by a German record company in the 1970s and again in Israel twenty years later. Moreover, some rabbis continued to use selections from the liturgy after 1933 when they led new congregations in Australia or the United States. This liturgy was perhaps the only real bond with my youth left to me—much to my amazement, I heard parts of it when I attended a synagogue in Madison, Wisconsin, some twenty-five years after I had left Germany.

The greatest tribute to this liturgy, however, came when the German racial laws were in place and the Jewish Reform Congregation passed through dark times. The president of the congregation wrote to my father, at the time a defamed exile, to send him best wishes for the Jewish New Year of 5697 (1936) and to tell him that the liturgy had given comfort in the midst of destruction, that the recordings had proven themselves.

My father's interest in the Reform Congregation also affected me indirectly through the rabbi who led the congregation during the Weimar Republic. Joseph Lehmann was a charismatic personality who played an important role in my family as a valued counselor; and for my sister

Hilde during her adolescence he seems to have been something of a father figure. When at the age of seventeen she experienced the usual traumas of adolescence her first thought was to turn to Joseph Lehmann for comfort and advice, even though she confessed in her diary that she did not believe in God, that she was too materialistic to accept religion, and that, in any case, religion provided feeble support for a life lived under intolerable conditions.

Typical of the important role Joseph Lehmann played in my family, and especially in the lives of us children, was his function as instructor in sexual matters. Neither my father nor my mother could ever bring themselves to speak about such a topic. To be sure, my father made an effort in 1930 when my sister had joined a coeducational social-work movement which maintained childhood nurseries in a Berlin working-class neighborhood. He began by trying to find out indirectly whether she already had a boyfriend (the answer was "no," to his great relief), and ended by warning her that all boys were only after her money.

As for myself, my parents waited too long to tackle the distasteful task of sexual enlightenment. I had already been to a coeducational boarding school for several years when, instead of confronting me directly, they sent me to Lehmann. This was not to my advantage: as a very impetuous youngster I took the initiative, even before he got started, and with the proper embellishments told the rabbi, as he sat behind his desk, stroking his long beard, all I had witnessed in the bedrooms and bathrooms at school, and in which sexual practices I had actually joined. This could not have been so shocking, dealing mostly with masturbation, which, however, was considered serious enough. I do not remember any details of the rabbi's response; his stern admonishment must have made very little impression. Lehmann was convinced from then on that I was the black sheep of the family, shameless if not worse, and I had no more encounters with him. Indeed, I was banished from the Reform movement's religious school because of my bad behavior. Although I can no longer recall the incident, it may have been one of the so-called mouse-rabbles with which I made my name in school. In the middle of the lesson, I would throw my notebook to the wall with the cry "mouse" and then all my classmates would do the same. Chaos resulted. After I stopped attending religious school, my association with the Reform Congregation was confined to annual visits to the synagogue.

I am sure that my sister's and my own experiences with attempts at "sexual enlightenment" were far from unique. Such matters were best left unsaid. Respectability still held sway among the bourgeoisie during the Weimar Republic, and the so-called loose morals which respectable men and women could enjoy shown on the Berlin stage every evening or could see represented in the arts were kept totally separate from the private sphere. Here there was no connection between life and art. Young people were sheltered and kept from temptation, so that they would not go wrong in later life. This precaution did not apply to those who, supposedly mature in age and mind, would not be tempted to draw false conclusions from what they saw on the stage and to make life imitate art.

When, for example, the play *Revolt in a Juvenile House of Detention* (*Revolte im Erziehungsheim*) by Peter Lampel opened in Berlin in 1928, my sixteen-year-old sister with her interest in social welfare was keen to see it. The play depicted juvenile houses of detention as places that brutalized youths, and it contained some rough language. The topic itself was considered provocative, but for all that it did not include explicitly sexual scenes. Our Quaker governess thought that my sister might see the play, but my parents were opposed. As usual, my mother did not address the theme of sex directly but said instead that a girl from a good family could not be seen watching such a play. Moreover, she continued, one must know something of life before one gets to see its seamier side, while my father added that he hoped that she would never know life's darker aspects. Such reactions could have been duplicated in most respectable Jewish or Christian homes.

My father's love of technology, which played its part in his work for the Reform congregation liturgy, also led him to help finance a new kind of car, pear-shaped, whose motor was in the rear—something unheard of at the time. The car was called the "Rumpler teardrop car" (*Rumpler-Tropfen-Auto*), after its peculiar shape and the aeronautics engineer who helped design it. I sometimes rode in it with my father and I remember the astonishment of passers-by. The car was produced in small numbers only between 1921 and 1925 and ended up as a prop for Fritz Lang's famous film *Metropolis*. The family made much fun of this venture, but also deplored its cost.

The fascination which the new held for my father had more serious and much more painful results for me when I had to have my tonsils removed. This was usually a routine operation in those days (as was the removal of the appendix), but my father decided to take me to the doctor he considered most appropriate. The very small, largely bald man grasped what looked like a blowtorch and proceeded to burn out my tonsils. This was Dr. Wilhelm Fliess, who gained fame in the future not for his own abstruse theories but for his deep friendship with and influence over Sigmund Freud. I suppose that if Freud himself for a long time believed in his theories, I cannot blame my father for doing likewise. Fliess held that the rhythms of nature determine the rhythms of life and so must be used to cure illnesses. Nature itself must be directed to provide the cure—thus the use of fire in order to get rid of my tonsils. He also held that the dates for cataclysmic events in one's life, such as medical operations, must be set according to the menstrual periods of the mother. The latter theory did not affect me, but to this day I can taste the burnt tonsils in my mouth, and when the stumps had to be removed a short time later, the operation proved singularly painful and difficult.

It was, however, my father's musical interests that affected me most significantly. The conversations I heard at the dinner table were all about music, especially when Wilhelm Furtwängler's secretary-manager, Berta Geissmar, was present, and she was a constant guest. When the Nazis came to power she became Sir Thomas Beecham's private secretary in London. In one of the bizarre scenes of the Third Reich, she returned to Berlin with Sir Thomas in order to supervise some recordings of the Royal Philharmonic Orchestra. A photograph of Hitler kissing her hand on that occasion has always impressed me as a good example of the hypocrisy of stereotyping, for Berta Geissmar exemplified the Jewish stereotype exactly as the Nazis described it in their hate-filled newspapers.

Berta Geissmar personified complete devotion and loyalty to her "chief," whether Furtwängler or Sir Thomas Beecham. She never faulted Furtwängler for remaining in Germany and putting his prestige at the service of the Third Reich, which had expelled her, just as she bravely returned to Germany when Sir Thomas required it. I wonder whether such utter loyalty of employee to employer still exists today, of an unmarried woman devoting her life to her boss. Her memoirs, which she wrote during the Second World War, read today almost like those of a naive and star-struck adolescent. She was, for example, thrilled to meet Winifred Wagner, the queen of Bayreuth, but she did not even hint at Wagner's extreme anti-Semitism or her worship of the Führer. Berta Geissmar was a period piece, though I had no intimation of that as I listened to the talk of the adults at the dinner table.

I was taken to hear the young Yehudi Menuhin play, perhaps in the hope that it would spur me on to greater effort in my own musical education. I took cello lessons as a child, and then piano lessons. I remember both as torture, though at a student recital in 1932 I once played a piano solo by Diabelli, a composer famous for his finger exercises. I might have gotten at least a taste for such instruments if someone had forced me to practice, but this was not the case, and I have often regretted the leniency of my parents and governesses.

My father's interests meant that most of the private dinner guests in our Berlin house were connected to the artistic world. By contrast, much of my parents' large-scale entertaining was more or less official, connected to the publishing house. I was not often allowed to take part in these receptions and dinners, and one of the few times I was permitted to go downstairs, I disgraced myself. I stood before the Soviet Foreign Minister Chicherin, who was wearing a tuxedo, and proceeded to ask him in my usual loud voice how a Communist could possibly wear such a bourgeois garment.

Like the unhappiness of my mother, the importance of all my father's activities became clearer to me only in retrospect. At the time I had little understanding of his important contributions to Berlin cultural life. My father made it a point never to talk about himself, and he told me often enough that one must never talk about oneself, other people, or matters of health. Not very much remained to talk about, and I was hardly a good disciple. (He would have thoroughly disapproved of my writing my memoirs.) I heard only indirectly, for example, about his courage during the stormy beginning of the Weimar Republic. In 1919, two months after the armistice, the rebellion by the Spartacus League, which became the core of the German Communist Party, shook Berlin. They made the Mosse Haus, our publishing house, their headquarters. My grandfather, still alive at the time, was not up to negotiating with them, and so my father went into the occupied building and talked all night to one of their leaders, Rosa Luxemburg, who wanted to prevent the publication of the *Berliner Tageblatt,* scheduled for the next morning. He managed to keep her in conversation until the paper actually appeared and was delivered in the early morning hours. For the rest of his life, this committed liberal and capitalist was fond of saying that Rosa Luxemburg was the most intelligent woman he had ever met.

Despite my father's preference for the cultural realm, politics occupied the forefront of our consciousness as the Weimar Republic was coming to a close, and here, young as I was, I found fault with him, though not as violently as did my older brother and sister. Though I was only between thirteen and fifteen years of age during the death throes of the Republic, when I was in Berlin the drumbeat of events did not pass me by—my father's comings and goings and the constant unrest on the streets, with their demonstrations and frequent display of anti-Jewish slogans, were enough of a reality check. However, being at boarding school most of the time, and then in Schenkendorf rather than in Berlin, unlike my politically engaged and much older sister, I was more of a witness than an actor in this drama.

I remember well that when after 1928 my sister broke with the liberal

Spartacists occupying the Mosse Haus, Berlin, 1919

family tradition and voted for the Social Democrats instead of the moribund liberal Staatspartei, my parents' indignation was boundless. While my father, pointing to the Socialists, asked her how she would like to share her toothbrush, my mother began to talk about illegitimate children. I have always wondered about that shared toothbrush, with which I was also threatened during my various radical phases, but I suppose that it is the only implement used on a private part of one's body which could be mentioned in polite society.

Like many liberals of his generation, however, my father could bring himself only with difficulty to take the Nazis seriously. He used to say that Hitler did not belong in the front part of the newspaper, but in the *Ulk,* the comic supplement. More telling, and demonstrating the serious underestimation of the Nazis which was so widespread at the time, was a passage in a letter which my father wrote to my sister in February 1933, after Hitler had been Reichs chancellor for ten days. He asserted that since that time

41

the sales of "our newspapers" had increased considerably; if sales continued to increase, the influence of the newspapers would grow, and in any case, the movement which brought Hitler to power would fail because of the dissatisfaction of the masses who would not get employment. And though he wavered at times, he hoped nevertheless for several weeks that the *Berliner Tageblatt* would again be given the right to criticize and become a leading newspaper once more.

We cannot look into the future, but even so this seems excessively naive; however, it was in keeping with one of my father's favorite sayings, that, as he wrote to my sister in that fateful month, one must always put the best face on all that happens. Moreover, he had not remained entirely passive during the Great Depression which led up to Adolf Hitler's chancellorship. He organized a world economic conference which met at the Leipziger Platz in May 1932, and ever since 1930 the publishing house had sponsored food kitchens for the impoverished. Much more typical of his cultural orientation and love of novelty, though, were the so-called *Lach-Abende* (evenings of laughter) which he initiated during the depression in one of Berlin's largest theaters. The chief entertainer was Claire Waldoff, a folksy and extremely popular Berlin cabaret singer. At one of these performances I myself was present, dressed as a vendor of the *Berliner Tageblatt*. These evenings of laughter were a resounding success.

In this last year before Hitler came to power, however, the deadly seriousness of the political situation could no longer be ignored, and in April 1932 my father wrote to my sister that these indeed were terrible times and that the Nazis could not be fought with mere logic. But this was a momentary cry of despair and did not touch his Enlightenment worldview, which remained intact throughout his life. Today I realize that my father's attitude toward the approaching storm was typical of many, perhaps most, German Jews of his standing, that they shared the illusions which for them presented the best hope of being truly accepted in Germany. After all, the Enlightenment and its rationalism had led to Jewish emancipation. My sister, of a different generation, told him more than once how the Nazi influence made itself felt even at the left-wing social-work organization where she worked. I eventually went to at least one Nazi mass meeting and witnessed the enthusiasm and élan of the crowd. But for my father, the irrational, like all religion, was "humbug," as he used to tell me, without substance, nothing but smoke and mirrors. Here political tensions were added to the family's other problems.

My father has had very bad press since the end of the Second World War. His indifference to politics and his attempts to save money in the editorial department of the newspaper even while he was involved in other apparently unprofitable ventures like the housing project in the Kurfürsten-damm made for bad blood, but also his stiffness and austere manner must have added to his unpopularity among powerful figures working on the editorial staff of the *Berliner Tageblatt*. When these editors wrote their autobiographies after the war, a very one-sided portrait was bound to emerge. Only hostile voices were heard, and they blamed my father for all the financial difficulties the firm experienced in the years before the Nazi takeover, disregarding the havoc wrought by ever-increasing right-wing pressure. The rumors about the firm's supposed bankruptcy, spread at the time and taken up again by journalists after the war, would have collapsed upon closer examination. The vast real-estate holdings of the family alone more than matched outstanding debts.

Moreover, there were those, like the longtime chief editor Theodor Wolff, who thought that the newspapers were theirs to control, though, in the end, their own underestimation of the Nazis was not much different from that of my father's. They shared the attitude of most liberals, pitting faith in the Enlightenment against "the exaggerated sense of power" of the Nazis, which, according to Wolff, was bound to provoke resistance in the end. Nevertheless, the *Tageblatt* under these editors never compromised with National Socialism, a very proud record in contrast to the rest of the liberal press.

I do not want to gloss over my father's lack of interest in politics and his very Prussian comportment. He was the wrong man for such a position at that time. Still, it is only fair to judge him not just as owner of the Mosse publishing enterprise, but through the entire range of his accomplish-ments, which were concentrated in different public spheres. To be sure, it is difficult today to imagine how someone in my father's position could essen-tially disregard politics, when racial hatred seemed to be exploding all around him. But it never occurred to him at the time (nor to most German Jews) that the Jews' very emancipation was in danger, that they would be ghettoized once again.

My family, like most other Jewish families, considered themselves Ger-man without giving it another thought. What else could they have been? The isolated cases of Zionists who settled in Palestine before 1933 or even 1934 seemed exotic and self-destructive. I did not even know about the existence of Zionism until I had left Germany. Even then my interest was fleeting, which is slightly ironic given my seventeen years of close associa-tion with Jerusalem and the Hebrew University more than thirty years la-ter. But this lack of interest was typical for the vast majority of German

43

Jews; indeed, my family remained hostile toward Zionism all of their lives. When eventually I lived in Jerusalem for long periods of time, my mother, then in her eighties, could not understand how I could live only among Jews. I explained it to her in a way she would understand: "Mother, they don't look Jewish." I myself never doubted that I was German, until well into exile. That I feel compelled today to state this fact seems to me an example of how looking back from one time to another can distort history.

Because I was mostly in boarding school and on our estate in the country during the crucial time in Germany, I was not aware of the immediate menace with which I was confronted, though I was shaken when I once attended a Nazi meeting in Berlin's Sport Palast (sports arena). Becoming aware of my Jewishness, however, did not mean that I felt any less German, even when racial epithets were quite common around me. There was until 1933, after all, a vast though narrowing section of German political life which fought racism. Before 1933 the issue was still open, an important fact which influenced the stance of many Jews, like my father and myself, who considered themselves an integral part of Germany and, besides, were optimists in the spirit of liberalism and the Enlightenment.

While the consistent attacks on my father did not touch me immediately, eventually I was hurt by the criticism made in equally harsh language first by the Nazis and much later by those whose advice had been ignored or who had sought a more active political role for our press. In our case the accusations against my father had a special edge, for the takeover of our publishing house had not been straightforward. Rather, the Nazis, as in all such matters during the first years of the regime, attempted to give it the appearance of legality, as though everything had been done in good order. In reality my father was forced at gunpoint to sign over our German assets to a mock foundation which was supposed to benefit war veterans. Extortion was made to seem lawful and lies could be believed to be true, as when, for example, in the village of Schenkendorf the rumor was spread that we had fled because of tax evasion.

I heard only later about the events that occurred after my father fled to France, when he secretly crossed the border back and forth into Nazi Germany. Hermann Goering himself, in March 1933, summoned my father back to Berlin from Paris, assuring him of immunity (and one knew what such assurances by the Nazis were worth); he took the plunge because Goering had hinted that our Jewish employees who had been dismissed might be rehired. That this sounded plausible in the first months of the regime shows the success of the Nazis' attempts to disguise their real aims, their true commitments.

44

Der edle Spender

Otto Flechtner

Lachmann-Mosse: „Ich will nix profitieren. Alle Früchte, die dieser Baum noch trägt, sollen den hungernden Kriegsopfern gehören!"

"The Generous Benefactor" (anti-Mosse cartoon from *Die Brennessel*, May 1933).
The legend reads: "I don't want to be a profiteer. All the fruit that's growing on this tree will go to the starving victims of war."

My father never talked, at least in my hearing, about what transpired on April 28, 1933, between Goering and himself, but he gave an account to my sister immediately on his return from Berlin. According to her, Goering asked again and again what my father knew about the Reichstag fire, which had provided the Nazis with an excuse to establish their dictatorship. This account is puzzling, though. It is by now well established that the Nazis themselves did not set that fire; did Goering want to find out who did burn the Reichstag? A more likely topic of conversation would have been Wilhelm Ohst, a storm trooper who was the point man in the Nazi takeover of our firm. Wilhelm Ohst was a thug, like so many early members of the SA, and in 1934 he would be expelled from the party for starting barroom brawls, for loose living, and for murder. I could never find out what happened to him later; even though ousted from the party he may have been a victim of Hitler's purge of the SA leadership.

Perhaps my father's conversation with Goering centered on Wilhelm Ohst's relationship with the soothsayer Erik Jan Hanussen, the "prophet of the Third Reich" (as he has been called). Ohst apparently led the commando unit that murdered Hanussen. The proceedings against Wilhelm Ohst before the Nazi Party court do not address the reason why he helped murder Hanussen. The soothsayer, of Jewish origin, was probably involved in corrupt financial transactions with some of the more shady Nazi leaders, but there is no sound evidence to confirm the rumor, current at the time, that he counseled Adolf Hitler, however much the Führer himself believed in the reality of occult forces. I remember that my father mentioned Hanussen a few times, but I no longer remember the context. My own knowledge about Wilhelm Ohst, whom I met only once, comes from the file which deals with his trial and expulsion from the party and which I read in the Berlin Federal Archives some sixty-four years later.

When he met with my father, Goering, according to what my stepmother later told me, may also have offered him Aryanization, which in the context of the times would not have been so surprising. Goebbels, for example, had urged our chief editor, Theodor Wolff, to return to the *Berliner Tageblatt* from France, where he had taken refuge. The Nazis needed prestige abroad at the beginning of their rule, but both Wolff (after some correspondence with Goebbels, copies of which were, for some reason, among my family papers) and my father refused such offers. My father was accompanied back to Paris from Berlin by Wilhelm Ohst and Rudolf Diels, the first chief of the Gestapo, the secret police. Was he supposed to be assassinated? My father later wrote to my sister that either Diels or Ohst was taken into temporary custody for having let him pass the French frontier.

Perhaps this is an over-dramatization of a dramatic episode—at any rate, both men survived. My father's brief return to Germany under those circumstances was a rather courageous act, and it is almost unnecessary to mention that no Jewish employees were ever rehired.

Surely, my father's experiences in interwar Berlin would have provided more than enough material to have fascinated a young boy out for adventure, and who had been brought up in school to look upon personal courage as one of the highest virtues. But all this was buried by my father's iron self-control and self-abnegation.

I do not remember having a truly personal conversation with my father, just as I could never build a close relationship with my mother. They both in their own ways wanted to reach out to me, and as I see it today they were much too lenient parents. My father never made much of an attempt at discipline; rather, he lamented about what was to become of me in later life. Indeed, he did sometimes take me through the halls where the newspapers were printed on huge rotary presses, but a more personal approach might have helped to destroy the distance between us. Even in the less charged atmosphere of exile we did not draw closer. Our conversations were usually about public matters rather than private concerns. But I must also have been distant, involved with myself. My stepbrother, who spent his youth and adolescence with my father, had a quite different impression of him as warm and loving. A relationship needs work by both sides.

My father, from my own point of view, was as remote as my mother. He had no real gift for friendship; in fact he had no close friends that I can remember, and he was constantly plagued by the suspicion that, given his position, anyone who came close wanted something from him and did not offer friendship for its own sake. That is why the family was so important to him. As this did not function properly until he lived with my stepmother in Paris and his moment of wealth and power was past, he must have been a very lonely man.

His only companion on his frequent weekend visits to his beloved Schenkendorf was old Aunt Berta. I say "old" because she seemed to me old and stooped over, familiar as a constant and lively presence in our house, though I remember her as rather a busybody. A sister of my Mosse grandmother, she had been married to a doctor who got the title councillor, or *Rat,* before the First World War, so she was always known as the *Rätin,* even though such titles were no longer officially recognized by the German Republic. Aunt Berta must have had social ambitions, for she held a weekly tea in her small apartment to which my father was invited. And here she played a much greater role in his life than accompanying him to

Schenkendorf, for at one such tea she introduced my father to the woman who was to be his companion. During the last four years of the Republic, they were to meet constantly, though always in secret, long before she became his second wife.

I am sure this introduction was made on purpose; Aunt Berta must have taken pity on my father's loneliness. This introduction, not astonishingly, led to a violent break with my mother once she found out what had happened. When we left Germany Aunt Berta was left behind, which seemed to me rather unjust at the time. She died a few years later, but my stepmother remained in contact with her faithful maid for many decades. I myself without knowing it had reason to be grateful to Aunt Berta for all that my stepmother was destined to mean in my life.

The family was fragmented; in spite of the efforts of my sister, each of us lived apart with his own unresolved problems, and that is why the family has played such an ambivalent role in my life. I was very close to my sister but not really to others of the immediate family. I had surrogates first in Miss Squire and, finally, in my stepmother. Certainly I was lucky. But in those early days I must have been a child in protest, up to no good most of the time.

My brother, Rudolf, was five years my senior and my sister, Hilde, almost seven years older than myself: they had their own friends and interests. That I was born at home just when they had their gymnastics lesson, which was held in a corridor of our Berlin house, may have contributed to my lifelong aversion to most athletics. Relations with my brother and sister were always excellent, however, even though at times my brother teased me good-naturedly, as older brothers will. After meals when we climbed up the rather narrow stairs to our living quarters in the Berlin house, Rudolf used to infuriate me: when I walked in front of him he said that dirt goes before the broom, and when I walked behind him it was the page going behind the master. I do not know why I have such a clear memory of these trivia, other than that at the same time I had a recurrent dream that I was standing on top of a mountain wanting to descend, and at the foot of each possible path stood a "man-eater," a *Menschenfresser,* as he appeared in some books written for very young children, thus giving me no way out. While my brother was always well behaved I myself was not; for example, during dinner, when the butler served the meat, I would take pieces of it from the platter to throw at my brother. My father became so desperate at one point that he took me between his knees at the dinner table, in order to mete out corporal punishment as he had no doubt seen it done in the books by Wilhelm Busch, famous in Germany as the creator of the naughty Max

48

On vacation with Rudolf and Hilde

and Moritz and in America as the inspiration for the Katzenjammer Kids. But I simply escaped, thumbing my nose at my elders, and no further attempts at such punishment followed.

My brother had a warm personality which reached out to people, but I was overawed by him and his real charm. In appearance he was tall and very handsome, and until his marriage was often surrounded by girlfriends. Our paths diverged in exile, and unfortunately he died of cancer in 1958, only forty-four years old.

I suppose he did not have the kind of motherly attitude toward me that I found in my sister and others with whom I was really close; nevertheless we regarded each other as firm comrades. He had a fine sensibility attuned to the arts, especially the theater, and he hated the business world which he was expected to enter. The brief span of exile that he spent learning the family advertising business, inspecting the branches which were left to us, was one of the most miserable times of his life. Eventually, having taken a doctorate in economics in Switzerland, he worked for the United States State Department, but his heart was never in his occupation.

My brother's relationship with my father was never good: he resented the pressure put on him to enter the firm, as well as on occasion my father's rough military way of speaking, and he came to question his business sense as well. Moreover, he kept accusing my father of having mishandled the confrontation with the Nazis, of bearing some responsibility for the end of the firm.

While we were still in Germany, my sister was more distant than my brother, occupied with her own adolescence and social work. This was hardly surprising. The difference in age was important: I was barely fifteen in 1933; at twenty-one, my sister was already a grown-up and her powerful personality was firmly in place. But this personality was mitigated by her compassion. When as children we had our choice among two healthy puppies and one lame one as pets, she without hesitation chose the lame one. She was not pretty in the conventional sense, but was nevertheless compelling, with a large circle of friends and male admirers, most of whom at that time met with disapproval from her little brother. All her life she was a very private person, and there were both in Germany and in exile parts of her life and her activities of which I never knew anything.

My sister, in exile, became a kind of surrogate parent. This was a role which, when our beloved governess left, she had wanted to play, as she wrote in her diary in 1931. That Hilde saw her place in the family in this light was part of her strong sense of social concern. When still a teenager, as I have mentioned, she had joined an innovative social-work movement which ran day hostels and provided social and emotional first aid to underprivileged children from Berlin's proletariat. The Zugscharen (the name meant migratory birds) was an offshoot of the large German youth movement; it had discarded the idea of roaming the countryside in favor of social work among the underprivileged. Hilde included all of the family and especially her younger brother in her strong impulse to educate, help, and repair, which later was to lead to a distinguished career in child psychiatry.

But what of the little brother? I contributed my part to the family's tensions, for I was an unruly boy. After primary school, about which I remember nothing and which must have been uneventful, I was enrolled in Berlin's famous Mommsen Gymnasium. There I came into immediate conflict with its strict discipline, but what brought this schooling to an end after only one year was my encounter with the Latin irregular verb. The classics were still the core of the curriculum, but grammar had taken over what was once regarded as classical learning, confirming the victory of the philologist over the humanist. Learning these verbs by heart took more discipline than I could muster. I promptly flunked, and would have had to repeat the whole year over again.

Why was I so disorderly and nearly out of control? That is how grown-ups saw me and how I have now described my behavior, but this is not how

At Schenkendorf

I saw myself at the time. I was a somewhat lonely boy with much energy to spare, and more than my share of arrogance, no doubt a consequence of the setting in which I was reared. I never had much patience except for those matters which fascinated me, and the very freedom which I had at home failed to give me the discipline I needed to mature properly. That I took to such discipline readily once it was provided by boarding school we shall see presently. My lack of patience, however, has accompanied me through life, but those areas such as writing or teaching in which I was engrossed were not touched at all by this restlessness. At home apparently no one knew how to arouse my interest; intellectually I was left largely to my own devices. I liked to read, but here too I needed discipline to make the most of it. All this was to change once I left for a very disciplined life. I remember this transition today as passing from chaos to light.

What, then, was to be done once I had proved that I was unsuitable for the Gymnasium? My father with his belief in technology thought that it was best to entrust such a boy to the hands of experts, as I heard him say often enough. This from a practical point of view meant boarding school, and the institution which I entered in 1928 and which was to dominate the next five vital years of my life was the junior school of the Schule Schloss Salem, whose headmaster, Kurt Hahn, had gone to school with my father.

4

Building Character in Salem

I T IS my firm belief that a historian in order to understand the past has to empathize with it, to get under its skin, as it were, to see the world through the eyes of its actors and its institutions. But in an autobiography I must analyze how I myself conceived of people and institutions, how they struck me as I lived among them, and all but ignore their own views of themselves, their own self-representations. This change of focus is no easy task, and at times the writer of this memoir and the historian are in conflict. As I now come to analyze institutions which determined much of the course of my adolescence, I have tried to see them as I saw them at the time, but also to look at them in the broader context of their aims and the influences which shaped them. Writing about the boarding school life which now engulfed me means linking the individual and the historical aspect and attempting to reconcile them with each other while not losing a personal focus. Without a broader historical perspective it is difficult to understand what actually happened to me and why, which in turn does have a bearing on my view of my own situation at the time.

If I had been born in England, not Germany, and into the same social class, I would automatically have entered a boarding school at ten years of age, and I was indeed ten years old when I entered Salem, already a famous boarding school. But in Germany boarding schools, apart from some military establishments, did not exist before the beginning of our century; they came into being as part of the effort to reform Germany's secondary education. This meant that such schools were usually based on the specific educational theories of the school's founder and were designed to shape the personality and character of their students. The boarding school which I entered was founded just after the First World War. Its founder, Kurt Hahn, had been private secretary to the last imperial chancellor, Prince Max of Baden, and it was in the prince's castle, and under his protection, that the school found a home in South Germany, near Lake Constance. Both the lost war as well as Kurt Hahn's time studying in England left their mark upon his educational theories and his school.

Being as young as I was, I did not enter the main school but what was then the junior school, the Hermannsberg, situated some miles away, on a hill in the midst of the wooded countryside. Salem itself had been a Cistercian monastery in the Middle Ages before it became the residence of the House of Baden, and the Hermannsberg had been part of a long-destroyed medieval convent. History was always present.

The buildings and the setting of the school were of great importance, not only for me but for most of my fellow students—much more important, for example, than the buildings and the setting of the English boarding school I attended once I had left Germany. That school was situated in the city of York, with its glorious minster, city walls and ancient churches, while the school buildings were nondescript. Perhaps the strong impression made by the actual buildings and the setting of the Hermannsberg and Salem (which we visited often) was due to our impressionable age. I myself awoke to the appreciation of the beauty of nature and ancient buildings during my time at this school. The buildings at Salem, mostly constructed during the seventeenth and eighteenth centuries, were decorated in the style of the South German baroque with its rounded forms, and the most glorious stucco embellished their large rooms and broad corridors. The highly decorated tiled stoves were still standing as well and were actually used for beautiful but unsatisfactory heating.

The Hermannsberg, by contrast, was plain, with thick walls and without much decoration: a rather spartan building which suited the school's spirit. Some of its rooms were spacious, however, or could have been had the school not been crammed into them. Yet the feeling of space which the old and solid building projected further enhanced my need for open spaces, such as I had grown accustomed to in the luxury at home. There were many churches and houses nearby constructed and decorated in the South German baroque style, and it is from these surroundings that I acquired a lifelong love of that style; indeed in the 1950s I often led friends on a tour of the South German baroque, specifically in its Lake Constance setting.

The landscape in which the school was situated became even more important to me than the buildings. Lake Constance was close by, but it was the hills and valleys as well as the forest which impressed me most. I cannot quite fathom why this particular landscape has remained with me for the rest of my life, as "my landscape," more than the many others which have impressed me. To be sure, it was important that it framed the baroque, and indeed the baroque and its landscape exist together in my mind, forming a whole. But the landscape also became so familiar because it was not merely an object of contemplation but was actually in constant use. We built huts in the woods, went on walks and runs, and played "war games" in which we tried to conquer a neighboring castle. Here again the landscape played a predominant part, for hide-and-seek was involved. Everyone got a number affixed to his forehead, and we were divided into attackers and defenders of the castle. If one of the enemy called your number three times you were out of the game. Those who survived were said to have stormed the ramparts (I was never victorious). Living within this landscape was very real, not only because of school activities but also because it was only when we were constructing our huts with our friends and sitting and reading in them that we had truly free time and more or less private space.

Moreover, the kind of romantic literature we were encouraged to read deepened our appreciation of this landscape and gave it a historical and emotional dimension. Thus I remember vividly how in our rest period in the afternoon—as we were lying on our backs on the hardwood floor—a teacher read to us Victor von Scheffel's *Ekkehard,* a book written in the middle of the last century which riveted our attention. The story took place on the Hohen Twiel, a volcanic cone-like mountain at one end of Lake Constance. The Swabian landscape itself plays a leading role in this tenth-century tale of the love of a monk (a blond giant) for a duchess. The patriotic motive looms large as armed monks fight the invading Huns. This was the legend of a native hero, a *Heldensage* retold according to ancient German tradition. Here was a story which was both patriotic and based upon the intertwining of soul and landscape. The effect of the book was enhanced when a school excursion led us to climb the Hohen Twiel itself. The landscape in which we lived was filled with history and had inspired many historical romances; books like *Ekkehard* were ready-made to inspire the youth of my generation, including myself, then in my early teens.

The landscape had its less desirable side as well, but I managed to keep this apart from the historic, still unspoiled nature. During my last years at this school, for example, we were required to dig up potatoes as part of doing our duty in hard times, or, more likely, as another character-building exercise. This was dreadful work, and my knees and hands still hurt thinking about it today. Moreover, a steep slope running down to a meadow outside the school building was used by the gymnastics teacher as the setting for punishment, an adaptation of the German army's "punishment drill": holding an armful of heavy logs, we had to run up and down the slope many times. Surprisingly, no one ever got a heart attack. But these were blemishes which could not diminish the love of this particular aspect of nature. Unlike the so-called "native landscape" of modern nationalism, it was not decreed from above, by some belief system, but came from the manner in which the school and the landscape related to each other, a theme of great importance to Kurt Hahn.

Kurt Hahn, the headmaster and founder, dominated the school, and though I came in touch with him only rarely because I was in the junior school, his educational theories nevertheless affected me, as they did all other pupils, whether in Salem itself or at the Hermannsberg. Kurt Hahn believed that in the chaos of the postwar and defeated Germany a new elite would have to be built which could help to rejuvenate the nation. He was impressed by English boarding schools like Eton as models of elite-building, applicable to the unstable and undisciplined Weimar Republic.

However, Hahn gave the English boarding school model a peculiarly national twist, as well as an emphasis upon discipline and personal tough-ness, which spoke not of England but of a Germany which had lost the war. As I went to an English boarding school after Salem, I will subsequently make some comparisons of the differences that struck me at the time. My earlier judgment of the Hermannsberg seems unduly harsh in retrospect, but just after the war, in 1950 when Kurt Hahn came to America in order to gather money for the school, I wrote one of the few letters I have ever written to a newspaper, in this case to the *New York Times,* warning against giving money to a school which had been dominated by the Ger-man aristocracy and was nationalistic to boot.

Kurt Hahn never published a reply to my letter, but he apparently planned an answer, for I have seen a letter in the Salem archives in which he tried to refute my attack by detailing his (belated) condemnation of the Nazis, defending the aristocracy, and making much of the one lone Salem alumnus who was part of the plot to kill Hitler in June 1944. Now, after the war, he wrote, Salemers must become good Europeans and defenders of Christendom. Thus there was still reason to produce soldierly men. Per-haps he himself in the end realized the inadequacy of this letter and shelved it. That the Second World War was just over was also reflected in my harsh letter; for in reality I had adjusted rather well to the school, quite different from my older brother at Salem itself, who, with his artistic and aesthetic sensibilities, had felt crushed there. To be sure, at first I was also plagued by homesickness, endemic to all boarding schools. It is difficult to be suddenly torn away from your accustomed environment when only ten years of age, and I often cried myself to sleep at night. Nevertheless, I adjusted to the Hermannsberg in short order. Certainly, the fact that I lacked my brother's artistic sensibility was one reason for my better adjustment. But much more important was the fact that my brother, five years older than myself, had already lived a full social life in Berlin, surrounded by friends, going to the theater, while I had been largely isolated from my peers. Boarding school meant for me my first real experience of community, while for him it meant just the opposite: a feeling of loneliness and isolation.

Character building dominated the thrust of the school, with an emphasis on hardening the body. Only one vivid memory of Kurt Hahn at the Hermannsberg has remained with me: during a game of ball, leaning out of an upstairs window, he called out *Schlappschwanz* (weakling) to various players, and especially to me. But Hahn was also said to be charming, a side I never saw. Still, he was an important educational figure, and after being expelled by the Nazis he went on to found Gordonstoun, a Scottish boarding school, as well as the Outward Bound movement, where, quite typically, character was built through leaving boys to their fate in the wilderness, where they had to cope with a hostile and barren environment.

Hahn himself came from a family of wealthy Jewish industrialists. This background was manifested in Salem only through the rich and influential Jewish patrons of the school (including my parents), who financed it, and through a representative of the Warburg bank who was supposed to control Hahn's chaotic financial management. Some of the pupils were of royal blood, for example Prince Philip (later, the duke of Edinburgh) and the princess of Hannover (later, the queen of Greece).

The school was run according to Kurt Hahn's educational theories, and though I might have deplored many of them at the time and even more in retrospect, they had their positive side, especially for a spoiled and self-willed child of my background. Salem was not supposed to provide a substitute family but to constitute its own little state largely based upon the model which Plato had provided (a part of the tyranny of the classics over German as well as English boarding schools). The prefects who were important in the governance of the school were appointed by the head of the school. At Salem the chief student officer was the phylax (according to Plato), here called the guardian, and other offices were held by the so-called color bearers. This was an orderly commonwealth, sparse as Plato had envisaged it, where the leader was supposed to be without family or property. Indeed, Kurt Hahn held that children cannot be educated properly in a modern family: the father is too busy and the mother too indulgent.

The hierarchy at the junior school was less formal than at Salem itself; there were no color bearers nor was there a chief prefect. However, there were prefects with set duties, as well as appointed "leaders" of dormitory rooms, a position which I held for a time—in fact, the highest position I ever attained in a boarding school. My other position at the Hermannsberg was most welcome: that of fingernail inspector before meals (while inspecting other boys' and girls' nails I did not, of course, have to clean my own). There was nothing really democratic about this structure as the term "leader" applied to many of the offices clearly shows, and it is small wonder that in the 1960s the students revolted against this arrangement and demanded a greater, elective share in the governance of the school.

Salem's aim was to educate "soldierly" men and women who had internalized those qualities of character which Hahn thought essential: a sense of duty, moral and physical courage, iron self-control, initiative, and compassion expressed through service to others. These are all laudatory aims and not so different from those of an English public school, and indeed Hahn wanted to set for Germany standards similar to those he thought informed the English nation. Yet, in practice, discipline became the chief educator, at least so it seemed—training in self-discipline and in obedience to the school. Character building excluded individual initiative: it meant instead conformity informed by those virtues which Salem held high. Conformity is part of the camaraderie of schoolboys in every boarding school, but at Salem the emphasis was upon supposedly voluntary conformity, which would become an integral part of the character of those who had passed through the school.

Life, as in all boarding schools, was regulated by the bell: it rang when you got up, went to sleep, ate a meal; it began and ended all your activities—always a bell would ring. That was no different in my English than in my German school, and it was the discipline of the bell I missed most when after living for eight years under its tyranny I finally left it. And though, as we shall see, Cambridge colleges also regulated their students, there was no bell, and so a period of disorientation was inevitable. The bell, however, simply regulated some of the outward signs of discipline. We were, it seems, constantly under restraint in order to mold our characters. As my brother wrote with some justification during his unhappy stay in Salem, "from morning to evening the word is 'you must.' "

Punctuality was an essential part of this discipline, in itself a good thing, but a handicap in a later life passed largely in the United States. Neatness was important; what seems on looking back the constant polishing and inspection of shoes provides an especially painful example. In order to bring home a lesson on cleanliness which was most impressive, the headmistress of Hermannsberg, Fräulein Maria Köppen, used to tell us about her visit to the British Museum. She saw the famous ancient Greek frieze from the Parthenon, part of the Elgin Marbles, being taken down for cleaning—and to her astonishment (and delight) it was carved in the back, where no one saw it, just as it was in front where it faced visitors. The lesson: you must be clean even in those parts of your body and clothes which cannot be seen by others (as, for example, your underwear). She was obviously a very educated woman.

But discipline meant much more than just what was necessary for the smooth running of such a school; it was supposed to be like an obstacle course, overcoming many of your instinctive reactions, fears, or dislikes, which, as part of reshaping your character, were not tolerated. Typically enough, Kurt Hahn wrote that adolescents were exposed to the forces of evil, which must be defeated. Thus, for example, he believed that the sexual drive could break through at any moment and take complete possession of a boy's or girl's spiritual energy.

Artificial obstacles were erected in order to test your mettle: the bad food served was certainly one of them (porridge cannot be burnt every morning by chance), and your plate had to be squeaky clean at the end of a meal. Even the pits of the fruit had to be eaten (to this day I still eat everything put before me at home or in a restaurant, though no one will punish me if I leave something on my plate and I may even be offered a doggy bag). Another example of the obstacles erected at the Hermannsberg easily comes to mind: at meals, as we sat on our long backless benches before the table, at times a long rod would be pushed through all of our arms so that we would learn to keep the proper posture while eating. (Certainly this was traditional Prussian posture, and it reminds me of the story told of my Lachmann great-grandmother: she was proud to have traveled from Berlin to Hamburg without once leaning back in her seat.)

Learning to overcome was all-important: it is typical of this spirit that in 1951 when I visited another branch of Salem where my former headmistress now ruled and she invited me and my American friends to lunch, I saw before me a familiar but happily long-forgotten dish. At the Hermannsberg it was called "heaven and hell," a kind of bread pudding; and she told me—now thirty-two years of age and whom she had not seen for eighteen years—that she wanted to find out if I could now eat it without complaining. Just so, and perhaps with greater justification, she noticed at school that I feared seeing the damaged limbs of those who were crippled, and promptly made me sleep several nights in a room with someone who had lost a leg in the war. This particular discipline was supposed to help me to overcome an irrational fear, but instead it left me traumatized. I must, however, add at once that neither did she compromise when the Nazis came to power: she refused to use Hitler's *Mein Kampf* in her classes or to swear an oath of allegiance to the regime. She was forced to move to a Salem primary school elsewhere in order to escape the wrath of the authorities in the locale where Hermannsberg was situated. But boys of my age at the time were not in a position to appreciate so upright and unbending a Protestant or Prussian character: it looked somewhat different when viewed from below. Indeed, for me at least, she was a source of fear, and all pupils carefully watched her changing moods: it was said, for example, that if she wore a reddish dress with a golden sash, this meant she was in a good mood. It says something of the school's atmosphere that I can recall this dress to the present day.

Punishment was more traditional, the same up to a point as in all German schools. Physical punishment was the norm, and usually involved having to stretch out your hand and being hit across the fingers with a ruler, or, in class, having the hairs at the nape of your neck pulled. This was not meant to be sadistic; it was taken for granted. Running up and down a hill and, more generally, runs of various lengths were also used as punishments. The punishment I could impose as room leader was to run several times around the large school building in any weather clad only in a nightgown. This could happen even when the crime consisted merely of not putting your slippers properly and neatly in front of your bed as regulations required. It is understandable that when on 72nd Street in New York I met a former roommate thirty years later, he still refused to greet me.

Sport was all-important, as in English public schools—it was believed to instill discipline and encourage team spirit. However, Hahn did not, as he claimed to do, imitate English models properly; instead he bent them in the direction of developing a soldierly spirit. He wrote about English sport as *Kampfspiele*—fighting games—while in reality in England any analogy to war was never intended. This difference was important because it points to a nationalist political agenda. These games at the Hermannsberg were mostly soccer or net games, which according to Hahn required presence of mind, initiative, courage, and proper physical comportment. Given the importance of sport for character building, I was a complete failure. Later, in England, I would make friends with the school nurse and thus from time to time get excused from sport, but in Germany no such good fairy existed, and anyhow, because of the seriousness with which sport was viewed, an excuse would never have been granted.

As with sport, the compulsory sessions in handicrafts were taught not for their own sake, but for the development of accuracy and patience needed to perform good work. I disliked sport, but at least I could play (though once at my English school, standing in the middle of the soccer field I forgot which goalpost was mine and which was the opposing side's, and started to kick a goal against my own team). But handicrafts were a lost cause as far as I was concerned, beginning with the board which had to be planed so that it was even, and which, by the time I was through with it, hardly existed at all. I am sure there was another ideological imperative at work here, though I was only barely conscious of it at the time: namely, to teach boys respect for the artisan, in German national consciousness always the foil for the city-dweller—just as working on the land and living close to nature was supposed to reconnect us to our life-giving roots. Many of us were essentially urban, after all, and had to be purified.

These applications of the school's educational theories struck me at the time as onerous but bearable; in fact I must have done rather well because not only was I appointed a room leader, but much more important, I achieved the honor of being quickly given the so-called Training Plan, the indication that one understood and accepted the school rules. Looking back, I believe that this plan was the best educational tool the Hermannsberg had to offer; indeed to my mind it makes up for many of the defects of the other disciplinary and character-building devices. All the duties of school life were listed on a chart: the morning run, the cold shower, brushing teeth, homework, cleaning the room, polishing shoes; indeed, whatever was expected of a boy or girl. Bad habits which were forbidden, such as nail biting or masturbation, were listed as well. Teenagers had to police themselves. If you accomplished the daily task or avoided temptation you put a plus, if you did not, you put a minus instead.

I describe the Training Plan so fully because during the time while I had the plan and even before, as I observed others, no one (with a few exceptions about which I heard many years later), ever cheated—it was just not done. And this though your own Training Plan was checked by a teacher every week, and too many minuses led to punishment. As I write this at the end of the twentieth century, today when cheating is rife, given the opportunity, it seems almost incomprehensible that such a spirit of honesty and self-discipline should have prevailed among teens. Some "honors" programs continue to exist, but even these, for the most part, go no further than monitoring cheating in exams and do not penetrate the school's daily life.

That the Training Plan was a coveted honor certainly encouraged such honesty, but the whole atmosphere of the school, based upon discipline and constant tests of one's moral as well as physical courage, seems important as well. I had not been above cheating in my elementary school, and had certainly never encountered such obstacles as the Hermannsberg placed in the way on the road to manhood. And now it never occurred to me that I might falsify the Training Plan and put a plus where a minus should have been, even when confronted with such hated tasks as the morning run, cold showers, and athletic exercise. Here was a true education in self-discipline, for which I have always been grateful.

Salem and the Hermannsberg contained one other innovation which I must reckon as part of a positive experience. I have already indicated that girls as well as boys attended the boarding school, and that was certainly unusual in the Germany of the time; unthinkable in state schools. Here boys grew up without the convoluted relationship between the sexes usually found in purely male schools. We took girls for granted as friends and comrades, and partners in flirtations, though at the Hermannsberg we were too young to go further than that. Dormitories and bathrooms were, of course, separate, except for one bathroom on my floor shared by boys and girls alike. Whoever got there first had to post the fact that it was now occupied by one or the other of the sexes. As can be imagined, we often changed the sign and burst in upon the supposedly horrified nude girls. Rather than risk severe punishment we then beat a hasty retreat amidst much laughter from both sides. Such pranks were common, as was to be expected of young boys, and I was often the ringleader.

Even in the coeducational setting, boys were treated differently from girls. We had to become true "men," as opposed to "*Schlappschwänze,*" and I do not remember having thought of the discipline and character training other than in male terms. But girls also became prefects and the discipline and character building, as exemplified by the Training Plan, held for both sexes. By and large, however, the conventional differences between the sexes with their different tasks were maintained though modified.

As in all boarding schools, sexual matters were much discussed among ourselves; we also found individual relief in masturbation, and often engaged in mutual masturbation. This was an unhealthy practice, not because masturbation itself is bad, but because we were conditioned to think that it was the beginning of physical and mental degeneration. I for one was often plagued by guilt feelings. At the same time the language in use among us emphasized virility, strength, and daring as opposed to the weakness and feebleness of sissified boys.

Controlling adolescent sexuality, preventing its breakthrough, which

Hahn had so feared, is part of the hidden agenda of all boarding schools. It was no different at Salem or the Hermannsberg: the morning runs, the cold showers, the constant round of activities could perhaps be interpreted that way. But such a single-minded interpretation would not do justice to Hahn's desire to build character, nor was it how the intent of the discipline struck me and others. We were impressed instead by Hahn's emphasis upon the grand passion a boy must possess in order to become a true man, and this passion meant love for the German landscape and commitment to German honor (a concept which combined German patriotism, honesty, sexual purity, and self-discipline). Kurt Hahn, from his point of view, was not wrong when he saw the fine and well-formed athlete as a proper hero among boys, a symbol for the ideals which must inspire true men—except that this hero-worship could traumatize for life those who thought themselves ugly and who did not love sports but instead liked artistic or intellectual pursuits which most boys considered decidedly unmanly. Kurt Hahn believed that a well-formed body—manly beauty—was an important sign of strength of character. (One example of the way in which this idea affected us was the rule forbidding pupils to drink more than five glasses of water a day because Hahn had somehow gotten the notion that drinking more water threatened to result in beer bellies.)

I felt no strong so-called perverse sexual drive as yet—that came with a vengeance in the quite different atmosphere of my English school. Kurt Hahn himself was a lonely figure, and though surrounded by women who adored him and played an important part in running the school, he was mainly interested in his male students. The image of the ideal Salem student and his athletic physique should make that clear. However, we never gave his homoeroticism a thought. We were not yet in an age when the private is public, and no intimation of scandal ever surfaced.

As I did not like sport, I would have suffered at any such school, and the Hermannsberg with its emphasis upon a soldier-like character could have been a nightmare. Indeed, artistically inclined young men like my older brother experienced Salem in exactly this fashion. Yet, I do not remember being put upon or bullied. That was all the more astonishing, for Jews and riches are often unfavorably associated, and my parents never hid our wealth. On the contrary, much to my embarrassment, they often provided special treats for the whole school. That I was left alone and accepted, unlike other Jewish boys, might have been due to my combativeness and decisive manner (and cannot have been due to my looks).

Nevertheless I suffered from an inferiority complex in both the boarding schools I attended, attaching myself in friendship usually to the least popular boys. I thought this only natural at the time and did not attempt to find an explanation. The age of incessant inner probings, of popular psychology, had not yet arrived. Looking back, however, it seems to me that both my feeling of loneliness and the pressure of an ever more articulate anti-Semitism in German society may have played their part. Almost unconsciously, any minority will, tragically, often measure itself against the dominant ideal—in this case that of an Aryan manliness. Here, I obviously fell short.

Anti-Semitism was a constant presence in the German-patriotic atmosphere which prevailed at the school, encouraged by the politics of the last years of the Weimar Republic—in spite of the fact that Kurt Hahn himself belonged to a prominent Jewish family. At least at the Hermannsberg those boys who were Jewish, and who in some way were thought to correspond to the normative Jewish stereotype, had a difficult time. To stand out, to be different from the run of boys in a boarding school, means being subject to bullying and ridicule. Boys among themselves are singularly cruel even without the added dose of nationalism which was part of Salem's definition of a soldierly man. None of us at the Hermannsberg readily admitted to being Jews, with one exception, and that boy was bullied and even at one time daubed with yellow paint branding him as a coward.

I did not have to wait for the Third Reich to become conscious of being a Jew and to see here the beginning of what later on would be a constant involvement with Jewish concerns. The fact that I witnessed the bullying and was too cowardly to come forward and aid my fellow Jew haunted me at the time and deepened my inferiority complex, which would end slowly only with the totally different atmosphere of Cambridge University. Conditions throughout my boarding-school life made it only too easy to internalize the Jewish stereotype.

Kurt Hahn's mother, who occupied an apartment at the Hermannsberg, was, in contrast to her son, a self-conscious Jew. Hahn had long ago disavowed his Jewishness; it was never mentioned except by the Nazis, and eventually in exile he converted to Anglicanism. The whole atmosphere of the school was Christian and Protestant, as were the morning devotions in the main school, held in a beautiful baroque "hall of prayer." But at the Hermannsberg Frau Hahn kept the Jewish High Holidays and insisted that Jewish boys and girls attend them, much to our distress, for we did not want to be singled out in this manner. I have often thought that I know no better education for conformity than life at such a boarding school, one where the boys themselves, whether consciously or not, act as its guardians. Not only creating an elite but also instilling social norms were princi-

pal aims of such education, wherever it existed. Conformity was emphasized through the school uniform: wearing it was, like the Training Plan, a
distinctive honor conferred by Salem; in my English boarding school there
was the special school cap which we all had to wear.

The cantor at the Jewish High Holiday services at the Hermannsberg
was a non-Jew with a good voice, Manfred von Pourtalès, whose subsequent history when viewed against this background is indeed ironic. Having enjoyed the hospitality and financial support of the Hahn family, he,
along with many alumni of the school, joined the Nazi SS and may even
have been involved in that organization's murderous activities. When the
war was over he did penance by becoming a monk—hardly a typical fate,
not even for those turbulent times.

Germany's defeat in the First World War continued to have an effect on
Salem; after all, the peace of Versailles was only ten years old when I entered the school. The character training, the discipline, was to steel boys in
order to compensate for the humiliating peace treaty. Hahn preferred ex-
officers as leaders of the school and as guides for the students. There was
some effort to provide free places in the school, mainly, but not exclusively,
for sons and daughters of officers and members of the local population. To
be sure, one of my best friends was the illegitimate son of Louise Schröder,
a prominent Social Democratic member of Parliament, but that was an
exception, and I cannot remember another case like it. Salem had acquired
even then the not entirely undeserved reputation of being a school for
princes.

The political atmosphere, then, in which the life of the school took
place was decidedly *Deutschnational,* close to the right-wing German National Party. Education for democracy existed only in the sense that self-
discipline, devotion to duty, and perhaps even so-called manliness were
virtues that could also benefit a functioning parliamentary system of government. There was no disguising the nostalgia for Wilhelmian Germany,
however, not perhaps for its outward form so much as—to cite Kurt
Hahn—for its supposed spirit of discipline, efficiency, and the exemplary
ordering of private and public life. Leadership was emphasized—the building of an aristocracy not of birth but of character which, so Hahn believed,
constituted a necessary leaven in every state.

However, being a member of an elite, being a leader, also included
obligations, not only those of honesty and self-discipline as taught in the
school, but above all courage—not military courage, which was taken for
granted, but courage to stand up for what you consider just. What the
Germans call *Zivilcourage,* which involved speaking out against injustice,

was constantly invoked at the school. This notwithstanding, some three hundred alumni joined the Hitler Youth, SA, and SS, the latter itself an elite organization, perhaps with the belief that they were expressing courage by supporting nationalism.

Individual teachers did depart from a nationalist commitment. I remember with pleasure to this day the lessons of Gertrud Kupfer, our German teacher, who read and discussed Lessing's play about tolerance and Jewish emancipation, *Nathan the Wise,* with us—certainly one of the few memorable purely intellectual experiences I carried away from that school. I have been told that there were also teachers at Salem who tried to instill tolerance and democratic principles in their pupils, but I doubt whether this was the rule. At any rate, it took me a long time until I could rid myself of deeply held prejudices against the French and the Poles which I had acquired not at home but at school.

The approaching storm cast its shadow over my school years. I remember seeing swastikas burning as fiery symbols on the hills surrounding the Hermannsberg, and the racist poison, though rejected by the school itself, had become so much a part of daily life that it penetrated the vocabulary of the boys and girls, aggravating the atmosphere of anti-Semitism. An awareness of the so-called Jewish Problem was everywhere in those years; why should it have bypassed the school? The blond girl to whom I was closest at school told me often enough to go back to Jerusalem, and this despite the fact that she used to visit Schenkendorf as our guest during the summer.

But there was another way in which the turbulence of the times was brought home to me personally. One evening, quite suddenly, late in 1932, even before the Nazi triumph, my father appeared at school with a lady who was eventually to be my stepmother and whose son was also at school. I threw myself on the floor with delight and astonishment; homesickness was always latent under the discipline of the school. My father explained that he had sought refuge in Salem's famous inn Der Schwan (The Swan) because the general who was in command of Berlin, in accordance with the emergency decrees then in force, had forbidden the appearance of our newspapers for a time, and Berlin apparently had become too dangerous. He said nothing about the demonstrations which had taken place against us as ready-made symbols of the so-called Jewish Press. My mother had left Berlin on one of her numerous travels abroad, which seemed now to absorb much of her time. Such surprise visits were repeated several times.

Still, I was not unduly alarmed. We were too far removed from the daily happenings of the world around us—we read no newspapers and did not possess a radio. Living in a well-regulated school "state" was indeed like living on an island in the midst of a stormy sea; it was bound to make the eventual transition to the real world rather difficult.

How typical for the school's German national orientation that Hahn himself did not wake up to the menace of National Socialism until August 1932 (Weimar Germany had only some five months more to live), when Hitler sent a telegram pledging solidarity with his "comrades," the storm troopers who in the Silesian village of Potempa had brutally trampled a Communist worker to death in front of his mother. Hahn believed that the Potempa murder had sullied the honor of the German people, and it was now inconceivable that Hitler could ever become chancellor. This reaction, once more, emphasizes the basic principles of the school: Hitler had soiled the "honor" of Germany in condoning such a brutal political crime; he had violated the ideals of honesty and the clean fight for which the school and the German officer corps presumably stood. Given all that the Nazis had done previously, this attitude is a little like the insistence of the Hermannsberg's headmistress that she would not teach Hitler's *Mein Kampf* because it was written in bad German.

My final departure from the school at the beginning of March 1933 again illustrates how distant it was from the reality of the new Germany whose time had now come. Hitler became chancellor on the 30th of January 1933, and immediately began a campaign of intimidation which culminated in the coincidental burning down of the Reichstag on February 27, 1933, a fire which he used as the occasion to silence his political enemies once and for all and to begin his dictatorship. Soon after this my mother, brother, and sister left the country, warned by the violent anti-Semitic demonstrations. Earlier, on one of her visits to my brother and me at school, my mother had been cursed as a "Jew-bitch" as she walked on a street in the nearby city of Friedrichshafen. Indeed, at home my father had feared for some time that my sister might be kidnapped and held for ransom, and an elaborate security system connected to the police had been installed in her bedroom and bathroom. I was not impressed, and one day while she was taking a bath, I set off the alarm, with the result that a police-commando stormed up the stairs and into the bathroom. But the danger seems to have been real enough. It is typical that no one seems to have thought that my brother or I could have been kidnapped; kidnappers would, it was assumed, go after the "weaker sex," though, in reality, my sister was the strongest member of the family.

My father fled to Paris in March 1933 after he had been rudely expelled from his publishing house; this indeed was a different sort of occupation from that of the Spartacists with whom he had dealt so easily after the

First World War. I was left behind at the Hermannsberg, an apparent hostage to fate.

The Nazis, soon after coming to power, had started to limit Jewish mobility. One of the deadlines affecting me was March 31, 1933. On April 1, further anti-Jewish laws came into effect, the Aryanization of Jewish businesses commenced officially, and in some German states all Jews had to hand their passports to the police. Therefore, I had to be out of Germany by midnight of March 31.

The time when I had to leave was drawing nearer and nearer and if I had missed it, the Nazis would have gained a valuable hostage, enabling them to pressure my parents to legally sign over our important foreign holdings, the European branches of our advertising agency which had escaped their grasp. Moreover, they might have blackmailed my father into lending his name to the Nazification of his newspapers and keeping quiet about the setting of the Reichstag fire, about which Goering at least assumed that as a press lord he had some knowledge. I might have ended up in a concentration camp, and these memoirs would probably never have been written. Why, then, had I not left in good time? To be sure, my parents left it to the last minute to ask me to join them. But another circumstance was decisive. I had, as usual, flunked several lessons and misbehaved in addition, so that I was required to stay after class and finish a paper which had been set for me as a punishment. Desperately my parents phoned the headmistress, but there was no relenting: the punishment had to be carried out and, besides, the term still had a few weeks to go. Duty came first if a boy was to become a responsible citizen—character building at the edge of the abyss. No ill will was involved; on the contrary, the best intentions were displayed and the political situation ignored. The Hitler government was simply regarded as another normal and lawful regime.

I myself at the Hermannsberg was only vaguely conscious of what was at stake. Of course, the main school had not yet been sealed off by the Nazis nor Hahn arrested, and the Nazis had not yet shown of what they were capable. However, as far as my family was concerned, the danger should have been plain enough. My own complacency would change dramatically when I finally left, only a few hours before the deadline of midnight of that same day. Then for the first but by no means the last time I would encounter politics not as an abstraction but as a very personal menace.

The quickest way to leave the country was by ferry from the German to the Swiss side of Lake Constance. As I walked to the ferry, both sides of the approach were lined by storm troopers in their SA uniforms, scrutinizing those who boarded and examining their passports. When my turn came my passport was duly taken, the name noticed, and with meaningful looks and much nodding the passport was handed down the line from one to another of the troopers. I must have been extremely scared, but hard as I may try, I do not recall my exact feelings at this critical moment, though I can remember the experience as if it were happening today. This must be the result of a very serious shock and fright. But I was at the same time impatient to finally get to see Paris, and that might have given a "sleepwalking" quality to this confrontation, as my thoughts raced ahead.

Yet, though I was convinced that I would be detained, to my astonishment I was allowed to board the ship, the last ferry before midnight. It was clear to me then, and today in retrospect, why I was allowed to depart even though the storm troopers had obviously recognized my name. Surely it would have been easy to find a pretext to detain me for the very short time (my memory tells me it must have been some fifteen minutes) before the ferry departed. I was saved by the often despised German conscientiousness and obedience to orders: the law took effect at midnight, and midnight meant midnight and not a quarter to twelve.

Though this episode has remained with me in blinding clarity ever since, I soon overcame my fright in joyful anticipation. This was to be my first trip to Paris, where I was to meet the rest of the family, and it cannot be overestimated what Paris meant to a Jewish boy who had been brought up in admiration of France, with tales of the glitter and beauty of its capital. French had been my second language, and since I had learned meanwhile that France was not ruled by a king, its history of tolerance was all the more familiar. This anticipation was surely one reason why I remained so calm during my departure: my thoughts were already at the banks of the Seine. I was not aware at the time that escape meant exile—how could I be when it was a generally held opinion among my elders that the Hitler government could not outlast the winter? Nevertheless, the ride across Lake Constance separated what I have come to experience as the two distinct parts of my life: the first one, up to this crossing before I was fifteen, is so distant that when after many decades I once more visited the scenes of my youth, I experienced no deeper feelings than those for the baroque and Salem's Swabian landscape, which, as I have said, I consider my landscape to this day.

Yet the Hermannsberg left a deeper mark than I realized at the time. It gave me some backbone—all that character building for one of my background and behavior had not been in vain, even though it meant a certain rigidity when it came to punctuality, efficiency, and order, as well as intolerance for slovenly types; it was counterproductive, however, as far as an inclination for physical exercise was concerned. The school also gave me a first taste of nationalism, which at the time I found congenial; there was a danger that it might provide the belief system I so sadly lacked.

The school was decidedly not Nazi but it was nationalist all the same: German "honor" had to be vindicated and maintained. Kurt Hahn was briefly arrested by the Nazis (here his Jewishness played the decisive part); he then fled to England and Scotland, where he started a new boarding school at Gordonstoun. Salem was kept open because there were new headmasters who managed to get along with the Nazis, and, probably just as important, because the government realized that Salem pupils made good army officers. That many old Salemers joined the SS seems not too astonishing, in view of that organization's claim to be the new German elite, for the virtues which Salem taught were also those praised by the SS. That these soldierly virtues could be bent to murderous purposes had surely been inconceivable, as contrary to all German honor, to anyone within the Salem tradition.

At the time when I was at the Hermannsberg, thoughts of so-called militarism never entered my mind. The war games were fun, the sons of famous World War generals and heroes were part of the school, and so were the stories and legends of the German past: one lived close to history and nature at the Hermannsberg. When as a historian much later I wrote about German nationalism, I did have an insight into its truly seductive nature.

The contrast between the Hermannsberg and my English school was great in spite of the fact that both boarding schools shared a similar structure. But I myself was more mature as well, looking at my surroundings with a critical eye and taking part in politics, which now seemed to determine my fate. But then, exile at that age makes one mature more quickly and sharpens one's senses. I suppose that leaving Germany was one of the chief defining elements of my long life, which would never be the same again.

5

Experiencing Exile

IFTEEN years would elapse before I saw Germany again. I was almost fifteen years old when I left and thirty years old when I visited
Germany once more, but for me a whole world lay between those
dates, and I was to feel no nostalgia, no real emotion, when eventually I
revisited the scenes of my youth, including Schenkendorf, where I had had
so many happy times. This was no doubt because I was so young when I left
and because, as I see it, my real growing up took place outside Germany.
Being forced to leave at the very start of the Third Reich, I never experienced the oppressive environment under which Jewish boys like myself had
to live in the new Germany. This fact undoubtedly was responsible for my
unsentimental attitude toward postwar Germany in general; it enabled me,
later on, to gather historical material even from those who had been committed National Socialists.

The end of our existence in Germany did have its effect for a long time,
and I will have cause to refer to it often throughout this book. The way in
which we lost our publishing empire was difficult for me to grasp at first,
and at the time I could not have cared less. But later, after the end of the
Third Reich, all sorts of nasty rumors about my father's role in this process
were circulated and books, some of which collected every rumor that had
been current in Berlin's newspaper circles, were published. As a result, I
reconsidered these events and tried to correct false reports. Such accounts
seemed to begin where the attacks of the Nazi press had left off.

My father's lack of judgment about people was perhaps his greatest
failing, and it pursued us even in exile. I was not directly involved, but
merely a spectator in 1930 when he installed a former publicity man and
one-time editor, Karl Vetter, as general manager of the firm. In the family

71

Vetter was regarded as an evil genius; he was no doubt ambitious and somewhat of an opportunist. The appointment a little later of a general counsel for the firm did affect me, however, for he went into exile with us, became a family friend, and took over the litigation for the restitution of our German properties at the end of the war. Ludwig Levy was a distant relative and good friend of my stepmother, who had recommended him to my father. I admit that I rather liked him, and after the war gave him my trust, out of laziness rather than judgment of character. Levy had told me, long before any restitution proceedings were thought of, how much he hated my father for some apparent slight, a fact which should have been reason enough to sound an alarm. I knew, of course, how important our large restitution claims were, but I have always been focused on my own work, and have tended to brush aside all else as basically uninteresting. Moreover, I seem to have in common with my father the tendency to avoid painful realities and to sidestep that which might turn out to be disagreeable.

As it turned out, my brother was the only one who gave any warning; but we discovered in the end that Ludwig Levy, through dubious real-estate transactions, had misappropriated considerable sums of money. While he was negotiating on our behalf, he was also receiving money from our opponents.

The restitution claims were at first clouded by the difficulties the publishing house had faced because of the Great Depression and the growth of a political and racist Right whose newspapers were surging forward. But as judgments by German courts after the war stated repeatedly during the restitution proceedings, it would have been impossible in 1933 to resist successfully the pressure to abandon the publishing house—after all, the Nazis used all possible forms of coercion to force the Lachmann-Mosse family to give up, since Mosse functioned as the symbol for the hated "Jewish Press."

The actual expropriation took place on March 21, 1933, when Wilhelm Ohst became the Nazi administrator of the firm. His tenure was destined to be short. Brandishing a revolver, he forced my father, as I have recounted earlier, to sign over the publishing house to a foundation that supposedly aided war veterans. This foundation, however, was actually a front for a takeover which would integrate the newspapers into an emerging Nazi Party publishing empire. Wilhelm Ohst accomplished the expropriation, but it was Max Winkler who orchestrated it. This financial expert was responsible for the mass expropriation of German newspapers and publishing houses which, through his manipulation of specially created

72

foundations or trust companies, became the property of the government or the Nazi Party. The manner in which we were expropriated seems to have been a standard procedure. There never was a "clean fight" as far as the Nazis were concerned; they always used deceitful means to project an image of order and respectability and fool the world.

After taking over the newspaper the Nazis appointed Paul Scheffer, who had been the *Berlin Tageblatt*'s correspondent in Russia, as chief editor. If Wilhelm Ohst was a murky figure, so was Paul Scheffer. He turned up in America during the war, and I remember my father being consulted by the FBI about his past. (Cataclysmic events tend to bring dubious figures to the fore.) At the newspaper, respectable appearances were kept up a little longer, until it was liquidated in 1936 and the firm came to an end.

This untidy end caused dissension in the family, and though I myself took no sides, the tensions were palpable enough to affect me indirectly. My sister thought that my father had not fought hard enough, and my brother accused him of lacking business sense and betraying the heritage of our mother. My father later wrote, in a letter in 1937, that he felt deeply offended by the accusations made against him by a boy he considered not yet grown up (my brother was then twenty-four); after all, he went on, it was not his fault that he was considered one of the most dangerous adversaries of the Nazis and therefore was one of the first to suffer the consequences of their rise to power. Indeed, the Mosse enterprises had weathered the inflation and deflation which had ruined others, and it seemed as if they might also weather the "Hitler crisis" in good order. This letter seems almost an admission that he had underestimated National Socialism, as well as a defense against the criticisms of him. More important, these were the kinds of controversies which surfaced continually, not only involving my father but involving all of those who had once been in public life. Exile meant recriminations, a soul-searching of what could have been, had one fought harder.

When we left Germany I did not know, nor did I suspect, that my father and mother were going their separate ways, and it was only much later that I learned that my father had a new companion. He never talked of her, though I had met her at the Hermannsberg when she accompanied him on his sudden escapes from Berlin. I could not have guessed the large role she was to play in my life. My mother went to Switzerland, to the resort of Pontresina, and took to her bed, blaming my father for undoing what had been accomplished by her father, Rudolf Mosse, whom she worshipped all her life. Eventually she settled in Juan-les-Pins on the French Riviera, while my father lived in Neuilly, then a near suburb of Paris. As both my sister and brother had started their studies in Switzerland, and I was in school in England, the family was effectively broken up—the fate of many refugee families. But I must repeat that all the turmoil connected with this resettlement and the attendant tensions did not really affect me firsthand, for I was again in boarding school, first in Switzerland and later in England.

If this account seems singularly detached, this mirrors reality. I had been away from the family for many years, except during vacations. And even then I had not seen much of my parents, busy in public life, unable to reach out to me in a manner to which I could respond. I looked on our leaving Germany as a rather exciting adventure, without bothering about the future. Still, we were now exiles, part of the stream of Jewish refugees, and it is from this angle that we faced the next years.

I may have been complacent about the family's collapse and experienced exile differently from most others, but I was still conscious of being a German Jewish refugee. The fact of statelessness now defined my place, or rather non-place, in the world; one Italian fascist described the stateless as "the bastards of humanity." As I think back, there was never a time when I denied being a Jew, even when many others, refugees or not, did their best to hide this undesirable condition. I suppose that I not only had a sense of belonging, but also of having an extraordinary semisecret bond with other young Jews. The handicap of being an outsider is often compensated by the establishment of a secret and meaningful bond with those who actually or potentially share your fate.

No group of exiles in modern times has been as eager to communicate their experiences as the refugees from Hitler's Germany. Through autobiographies, published diaries, and novels they have sought to make sense of what seemed to them senseless, to justify themselves and their failure to prevent the German catastrophe—or as Stefan Zweig in his autobiography, *The World of Yesterday,* put it, just to look back at gentler and quieter times. Those men and women who wrote down their experiences and feelings as they left their homes, their native languages, and their professions behind had as a rule already made their mark during the Weimar Republic. I know of only a few autobiographical writings by those who were still children or adolescents at the time. Going into exile is obviously experienced differently by those, let us say, fifteen years of age (as I was in 1933), than by those twenty, thirty, or even just ten years older.

I never felt the need to justify my exile as did those grown-up intellectuals. I am often amused, as I have said, when young people in present-day German audiences ask me what it had been like to live in the Weimar Republic, hoping to hear about its culture, and perhaps to get a personal insight into the great figures who became its symbols, men like Bertolt Brecht or Thomas Mann. My experience was quite different from that of adults, and those who ask this question today do not want to hear about German nationalism or boarding schools.

Moreover, and still more important, exile has become stereotyped, for most accounts emphasize loss and deprivation. Those exiled lost their way of life; in extreme cases, for example, formerly wealthy housewives became housemaids working for others, and those who had lived opulent lives at home found themselves turning over every penny before spending it. This was a harsh reality, but one, in truth, neither I myself nor my family ever experienced. My parents' standard of living dropped, to be sure, but throughout her life my mother had a personal maid or, later on, a companion, and was never forced to do housework, dress herself, or even cook. As for myself, what could be more spartan than Salem or subsequently my England boarding school? I have always been grateful that my education accustomed me to such a lifestyle, for it has been easy to make do without much comfort when necessary.

I never experienced the personal and mental deprivations of exile; on the contrary, exile energized me and challenged me as nothing had ever challenged me before. My existence had been secure, my future programmed, and I would eventually have entered the family firm and stayed there. As a result, I was a youth without direction, without much of a purpose in life, except for such individual challenges as the Hermannsberg provided. Character building might have taken place, but it would have had to cope with the arrogance and apathy which an opulent and secure lifestyle brought. There would have been no need to use my own resources in order to create something important, to make something of myself. I was, so to speak, ready-made already.

But now I was thrown into a void, faced with an entirely new set of circumstances, though I was deliberately kept in the dark about the family's precarious financial situation. Now I had to cope with a new country, the use of a different language, though one with which I had some acquaintance, and a future which I had to shape for myself. For me there was no easy transition; my parents' closest friends were and remained fellow refugees, but I suddenly entered a different world: there were no German speakers at Bootham, my English school, and no other refugees.

I did despair at times, especially in the first year of exile. At that time I had a brief encounter with the synagogue, perhaps in search of a firm footing. I wrote to my future stepmother in 1934 asking her to tell me if there was a synagogue in Ostend I could visit on the Jewish New Year, on my way from England to Paris. I do not remember what became of this request, but I have vivid memories of the Jewish New Year the year before, which I spent in Zurich. Then, in the face of the stark reality of National Socialism triumphant, there was much heart-breaking crying and lamentation by men and women usually hostile to such unrestrained expression of sentiment in public, and this in a Reform congregation unaccustomed to raw emotion. Though my own experiences with Judaism have proved to be merely interludes, I have never forgotten the emotional shock of that New Year in 1933.

My parents at first could not decide where I should go to school, and for less than a year put me in a Swiss boarding school not far from Zurich. I have almost no memory of that school except that I hated compulsory handicrafts more than ever, and I have not forgotten my one triumph in the classroom. From my desk I could see down into the valley below, where trains entered a tunnel, then came out at a much higher level. During class many of us followed the trains rather than the teacher. So, when I raised my hand one day and said that a train had entered the tunnel and had not emerged, I was punished for not paying attention—yet I was proved right, and there had indeed been a terrible accident. My lack of memory about this school may be because of the shock of adjustment, but perhaps also is because all now seemed so unsettled, so temporary. This feeling changed once I entered Bootham School in York. But even there I was apparently prone at first to changes of mood between happiness and despair.

Shortly after my arrival at Bootham in 1934, I wrote to my sister that I should, after all, have gone to the new school Kurt Hahn had founded in Scotland, for "I may well feel more at home with Kurt Hahn. One cannot manage completely without the help of one's own." The contrast of these words with the picture of Kurt Hahn and his school which I have painted in the last chapter springs to mind; at the Hermannsberg I would hardly have thought of him as one of my own. However, this sentiment must have been transitory, for only a week earlier I had written that the boys at Bootham were very nice; one immediately feels a part of the school. And two days before this praise of Bootham I had asked her to send me some German classics because "I would like, once again, to read something in German." Such alternating moods are, I suppose, only to be expected in the process of adjusting to a radically new environment. They were not destined to last—at least I have no recollection of such nostalgia or despair. My memory of such unhappiness might have been more vivid had I been older, but at sixteen adjustment was swift and successful, and I, for one, never looked back wishing that I had not been forced to leave the old country. Here the difference between generations stands out in sharp relief.

And yet, being an adolescent also constituted a handicap. While those who were fully conscious of what had happened in the Weimar Republic also faced an unknown future, they were sometimes strengthened by an unchanging political or cultural commitment. I myself knew better what I disliked than what I liked and as yet had no firm outlook upon the world.

My sister, on the other hand, beginning medical school in Switzerland, carried over the social and political ideals she had gained from volunteer work in a Berlin working-class district and the left-wing antifascist struggle. This gave her an enviable stability amidst all the change. My brother, who had been interested in the arts but not in politics, continued his studies in Switzerland as well, but for him personal considerations were foremost; he had at first no sense of the drama that was being played, but worried, for example, about whether his tennis racket had been forwarded to his new Swiss address. However we might characterize and classify emigration, such personal detail is very much a part of the experience. Emigration—being a refugee—is in the last analysis always a personal as well as a collective experience, the former depending upon the degree of a person's political and social and cultural consciousness as well as financial resources. Here all previous experiences reach a crisis point.

As I crossed Lake Constance at the end of March 1933 I engaged in no such speculations, and did not give politics much thought. My enthusiasm was centered on Paris, where my mother had found a temporary home, but first I had to see my father, who was in Zurich. It was there that I awoke to the fact that this journey was special, that it represented a further stage of my father's unannounced visits to Salem, fleeing from the consequences of military censorship.

The Hotel Dolder where my father was staying was one of the better hotels, though not as luxurious as the Grand Hotel Dolder further up the mountain where he would presumably have stayed in earlier times. But it was here that I first tasted something of the atmosphere of the uprooted, an experience which remains vivid even today. The lounge was packed with Jewish and Christian refugees, though this term needs elaboration, for today we think of refugees as inevitably poor and ragged. While these refugees might have lost many of their possessions, they were hardly ragged or shabby. This was an overwhelmingly middle-class emigration, educated and articulate. In 1933 the dictatorship was only beginning, and its confiscatory and repressive measures were not yet completely in place. Moreover, many people thought that Hitler would not outlast the next winter. I remember being struck not only by the atmosphere of bewilderment and uprootedness in that hotel lobby, but also by the tentativeness of it all.

Apart from my father, I remember only two of the men whom I met: Alfred Kerr, the famous literary critic of the *Berliner Tageblatt*, was one of them. The reason I remember him relates to that mixture of the serious and the ludicrous which seems to have been a hallmark of my life, and which has largely determined my own sense of humor—I have never been able to take myself or indeed almost anything else with studied seriousness. As I was ascending the staircase to the lobby a huge sheepdog came down and in passing bit me in the leg. That was Kerr's dog. I immediately became the center of attention in the midst of all the no doubt weighty conversations about Germany's future. Bandaged up, I rejoined my father, who was in deep conversation with Wilhelm Ohst, whom I have earlier described as the point man in taking over our publishing house (probably enriching himself in the process). I do not know what they talked about, but here he was, the committed Nazi, in the midst of all those refugees. He should have stayed, for a few months later he was expelled from the Nazi Party.

Did these experiences of exile raise my own political consciousness, which until then had been more a matter of curiosity than commitment? This is an important question, given the preoccupation with politics that has characterized most of my life. All I have done since and all I have published has had a political agenda. I was and am convinced that there is, in fact, no action, however personal and supposedly neutral, which will not have political consequences. To call someone "unpolitical" is a typically conservative statement, on a par with the maxim, which used to be a favorite of European conservative parties, that youth should keep its nose clean and find joy in sport.

Yet my preoccupation with politics had been latent ever since birth. I was born, after all, into the stormy beginning of the Weimar Republic, and the few memories I can recall from my very earliest years are all political: the death of President Ebert, my mother's soup kitchen on the Nollendorf Platz, political tension at home. But then it does not take such focused memories to recall the turmoil of the times. Youngsters of my generation, for example, collected as a hobby the million-mark or even larger notes printed during the German inflation (I carried an album of such currency with me into exile).

Moreover, the consequences of the war and of economic hardship were part of our daily environment. Their legacy was imprinted upon the Berlin street scene: young men without legs, or without a leg or an arm, or blind, all begging for a living. Today, after another world war, society does better in hiding its war-wounded in hospitals or other institutions or helps them to have an acceptable lifestyle. But during Weimar one could not escape such confrontations with the legacy of war. That urban landscape left a more lasting impression upon me than the ever-present political propaganda, perhaps because it combined physical deprivation with poverty, in contrast to my own surroundings.

That I took such street scenes for granted at the time is not astonishing. After all, few Berliners became pacificists as a result of these sights, but they were, at least for me, a barely conscious preparation for later political action. This did not come to fruition until I entered Cambridge University; it is there that my true political awakening took place. However, it is remarkable that so little has been written about the effect of this urban post-war environment, perhaps because those living outside Germany, with the exception of Italy, did not experience such sights in the same manner.

Exile did confront me with the reality of the new Germany, and gradually I was drawn into the antifascist struggle, though it was not uppermost in my mind until the outbreak of the Spanish Civil War focused the political energies of my generation. Shortly after my visit to the Dolder, as an interim arrangement I was sent to the Swiss boarding school I have mentioned already. My father wanted to send me from there to Scotland, to Gordonstoun. But at this point I rebelled and, so it was reported later, said that I wanted finally to learn something. I am sure that this must have been a tactic: faced with more Salem-like character building I simply took the opportunity to escape.

Now another school had to be found for me, and England was not necessarily a logical choice, as my parents remained in France. But English boarding schools enjoyed a high reputation in Germany; after all, they had provided part of Kurt Hahn's inspiration. Moreover, through my father's activities in the Jewish Reform movement we had some highly placed English acquaintances. The family turned to Miss Squire, now settled in Belfast, for immediate counsel, and she recommended Bootham, one of the best of the schools run by the Society of Friends. This was to prove a very lucky choice, largely because of the presence of some superb teachers.

The surroundings of the school were fascinating—this time not a historic landscape, but the medieval city of York with its minster, city walls, and old churches. The school itself was named for one of York's ancient city gates. (When we wanted to annoy our parents or other visitors we made them tour the city walls and visit many of the thirty-eight medieval churches.) This was, however, a modern boarding school, where physical exercise was also compulsory, even if it bore much less ideological freight: there was the daily run, not at full speed as at Salem, but pleasant and relaxed, providing an opportunity for conversation. Nevertheless, cold baths took the place of cold showers before breakfast, and the living arrangements were spartan at best.

Character building was also a goal of all English public schools, but without the crude discipline of Salem or the intrusion of the headmaster's private quirks. Much was nevertheless forbidden. We were, for example, allowed to walk down Bootham Street only as far as Bootham Gate. But on that street there was a so-called tuck shop, which specialized in tea and snacks. Here much of our socializing took place, and what is more, here we learned to smoke cigarettes, precisely because it was strictly forbidden. (I was to continue to smoke quite heavily for the next thirty-six years, first cigarettes and then a pipe, which was said to be healthier, and in addition looked more academic.) The cold baths every morning were, if anything, even more disagreeable than cold showers. Punctuality was prized here as well, and this meant hurrying through the morning toilette (I can still hear the call "five minutes more"). At meals one hurried as well, mainly so as to get second helpings. To this day I gulp down my food as if I were sitting at one of the plain tables of my boarding schools. The character building certainly did me some good here as well, giving me discipline and focus, but also giving me some bad habits which were difficult or impossible to shake off.

A hierarchy existed among the pupils at British public schools through the system of prefects, who had disciplinary powers, and the fags who had to serve them. The system was supposed to teach how to command and to obey. But fags had been abolished at Quaker schools, and I never became a prefect. At Bootham, as I remember it, a certain civility prevailed and there was no physical punishment.

But the greatest distinction between the Hermannsberg and Bootham was the fact that the quality of both teaching and academic work counted much more at Bootham, not only in class but also in debating and essay societies (which Salem did not have, to my knowledge). Every former schoolboy has his favorite teachers, and at Bootham two teachers in particular not only were my favorites but vitally influenced my intellectual growth and development. They did this not by teaching as it was generally understood—lecturing, explaining, testing—but, at least in my case, matching the assigned reading to the student's intellectual development.

Mr. Grubb was the English teacher, and his method was simple: he gave us a list of the most famous English novels from Jane Austen through Charles Dickens and interspersed our private reading with classroom discussions. We all read these novels and more besides; I devoured Austen, Dickens, and everything the Brontës ever wrote. There was, apparently, a perfect match between these novels and us teenage boys: no hectoring was needed for discipline; the class taught itself. This is how my intellectual curiosity was first awakened, and I have been grateful ever since.

The other teacher, Leslie Gilbert, is better known. The historian A. J. P. Taylor has erected a monument to him in his autobiography, and I must do likewise: he was an inspired, though compared to Mr. Grubb, a traditional teacher. He made history come alive, and like Mr. Grubb he had a way of sizing up his students correctly. When I had to do some reading outside class he assigned G. M. Trevelyan's *History of England* as a book which might interest me. Reading it, I was on the way to finding my vocation. I cannot explain today why Trevelyan's *History of England* had this effect upon me; to be sure, it is a popular history, vivid and fluently written. But at the same time I read many of Trevelyan's other works, and they did not leave much of an impression. Bootham had a school library which had been stripped of most works of fiction, and we were advised to read Trevelyan's books instead—a recognition of his skill as a writer of sound yet popular history. Was this a remnant of Quaker puritanism which confined fiction to the classroom? Or an attempt to accustom us to good reading? I am only one of the historians Leslie Gilbert created, and given my continued poor overall scholastic record, he would in my case have been rather surprised by the result of his teaching.

The worst aspect of any boarding school life, as far as I was concerned, was the utter lack of privacy, aggravated at Bootham by the cramped quarters of the school. We were not allowed to stay in our dormitories during the day, and that meant staying in the classrooms or using the gym. However, I did find a way to be by myself during the last years at school. Like all such schools, Bootham stressed hobbies, and I took up astronomy, not because I was interested in the stars, but because the observatory offered some private space. At any rate, I was more successful in my hobby here than I had been at my other schools: I won a prize of sixpence for the astronomical diary I kept.

Perhaps we were not allowed to stay in our bedrooms because of the "unhealthy thoughts" that might occur to us. Bootham, unlike the Hermannsberg or Salem, was not coeducational, and only one yearly dance was held, under strict supervision, with a Quaker girls' school in York, The

Mount. The dance took place in the Cocoa Works, as the Rowntree choco-late works were called, for the Rowntrees were regarded as the patrons of both schools.

A Rowntree also presided over the Quaker meetinghouse in York at-tended by both schools. Bootham boys marched through town to attend the meeting—a word which describes the silent Quaker service—on Sun-days and once during the week, the so-called Fifth-day Meeting. The si-lence at the service was interrupted by those who wanted to communicate a spiritual message. School boys could have spoken like anyone else, but almost never got up to do so, and neither did the girls of The Mount. The Quaker meeting could be abused by those who gave what we called "well-prepared illuminations," and indeed on one occasion I got up on a bet with a fellow pupil and recited a short Tennyson poem. This is one action of my youth of which I am still ashamed because in reality I found silent contem-plation, shared with others, a true spiritual experience, and if I were reli-gious it would still be my favorite form of service.

We lived within a male camaraderie, and like most of the English upper-middle and upper classes at the time, would do so through univer-sity at Oxford or Cambridge until our early twenties. I had my sexual awakening within this camaraderie, not, of course, literally, but in terms of the consciousness of my own sexuality. The sexual inclination toward one's own instead of toward the opposite sex is not turned on and off because of the environment in which one lives. I can trace my own inclina-tions back to a very early age when I still lived at home, but it was here, at Bootham, that I first experienced conscious attraction and temptation, and fell in love.

All the sexual activity which actually took place at school as far as I could observe—and as far as I was concerned—was still the same as at the Hermannsberg: some horsing around, a very little cuddling, and that mu-tual masturbation which no threat of dire punishment managed to stop. Boys are very proud of their manhood and fear any intimacy which could be regarded as effeminate, an attitude which was encouraged by the role which sport and athletic competition played in school life. I shared this attitude in spite of my dislike of sport, and never even thought of what today is called coming out. Conformity is the rule not only in society at large, but especially among teenagers living together.

Any marked difference in such a society is the occasion for bullying and persecution. And, once again, it was the two English Jewish boys who were given a hard time, treated as outsiders according to the anti-Semitic stereo-type. I remember, for example, one occasion when they were made to climb ropes in the gym to the jeers of their comrades, or on another made to dive for pennies in the swimming pool (in accord with the Jew's supposed love of money). Yet the difference from the treatment of the Jews by their fellow schoolmates at the Hermannsberg was real enough and struck me at the time. There was some good humor about such treatment at Bootham, as if it were really a joke and not a serious matter. This impression was reinforced when one of the Jewish boys handily won a mock parliamentary election at school. Moreover, the two boys were proud Jews who accented their Jewishness, even though this came near to confirming the stereotype (as in greasing their hair and parting it in the middle). Today, as a historian, I would say that the barriers erected against brutalization were much higher in England than in Germany.

I myself was not affected by this kind of outsider status, just as I had been left alone in Germany, but at Bootham it was easier to explain. I was, as far as I know, the only foreigner present and thus an outsider of a different kind, not hedged about by the same prejudicial stereotypes as native Jews.

Though I was fully accepted at Bootham, still I carried an inferiority complex around with me; I suppose that I had internalized my Jewishness, shocked by the treatment of Jewish pupils and by my own failure to declare my solidarity with them. Moreover, I was bad at sport and hobbies, both of which counted. My sexual inclination had to be kept hidden in any case— the role which it played in my comrades' vocabulary was enough of a warning. However, no one was bullied because he seemed gay. Quite a few boys secretly shared this inclination, as I soon realized.

I was not able to give expression to two basic facts about my personality; the pressure for conformity could not be resisted. It was as if I were the carrier of unsavory secrets. The atmosphere of the boarding schools encouraged this belief, and though much later, in the United States, I came to joyful terms with my Jewishness, more than two decades would pass before I could halfway acknowledge my homosexuality. The differences and similarities between the two in my life were clear: I could not really hide my Jewishness; it had determined my fate (why I was a refugee in the first place), as well as my name, but I did not have to parade it in a society which discriminated against Jews. As to my homosexuality, had I revealed it at this point, not only would I have exposed myself to persecution, but I could never have aspired to a respectable position in society or in any profession—quite apart from the reaction of my family. One of my "secrets," as I thought of them, could be partly revealed and the other not at all. As far as my sexual orientation was concerned, I made up for my inability to find fulfillment outside of myself through a rich and highly romantic fantasy life.

While I was at school in England, Bootham did not occupy my whole life. Vacations were quite long and stretched over several months of the year. I spent those not in England, but in France with my family. But here too there was a considerable change which affected me deeply and indeed was to change my life for the better. On the first vacation I went to Paris to meet my father and to accompany him on the train to Juan-les-Pins, where my mother had rented a villa. Much to my astonishment, once on the train, my father unpacked some delicious sandwiches that I knew could not be bought in a shop and that, as I also knew, he was incapable of creating himself. It emerged under intense questioning that they had in fact been made by the woman friend who had joined him in Paris, my future stepmother whom I had met only briefly at the Hermannsberg. Although she had accompanied my father on his visits to Salem, I was much too innocent to draw the inevitable conclusions. I had liked her very much, for she always brought a present and had kind words for me.

The father of Carola Strauch-Bock was Alfred Bock, a Hessian novelist, well known in his time. Carola had been married previously to a Lutheran minister who had died after a few years and left her a widow with a young child, later to become my stepbrother. She had subsequently studied Protestant theology, and much later her library was to be useful to me in my own studies. My father and his new family took a flat in Neuilly facing the Seine, only a few steps from the Bois de Boulogne, Paris's huge wooded park. For the next few years I spent half my vacation time in Paris and the other half with my mother. The Paris apartment was commodious and I remember it as elegant. Though the standard of living of neither of my parents could be compared with Berlin's luxuries, each household had a maid (and my mother a companion besides); moreover, the usual routine was kept: to go skiing in the winter and to a resort in the summer. Exile for me never meant deprivation, and indeed the change of environment was only a matter of degree. I, for one, never missed the past.

Carola, a rather stately woman, brought a new feeling of security into my life, of being protected, of being enveloped in a motherly care whose immediacy I had never known before. She was an open and simple soul, in the best meaning of those words, and we all trusted her and used her as our confessor—even my sister, who was alienated from both her parents. With all these qualities she was of her times: naive about many aspects of life, she was highly conventional in her attitudes and reactions. (I never discussed with her my feelings of outsiderdom; indeed I could not discuss them with my sister, either). Carola was not an intellectual, and that in my eyes may have given her a special kind of openness and charm. She was born and brought up in the provincial German city of Giessen, and whenever she voiced an opinion we thought naive, or with which we disagreed, we would say, "But we are no longer in Giessen."

My sister, who after Carola was the family member closest to me, in contrast had definite opinions on many matters from the fate of the Jews, whose history she hoped would end once and for all with the coming of socialism, to homosexuality, which she thought of as degenerate. She was, during much of her life, an admirer of Trotsky, and therefore a discussion of politics, on which we would never agree, was out of bounds and indeed remained so to the end.

Carola and my father lived among German refugees in Paris (as they would in Berkeley, California, during and after the war). We had been pro-French in Germany, and many of the important French newspaper magnates had been entertained in our house in Berlin, but now they—like so many French Jews, in contrast to English Jews—turned their backs on the new refugees. Indeed, while living in France in the 1930s, neither of my parents had any French friends. But there were exceptions to this indifference: François-Poncet, the French ambassador in Germany, was aware that father had expressed pro-French attitudes when it counted after the First World War, and Carola was acquainted in Paris with Pastor Boegner, a courageous Protestant minister, who has gone down in history as a beacon of light for refugees in the surrounding darkness.

My mother's villa in Juan-les-Pins was quite large and very close to the beach, and while there I swam, drove up and down the coast, and gambled a little at Monte Carlo. But here also we lived in virtual isolation, and apart from my mother's companion it seems to me that only refugees entered our house. I did become slightly acquainted with a French Jewish family and their son, who owned one of the better hotels, but otherwise my time spent there does not yield any specific memories, except of the beach. Not only was it an ideal place to swim, but it also contained its proverbial "mad Englishwoman," who ran around muttering to herself, disheveled and half-crazed. Was this a reflection of the fact that the English were the rich tourists at that time, figures of fun, as subsequently the Americans and today the Japanese? Juan-les-Pins, at any rate, was still not built up, as it is today, but was a place of trees, lawns, and villas.

During the first months of exile, while my mother, in despair, hardly left her hotel room, at the same time she had confessed herself thrilled that now she might be able to realize her dream of owning a small fairy-tale house with a garden. Needless to say, neither the villa by the sea, nor later the house in the mountains, bore much resemblance to the dream (and neither did the New York apartment of the future).

My mother moved to Nice during her last years in France, and from that time one episode in particular was to have some effect on my life. I have traveled a great deal and only once did I witness a spectacular accident. My mother and I decided in 1936 to visit the island of Corsica, and for that purpose took a boat from Nice. This was the *Beauté de France,* a rather ironical name considering what happened. The passage from Nice to Corsica is usually stormy and this time was no exception. The ship, once it had lurched dangerously to the right and left, usually righted itself; but there came a time when it seemingly refused to do so. The passengers rushed to the lifeboats: not a member of the crew was to be seen (they had left already), and a passenger who had kept his head saw to it that it was women and children first.

Meanwhile, there had been severe injuries when the grand piano, which had not been bolted down, careened through the ship's lounge to cries of "*Voici, le piano.*" Luckily my mother sat safely on a couch, while I lay, being sick, behind it. We missed the few lifeboats the crew had left behind, but for some reason at that point the ship decided to stay afloat and limped into the harbor. There, several more persons were injured when the landing bridge to the pier collapsed. That my mother's companion had been raped by a member of the crew in the midst of the storm came to light only when we were safely on land.

This shipwreck was a frightening experience, cushioned only by my seasickness, which took up all my energy. I did not have the feeling of having looked death in the face, though the fright was big enough to keep me from traveling by ship whenever possible. Small wonder that I took an airplane across the Atlantic as soon as that was possible.

Winter vacations have left long-range memories, perhaps because I enjoyed them most. For years the whole family went to St. Moritz in Switzerland, and I learned to ski at a very early age. Skiing was the only sport I really enjoyed, and I became good at it. I took a skiing vacation every winter until I emigrated to America, and then a few well into the 1960s. St. Moritz spoiled those who loved downhill skiing with long descents from the mountains; yet Davos, where we went after 1933, was even better: one could ski downhill all day and then take a train back to the village.

When in the last couple of years before we left Germany we transferred our allegiance to the Swiss resort of Arosa (I do not remember why we left St. Moritz), my parents got to know a very rich Belgian couple, industrialists, who also vacationed there, and they in turn played host to a count and countess from whom, so I was instructed, one could leave only walking backwards. I soon learned that the so-called count and countess were King Albert and Queen Elizabeth of Belgium, both admirable monarchs, the king a hero of the First World War and the queen a great patron of music. But for me this presented a temptation to encounter them, not out of any anti-monarchical feeling, but because I longed to engage them in conversation. Thus when I was in the hotel elevator with the supposed count and countess I pushed the stop button between two floors. We were stuck for quite a time amid general excitement, though neither the king nor the queen ever told on me; perhaps they liked our conversation (though I unfortunately do not remember its contents).

Most of the summers I spent with my mother in a villa she had rented in Chamonix which faced Mont Blanc and the mountains which surrounded it. This was a spectacular setting in what was then a small French alpine resort which could be reached only by train, and which had not yet been overwhelmed by traffic through the Mont Blanc Tunnel connecting France with Italy. I took advantage of the town in two ways, one pleasurable and the other not so agreeable. Cultural events used to come to Chamonix, and the event I remember best was the appearance of the dancer Josephine Baker. She came nude onto the stage except for four birds which covered her private parts, front and rear, and she was accompanied by a game-keeper with a presumably loaded rifle who stood guard in case any curious member of the audience wanted to shoot one of the birds.

As I was in constant danger of failing Latin in school, the local parish priest was enlisted in order to fill my summer with irregular verbs. I did go to the parish house next to the church several times a week, and after the first few meetings, where we had indeed struggled with Latin grammar, the lessons became quite bearable. The nice old priest usually fell asleep and I could go on reading a mystery story or a novel. Latin was forgotten until I made a noise; then he woke up, and it was time to go home.

Most of my days in Chamonix were spent climbing the jagged mountains and steep glaciers in the company of my brother and sister, tied to a rope and with a guide. I shared the climber's feeling of accomplishment when a steep mountain is conquered and one stands at the top, and that must have given me a feeling of empathy when, many decades later, I wrote about the Alps as cultural and political symbols. I never felt purified by the mountain, as the mountain-myth would have it, but I did feel stronger, more manly and proud.

Meanwhile, my future was on the line: What was going to become of

Switzerland, 1936

Chamonix, 1939

me? What would I study? Or would I enter the business world? These were open questions, for I had shown no particular interest in any one subject, nor had I thought about earning a living. After all, I never had to worry about the lack of money: I was no spendthrift—that I had learned through spartan boarding-school life—and there was always enough money for my own needs; nor had the family's standard of living fallen so much that we faced deprivation, let alone poverty. But like all refugees, rich or poor, we had sunk rapidly in the social scale.

The feeling of rootlessness, by contrast, was real. We had been stateless since December 28, 1933, when each of us separately had been stripped of German citizenship, not only confirming our rootlessness but making all travel a challenge. Moreover, it might well make gainful employment difficult. Passports, under these circumstances, became prized, almost life-saving documents. My parents obtained passports (my mother a Nansen Passport invented for Russian refugees from Bolshevism), and my sister owned a German passport without the dreaded "J" which the Germans put on Jewish passports at the request of the Swiss, who wanted to keep refugees out of their country. She obtained this passport through the German consul-general in Naples (and the father of a friend from Salem). Consul-General Breitling helped many refugees; he was a staunch anti-Nazi. At first I myself had an English identity paper—though another cou-

89

rageous consular official at the German Embassy in London, where I had gone to give back my expired German passport, had shoved a new one across the table while saying loudly that I was no longer a German. But it had the dreaded "J" and I never used it then; thus, whenever I went to Switzerland my parents had to deposit quite a large sum of money so that I would be able to leave the country again. Not really a confidence-building measure.

Eventually, my father bought a Luxembourg passport for me, forged by the prime minister himself, without an expiration date. I have kept this passport to this day in case of emergency, for anxieties about passports have never left me, and I still refuse to hand my American passport over to hotels for overnight registration. But such built-in insecurity was like an undertone which accompanied what seemed the normal routine, the hopes and dreams of daily existence.

My father had always thought that only the best and most prestigious schools were good enough for me, and before I went to Bootham had even toyed for a moment with the idea of enrolling me at Eton. I should not have resisted, for, considering the Anglo-Saxon snobbishness of the American academic establishment, as a former Eton boy I would certainly have benefited in my search for a position. Now, however, a Bootham tradition came to the rescue. In keeping with the Quaker tradition of that public school, the boys went on to Emmanuel College at Cambridge University, for this was the "Puritan College." Still, there was a great obstacle to overcome: my poor academic record, in which only history and English were exceptions. The Cambridge entrance examination required papers in Latin and in mathematics. I have already explained that I could not master Latin as it was taught: I was always easily bored, and I never had the patience for learning by rote, especially in subjects which lacked any interest. Mathematics passed me by, since it involved a great deal of abstract memorization.

Most seriously, and unfortunately, I never acquired the scientific knowledge needed for the Cambridge entrance examination. The teachers of science at Bootham were admirable and learned but not disciplinarians. And so I spent most of my time in the laboratory roasting chestnuts over Bunsen burners. Teacher and student have to cooperate, and I just refused to take part. There was no reason for such a refusal that I can remember, except a general lack of interest, a naughtiness which could have been curbed by the arousal of enthusiasm or the application of discipline; but neither happened in science classes. Thus, when a teacher tried to teach us the properties of magnetism, I went around the room with a hidden magnet, upsetting

The "J" passport

all the experiments. These are not proud recollections but rather memories of a failure that was to haunt me for the rest of my life.

I used to boast that one could apparently go through life without knowing how to calculate square roots (which seems to have been a favorite subject of my teachers), or even how to divide, multiply, or get percentages easily—there are calculators which do all of this for you. Ignorance of physics, chemistry, and even biology has more serious consequences, however. I did try to catch up a little later as a cultural historian (but mostly with now obsolete theories), yet never satisfactorily. To give a singular example of my biological ignorance, when a squirrel invaded the attic of my house in Iowa City, I was greatly disturbed. During a faculty meeting at the University of Iowa, where I was then teaching, in the kind of pause which sometimes occurs in these meetings, my voice burst forth addressed to a colleague: "Will the squirrel lay eggs in my attic, and what then?" That was almost the end of that meeting, but it had, believe it or not, been a genuine question, not asked in jest. As I said to atone for my ignorance, "One cannot know everything."

I myself may well provide an example of the results of a type of English education which stressed the humanities and not the sciences and which was at least partly responsible for Britain's slow industrial decline. At any rate, with the gaps in my knowledge, obviously something had to be done if I was going to pass the Cambridge entrance examination. I was sent to study Latin and mathematics with a private tutor, as soon as my last school term was over. He lived in Strensall in Yorkshire, and this remote spot seemed to offer few temptations which might distract me from my studies. This proved to be a thorough miscalculation. I took the opportunity to learn to play golf, while my teacher drank French champagne at all times of day, a habit in which I gladly joined. I learned very little, but I do remember a story my teacher told me about the death of his wife, a story on which I have dined out many times. She was picking flowers in a meadow when a cow came up behind her and breathed down her neck. She died instantly of a heart attack. This story would have added a new dimension to Karl Marx's observation about the idiocy of the countryside, a sentiment which I largely shared.

These lessons had been a failure, but luckily for me this was as yet an undemocratic age, and if you could pay, Cambridge entrance was made not too difficult; in fact, as I remember it, you could fail some three or four papers out of seven and yet pass. This meant in practice that I could omit taking science and try one of the mathematics papers only, which I failed; I failed both Latin translation and sight-reading as well. Even these failures could not keep me out of Cambridge. But because of them I entered not the prestigious college of my choice, Emmanuel, but Downing College instead, one of the newer colleges (founded in the eighteenth century), and therefore endowed with less prestige. When I myself taught at Cambridge some fifty years later, not much of this snobbery seemed to have remained.

6

Political Awakenings

ENTERING Cambridge I began a new chapter in my life. While I had been away from boarding-school restraints during the long vacations, I could now leave character building behind me for a new-found freedom. Moreover, I began to make my own friends (not selected from those I was forced to live with) and asserted my own tastes and intellectual priorities. But first I was confronted with the problem of what I should study, for I had no defining interests as yet, though I knew that I would specialize somewhere in the humanities. The choice of a subject to be studied had to be made immediately when I entered the university; there was no period of grace as in American universities, where one could shop around for two years before settling upon a major. History lay readily at hand, largely through the influence of Leslie Gilbert, who had given me a taste for it; this interest, however, had not yet become a full-blown commitment. Just as important, history was the course of study my English friends took at Cambridge when they did not know what they really wanted—a "gentleman's" subject—and I too drifted into it, rather than, at first, regarding it as a firm choice.

Such a choice was not to be uncontested. When I arrived to take the entrance examination I had an interview with the master of Emmanuel College, Mr. Welbourne. As we walked around the quad and I told him what I thought of studying, he said to me: "You people become journalists, not historians." Not even in tolerant England (and Mr. Welbourne was the most tolerant of men) could I get away from Jewish stereotypes. Indeed, it would be true to say that in those days, in whatever country he lived, the Jew carried his stereotype with him, considered by many—myself at this time included—as an indelible mark of Cain. I did not follow Mr. Welbourne's advice, but, as I was to learn in the United States as well, history and English were subjects reserved for so-called Anglo-Saxons. And if, because of your origins, you could never be trusted to understand the history or literature of the nation in which you lived, you certainly were not a full member of the community. Much later, I became the first Jew ever to teach history in two important American state universities.

Opposition to my choice of history came from my family, too; it was as strong as it was ineffective. It was true that some important German scholars had been part of my family, but they did not hold academic appointments; they lived on their own incomes as "private scholars," with prestigious accomplishments to their credit. The most famous, Felix Liebermann, the brother of the painter Max Liebermann, had married a Lachmann; at the beginning of this century he had edited and published the laws of the Anglo-Saxons, which had led to honorary degrees from both Oxford and Cambridge. Indeed, when it became known that I was a relation of Felix Liebermann (who in England was much more famous than his brother), it greatly increased my prestige and even gained me entrance to seminars to which otherwise I would not have been admitted.

A much more distant relation on the Mosse side of the family, Felix Makower, had done his life's work on the constitution of the Church of England; published in 1894, it was to be found in every English bishop's study. There were other scholars connected to the Mosse family as well, such as Hermann Blaschko, the Oxford specialist in Roman Law.

These scholars, except for Blaschko at Oxford, lived off their fortunes; for me, however, this road to respectable accomplishment was cut off, given our situation in exile, and I would have to earn my own keep. Knowledge of history was considered a necessary part of what it meant to be cultured and was even prized as an avocation, but it was not considered a money-earning profession. If I wanted to go on to study, it should be either a scientific subject like physics, or perhaps, as in the case of my brother, economics, which would be a good foundation for business. But in spite of some rather awesome scenes with my parents, I went on to study history, perhaps confirming my father in the despair he felt about my future—a despair fuelled by my mediocre school record and my failures in the Cambridge entrance examination.

When I entered Cambridge in the fall of 1937, the transition from boarding school was eased by the fact that Cambridge retained in its colleges certain features of boarding-school discipline. Students had to be in the college or in the residences licensed by the college by 10:00 P.M.; after that, gates and doors were locked. Gowns had to be worn in class and mortarboards and gowns in the street. This was a sort of continuation of the school uniform that I was accustomed to at Bootham. Moreover, here also, certain places of "ill-repute" were out of bounds, though this cannot be compared with the strictures at Bootham. There not only were we forbidden to go into the town proper, but when marching to the Quaker meetinghouse, which was in the center of town, we had to avoid certain streets. Cambridge had its own forbidden establishments, for example, a bar called The Rendezvous, which was out of bounds and fired our imagination, so that I still remember the name. My friends and I did eventually visit The Rendezvous, without being caught. We failed to notice anything particularly exciting, but I suppose that if we had seen a prostitute we would not have recognized her. The streets of Cambridge were patrolled by the university's own police, a tutor from a college in full regalia, accompanied by the "bulldogs," two college servants in top hats.

Cambridge was in session only half the year, and so the generally received wisdom in my time was that you took part in social life during the term and studied during the long vacations. I took full advantage of that custom. The social rounds became habit: lunch and dinner, and sometimes even breakfast, were taken with friends in one's own college or very often as a guest in another college. One went punting on the river Cam, propelling a pontoon with a long wooden pole, or bicycled to take tea in the countryside. This seems an idyllic lifestyle, looking back upon it, interrupted by occasional bouts of study in order to write the weekly paper for the tutorial. Social life, however, was soon accompanied by lively political discussions and came to include political action as well.

My close friends were, for the most part, fellow refugees, or students who had come up to Cambridge from Bootham. There was no hostility to foreigners that I noticed, nor was there any race prejudice. I went out for a short while with an African princess who was totally accepted among all of us. A nation with an empire could not very well discriminate at home against those natives who helped rule it, at least not in its university. Indian princes gave the most lavish parties: I was present at one, where, punting up river with the young prince, we smashed every window of Queen's College with our beer bottles; as far as I remember, no one was ever punished.

We all had a few friends in the two women's colleges, but on a daily basis this was a man's world, much the same as at school. With one exception, I subsequently lost sight of my friends of those days, for which the war was partly to blame. I was in the United States and most of them remained in Europe, and my subsequent nomadic lifestyle made it easy to become separated, especially if they did not share my intellectual interests. But the rule that Jewish refugees who volunteered for the British army had to change their names also played its part. This was a sensible rule, necessary in case they should fall into German hands as prisoners of war. Many, though, retained their English names after the war as did, for example, Hans Seligson-Netter, who had been a close friend in Berlin and in Cambridge, but whom I never found again. Another acquaintance took on the name of his best friend, killed in the war (a name change which was sanctioned at the time, though I have heard of no other such case). My immigration to the United States proved to be a real break with this past. Even so, I sometimes now get a note from someone who knew me at school or at college, especially when he has seen my name in print. Such recognition was not to be taken for granted, however, as I changed my last name from Lachmann to Mosse when I immigrated to the United States (the hyphenated Lachmann-Mosse had been dropped on leaving Germany).

Similarly, neither from my American college, Haverford, nor from my graduate work at Harvard did I, again with one exception, take away lasting friendships—those came later, when I was one of a coterie of young teachers starting their careers at the University of Iowa. To be sure, after I left school, I often fell desperately in love—usually in vain—and that may have distracted me from investing what was needed in other personal relationships. I did date women at the time and in the future, but as a friend rather than a lover. I was continent in matters of sexuality for almost another thirty years. Moreover, I became convinced early on that any distinction I might achieve in my work depended upon focusing those energies in the classroom which I might have expended upon a sexual relationship. Today, this seems a rationalization of a love that dared not speak its name, but at the time these were genuinely held beliefs. How matters would have turned out if the environment had been less hostile or, even more important, if my love had been overtly reciprocated, I cannot say.

However much one was involved with social or political life in Cambridge, the weekly essay still had to be written and discussed with one's tutor. Mr. Goulding Browne, my tutor, was based in Emmanuel (colleges sometimes had joint tutorial arrangements). He was capable but dull. I read my paper during my weekly hour with him and he then gave me his criticism. As I look over his comments on the written version of my essays, which I have kept, I realize, in retrospect, that this is truly a wonderful way of teaching—custom tailored, so to speak—painstaking and thorough.

What a pity that my thoughts were often elsewhere and the improvement in my papers minimal.

Lectures were not compulsory but I was interested enough to attend many of those offered. I attended, for example, the lectures of George Macaulay Trevelyan, whose *History of England* I had found so inspiring at Bootham. The disappointment was great. He was an imposing figure on the podium until he got out the proofs of his next book, spread them over the lectern, and began to read. The audience almost vanished, but I stuck it out and was rewarded with a conversation in his chambers. One remark he made to me at the time has obliterated in my memory everything else we talked about. When I asked him whether I should stay in England or go to America (which my father wanted me to do), he urged me to go because England was finished. This remark coming in 1938 from such a great and very English figure has remained with me ever since.

The other lecturers were not much more inspiring; they were usually dry dispensers of information. I took no lectures in what we would call modern history, for these hardly existed at the time; most instruction ended with the Victorian period in England. Practically all the lectures I attended were on medieval topics, with a few in ancient history. If one studied history at Cambridge and was interested in a modern topic it seems that one became perforce a medievalist. However restrictive this may have seemed at the time, it did give students in modern history an excellent foundation, a dimension to their studies which subsequent scholars specializing in more recent history often lacked.

Apart from my own tutor, one other teacher took an interest in me, because she thought at first that I was Felix Liebermann's nephew (in reality I was only a third cousin or so, by marriage). Helen Maud Cam was a distinguished medievalist, though her lectures on the medieval English sheriff at 8 o'clock in the morning were somewhat of a trial; her seminar was much better. Lectures and seminar both were dominated by her impressive personality, which was singularly austere. Helen Maud Cam seemed to me a typical woman don of Cambridge and Oxford; however, when after the war she became the first woman professor appointed to the faculty of Arts and Sciences at Harvard, a sea change seemed to have come over her: she drank cocktails, wore more modish silk dresses, and was a more relaxed person.

At Cambridge I was rather terrified of her. Eventually, as was the custom with dons whose seminars one attended, I had to ask her to tea in my own rooms. She arrived, we had tea, and then she went to wash up in the lavatory. Nothing extraordinary about that. But I had not reckoned with my nosy landlady, who soon enough climbed up the stairs, knocked on the glass door of the toilet, and called out for all to hear, "Young man, are you using all my toilet paper?" To say I was mortified is an understatement. Helen Maud Cam reminded me of this episode whenever I saw her, even twenty years later.

The institutional history which was her specialty seemed to me dry and empty, and the economic history which I heard with the then famous M. M. Postan seemed to be more interesting only because of his vivid personality. The history of political thought, of ideas, seemed much more challenging. The lectures by J. G. Sikes, the editor of William of Ockham's works on medieval theology, scarcely attended, were, as far as I was concerned, on a quite different level, even though he had Parkinson's disease and was at times not easy to follow. But it was George Kitson Clark who made the most lasting inspiration, both for the content and for the style of his lecturing, which was in stark contrast to our usual fare. Standing under the Holbein portrait of Henry VIII in the great hall of Trinity College, an imposing figure, he made Victorian history vivid and intellectually stimulating. When, many years later, I got to know him personally, he proved just as lively, exciting, and impressive.

My experience attending lectures at Cambridge, which was also my first real introduction to this form of teaching, taught me what to avoid and whom to imitate: the abiding lesson seemed to be that lectures, if they were not given solely for the benefit of the lecturer but kept the audience in mind, could be stimulating, a legitimate teaching tool. I became convinced even then that lectures must be something of a show if they were to hold large audiences, and that the usual academic lecture could command the attention only of those already interested in and somewhat knowledgeable about the subject. A college or university lecturer must be learned, but if he cannot hold and interest his audience, his and their time is wasted. Since I was to teach huge classes once I started my career after the Second World War, this lesson proved more valuable than much of the history I was actually taught.

There was one other course of lectures to which I went with a cousin of mine, Werner Mosse, who was also studying history (but, unlike myself, as a promising fellowship student). Those concerned the future, not the past. General (later Field Marshall) Archibald Percival Wavell lectured on the future of war. Later, during the war itself, an enterprising fellow student sold his notes of these lectures to the *New York Times*. All I remember is Wavell's statement that generals would direct future wars from helicopters flying over the battlefield—surely one of the many forecasts about the war of the future, popular at the time, which reflected the fantasy life of the author rather than the reality of combat. That we went to these lectures in spite of our quite busy daily schedule, lectures which were not part of our subjects and therefore not relevant to our examinations, shows that the possibility of war was always on our minds in those years. As a refugee from the Nazis, I was especially alert to the consequences of such a regime for the stability of Europe, and therefore for my own safety. All of us refugees believed that France was especially vulnerable: and I, for one, was much impressed with the prevailing pessimism about France's fate voiced by virtually all the French with whom I had contact (mainly shopkeepers). Because of the constant strikes and political turmoil, my belief in the presumably invincible French army was rapidly undermined. Britain was different, and I did feel relatively safe.

Politics could not be ignored in any case, and as I stated earlier, interest in politics was the fate of someone born as a Jew into the postwar world. One could not be an "unpolitical German," if indeed such a person had ever existed. Being unpolitical would mean in fact supporting all existing regimes, and that was hardly an option for me at a time when European governments, and the United States as well, were treating Nazi Germany as a "normal" nation. The policy of those governments was appeasement long before the word itself received the negative connotation it acquired with the signing of the Munich Pact in 1938 and the dismemberment of Czechoslovakia.

We were all deadly afraid of war in spite of our relative safety in England. Neither I nor my friends believed that we would survive the conflict, for powerful new weapons would destroy us and our world. Writing to my sister in 1936, I added a personal note to this fear: the next war would surely mean the destruction of Europe, and this would mean the end of our financial resources; we would be penniless. During the 1930s one seemed to live at the edge of catastrophe: we refugees were sure that Hitler wanted war, and we had a much better insight than contemporary statesmen who comforted each other that "the soup is never served as hot as it is cooked." But, then, no one listened to refugees, who were said to have their own prejudices and agenda—only this time the refugees were correct and the others were duped.

But living at the edge had its price for me—this period of waiting for a catastrophe, which seemed inevitable and perhaps even necessary if Hitler were to be overthrown, had long-range consequences. Ever since those years I have lived in expectation, if not of catastrophe, then of some accident or misfortune about to happen, and have, in my mind, planned how to meet such an imagined contingency. This attitude comes to the fore especially in travel (one reason I hardly ever check baggage on flights; it would surely get lost). However, these fears do not dominate my life, but are only bothersome on occasion; moreover in a real crisis I have been able to cope very well. Refugee life, then, has its effect: to give further examples, the fear of crossing borders, of losing one's passport, and the practice of buying gold as security (my sister even bought gold once she was settled in America when there was no more apparent need to do so).

As for myself, the menacing dynamic of the fascist regimes led to active membership in the Cambridge Socialist club, while the fear of war made me heave a sigh of relief when Neville Chamberlain returned from Munich in 1938 and the immediate danger of war seemed past. Somewhat earlier each student had received a gas mask, which gave substance to our fears (even before it became known that some of them leaked), while the military exercises of new recruits on the Cambridge commons hardly inspired confidence. My contradictory feelings, fearing war and yet accepting it as necessary to fight fascism, were widely shared by my friends in the antifascist movement to which my energy and my heart now belonged.

In some generations people can trace their political awakening to a crucial event. Recently this was the Vietnam War, which politicized the 1960s generation in Europe and the United States. This role was played for me and my generation by the Spanish Civil War, which broke out in 1936. It aroused our passions and engaged our emotions, determining our political attitudes for a long time to come. I was prepared for such a commitment. Politics had played a part in my life whether I liked it or not, and the menace from the political Right was a constant presence. The swastikas which were burned on the mountains near the Hermannsberg were a signal, and the frequent anti-Semitic outbursts and slogans which appeared in the village of Schenkendorf were constant reminders. Moreover, as I have mentioned, in our exposed position as so-called German Jewish press lords, politics was daily fare.

I had not been particularly political at the Hermannsberg, other than receiving the kind of nationalist orientation which the school fostered and Kurt Hahn advocated. At Bootham, however, this changed. There the students did take part in local politics and held mock elections among themselves. At Bootham, I became involved in a political process which previously I had known only through dinner table conversations at home. What are known as "grass roots politics" did not really exist in the Germany I knew, dominated as it was by political parties and their hierarchies. Now I

101

not only campaigned for the Liberal candidate in the mock election at school, but I also went door-to-door in the city of York campaigning for the local Labour candidate for Parliament; he was opposing Lord Halifax, who as a member of the British Tory government played a leading role in the politics of appeasement. I had a strong German accent at the time, but that apparently did not interfere with such political activity.

When the Spanish Civil War broke out I was still at Bootham. Now the lines between enemy and friend were clearly drawn: this war presented the first chance to fight openly against the fascists other than in newspaper articles and debating societies. If it was the Communist Party which mobilized Cambridge students and was largely responsible for more than doubling the membership of the Socialist club, as some historians have told us, I was totally unaware of this supposed fact when I was there. For most of us the fight against fascism was cause enough. The fate of Spain itself was a minor consideration as far as I was concerned. The democratically elected left-wing government had to be defended, but that its victory would provide the model for a new and better society—a future socialist society— never occurred to me or to many of my friends. About Spain itself we knew next to nothing.

I have always felt lucky that my first real political engagement was so clear-cut, that there was no ambivalence such as some who opposed the Vietnam War felt—a commitment to the Viet Cong can hardly be compared to our struggle for survival against the fascist tide. Looking back, I suppose that I also needed a cause in which I could believe; moreover, this cause was embedded in its own liturgy and mythology: the songs of the Spanish Civil War, the posters, meeting the men who had volunteered in the Oliver Cromwell Brigade, hearing the reports from the front.

The Spanish war was the first modern war in which propaganda was used on a massive scale. My friends and I entered wholeheartedly into what our opponents (and later historians) called propaganda, but for us was like any liturgy; it was an emotional and creative expression of truth, and the songs cemented our community. Here I received one more insight which I later elaborated in my own work on National Socialism and nationalism: the word "propaganda" is usually a hostile term which obscures what those involved felt about the self-expression such movements provide through their mass meetings, posters, dances, and songs—these were in fact an important expression of an attitude toward life as a whole.

I had been brought up without any strong emotional commitment in a decidedly liberal environment. The Hermannsberg had filled this void to a certain extent; there I was influenced by nationalism largely through the landscape and through a romantic vision which exile had now rendered obsolete—though a strong residue of this feeling remained for the rest of my life.

The Spanish Civil War gave me a focus, and at the time a commitment to the plight of the Jews threatened to vanish beneath the antifascist struggle, which we regarded as a struggle for the freedom from tyranny of all peoples, including the Jews. British neutrality in this struggle, the prohibition on furnishing arms to the Republicans, increased our urgency in seeking to help a beleaguered republic. All we could do was collect money in order to send milk to Spain, as part of a drive mounted by a prestigious antifascist coalition.

The archbishop of York, William Temple, collected money for the cause, and often boys from Bootham helped him in this mission. I myself joined him on one occasion, and for this purpose became the voice of British Youth. I found this quite normal at the time, even though it seems bizarre in retrospect. I was unfortunately much too young—seventeen years of age—to realize that William Temple, who later became archbishop of Canterbury, was one of the great progressive figures of the Anglican Church in our century.

At that stage, however, my involvement in Spain was sporadic; my energies were taken up with trying to get in to Cambridge, and, once I had attained this goal, with fighting my family about the subject of my studies. I could have involved myself in politics in France as well, where I spent so many months during my long vacations. But in France I was stigmatized as a foreigner, and it was better to abstain from political actions. I did witness the frequent disturbances and disruptions taking place in Paris. Because of a general strike, for example, one day when I arrived at the Gare du Nord from Britain there was no transportation whatever available for me to take to my father's and stepmother's flat in Neuilly, at the other end of Paris.

Still, in France, my curiosity once got the better of me. The French right wing, even if not quite so visible as the German, was covered exhaustively in the *Pariser Tageblatt,* the refugee newspaper we all read in Paris. The newspaper reported that amidst general unrest a huge gathering of the right wing, led by the political movement called Croix de Feu, was to take place in February 1934 at the square in front of the Chamber of Deputies. I went as a spectator and not as an active participant, in order to see what was going on and to listen to the speeches.

I got much more than I bargained for, as the crowd soon surged forward to storm the Chamber of Deputies, though it never reached that goal. I was carried forward by the crowd and was unable to disengage myself for what seemed the longest possible time. The dinner hour was approaching and I had to be home. I was not the only one; many others left the crowd at that moment rather than braving the wrath of Madame. This contrast to the German crowds I had known made a lasting impression upon me, and I could never take a French crowd quite so seriously again. This is the closest I would ever come to what was glorified and romanticized by many of my students in the 1960s as revolutionary action.

My political involvement in Cambridge, however, was no longer sporadic but marked my two years as an undergraduate. There I became active in the antifascist movement which had found its voice in Spain. More must be said about this movement because it influenced so many others of my generation and determined their outlook upon the world. The antifascist movement, despite its importance, has not yet found its historian, and those who have written about it have tended to look at it through the prism of the Cold War. Antifascism looked at in this manner turns into something like a Communist front, and the issue of whether or not it was dominated by the Communists becomes the central focus. This is looking at history backwards from a time after the Second World War when "antifascism" was no longer a true political movement but in effect became a Communist slogan.

I myself have a special problem looking back at the antifascist movement, for ever since I have studied fascism as a historian I have resisted using fascism as a vague term covering all the components which were supposed to form the movement. Such a use of fascism disguises the real differences among various fascist movements, and looks at fascism solely from the hostile perspective of parliamentary government—it does not help us to understand the force and attractiveness of the movement which made its dominance possible. But this consideration lay in the future: for now, antifascism embodied a political and emotional commitment, and not a historical problem which I wanted to solve. Moreover, for us in the 1930s antifascism was both a political and cultural movement in its own right, and one could join the movement, admire the Soviet Union for its lonely stand against appeasement, and yet reject communism and bolshevism as systems as well as for their materialist views of history.

Our energies were focused on defeating fascism, which threatened to engulf Europe, but beyond this goal antifascism also fulfilled a need which many of us felt strongly. This need was well summarized by the author Klaus Mann, in 1938, when he wrote that paradoxically the existence of fascism made it easier for us to clarify and define the nature and appearance of what we wanted. Belief in "the people" themselves was a constant refrain; it was they who supposedly fought against the fascists and who were commited to freedom and democracy. Such a belief in the people seems almost archaic today, but we were children of the Enlightenment who found legitimacy for our fight in supposedly executing the will of common people. That this belief was not so isolated at the time is proved by the fact that the arrival of "the age of the common man" was to be a recurring theme in Allied war propaganda during the Second World War.

Liberalism and antifascism coexisted not only in the thought of a poet like Stephen Spender but among most of those with whom I came into contact in the antifascism movement in England. Such coexistence was less likely among German antifascists because for many of them liberalism had proved a failure, but in England the liberal tradition was still largely intact. That the Soviet Union as part of the antifascist movement was itself a dictatorship was successfully ignored, with the aid of its own profession of freedom and democracy and the Popular Front, which united Liberals, Social Democrats, Trotskyites, and many others of the non-Bolshevik Left with the Communists in the common struggle. We knew nothing about the power struggle among some of these groups which took place in Republican Spain, and the eventual triumph of the Communists and through them of the Soviet Union did not affect us. We were engaged in a noble cause on behalf of the people, the struggle for freedom and democracy supported by a vibrant and creative culture which proclaimed the principles for which men and some women as well were fighting and dying in Spain. Antifascism was a totality which embraced the whole person, in itself an ideology to which I subscribed.

The war in Spain led to this commitment, but it was also fuelled by opposition to the present establishment, whose corruption was exemplified by its policy of appeasement. This opposition pushed me, and many others as well, toward socialism in our search for a newer and better form of government. Antifascism was hostile to laissez-faire capitalism, and it was skeptical of, if not opposed to, what we called the power of the bourgeoisie, which was not ashamed to compromise with evil. We focused upon the stereotype of the comfortable, complacent, and selfish bourgeois, while, paradoxically, praising true freedom, democracy, and respectability—which in and of themselves could also be considered middle-class aspirations.

Many of my friends were thus led closer to a Marxist, but not necessarily a Bolshevik, analysis of society. As for myself, while I never accepted the materialist conception of history, I did become a socialist, attracted to the model of social democracy, believing in the utopia of a society which would somehow put an end to the present establishment and the economic monopoly on which it was based, while at the same time preserving liberal ideas of freedom and parliamentary government. It may seem as if I am making very fine distinctions, but it is important to record as accurately as possible my involvement with antifascism at a time when terms such as "fellow traveler" are today applied indiscriminately to anyone sharing a common struggle with the Communists.

There was also a darker side to antifascist culture, though, again, we were not conscious of its dangers. The antifascists used some accusations against the Nazis which could have been taken from the National Socialist repertory itself. Thus it was repeated again and again, and believed, that in spite of its respectable front the Nazi leadership was a homosexual clique. The Communist-inspired *Brownbook against the Hitler Terror* (1933) was one of the main sources for this homophobia, but it was repeated by many different newspapers and journals published by German exiles. The Nazis were not the "real men" which many of the volunteers for Spain wanted to be, and about which Ernest Hemingway wrote so eloquently. Klaus Mann, who with good reason was especially sensitive to this accusation, wrote as early as 1934 that the homosexuals were the Jews of the antifascists. I, too, should have been touched by this accusation, but I was not, and unlike Klaus Mann I did not give it a thought. Perhaps this could be seen as an especially poignant example of gay homophobia, but in reality it is an example of suppression at a time when no one yet thought of coming out of the closet, when that door had to be kept tightly shut.

In addition, as it happens, our attitude toward our enemies in Spain was not free from racism either. Again, I was not conscious of it at the time; we were still far removed from the kind of sensibility on matters of race which came only after the Second World War. General Franco had sparked the rebellion against the Republic by bringing his army from Morocco to Spain, and that army was partially composed of Moroccan soldiers—"blacks" as we thought of them, the original "Moors." And this importation was branded as a crime against civilization. Though I myself was a victim of Nazi racism, I failed at the time to make the connection between anti-Jewish racism and racism against blacks. The indivisibility of racism was not yet widely accepted, and it was usual to regard anti-Jewish racism as somehow different from other racisms. But even here there were contradictions (which I, of course, did not feel as such)—for example, I dated the African princess for a while, and yet I took the separateness of blacks for granted, if I gave it any thought at all. I was, after all, a child of my time, and it seems wrong here to read a later sensibility back into this period. Winning the war against fascism was what counted, and one used all means readily at hand. Not until I encountered the antiblack racism in the United States did I proclaim my solidarity.

But what of the study of history? The lecture hall and even the tutorial were not as important for me as a series of books and the book club which published them. They were part of my political awakening. The British Left Book Club produced limp, clothbound volumes, through which, as its historian has written, it was easy to identify a left-wing, antifascist, anti-war, and pro-Soviet intellectual. As a matter of fact, the club adhered to no single left-wing ideology. Its publications followed the example of the Popular Front: it wanted to link labor, liberals, trade unions, the Socialist League, and the Communist Party. The ideology of the book club's publisher, Victor Gollancz, was close to a mystical Christian socialism—he wanted to provide the indispensable basis of knowledge without which a really effective united front of men and women of good will could not be built. The publications themselves mixed propaganda tracts with books of scholarly and factual analysis. Books by Arthur Koestler and Frank Jellinek, as well as by the Communist propagandist R. Palme Dutt, were part of the fare.

But a writer like Harold Laski was more representative in his attempt to balance Marxism and liberalism, a search which, as I have indicated, was typical for much of the antifascist movement in England. Harold Laski's books, which sought to revolutionize the establishment, had a great influence on my own thought, for he had a lively sense of history and anchored his political thought in what seemed a scholarly historical analysis. He also combined an unabashed intellectualism with active po-litical involvement (rising to the chairmanship of the Labour Party), a combination which acted as a kind of role model for both me and many others in the movement.

The book club was an enormous success, reaching some 60,000 sub-scribers and providing one of the most effective means of political educa-tion. But antifascism was not only food for the mind; action had to be paired with thought. As I look back upon it, what did we do? We held endless debates, which were useful for acquainting me with a dialectical mode of argument. To my mind, the Marxism of the Socialist club was not much to the forefront—though it was present, and some members of the club were, in fact, Communists. We were all firmly anti-imperialist and against all war, contradictory though this may seem in view of our engage-ment with the Spanish struggle. The highlight of our debates—when they received the most effective publicity—came when, in April of 1939, both the Oxford and Cambridge Unions—the universities' debating societies, arranged much like the House of Commons—debated the issue of compulsory military training. The government had just introduced a military training bill, to which we were opposed. In Cambridge, the military analyst Basil Liddell Hart spoke against conscription, but I do not remember the details of the debate, except that it was a grand occasion and my side won handsomely. I recall the sequel more vividly.

Both Oxford and Cambridge were training grounds for future leaders of Britain, and the supporters of the government's bill were concerned that this opposition would send the wrong signal to the dictators. When the Oxford debate took place, Winston Churchill's son, Randolph, was the leading speaker in favor of conscription. The hall was full, and I myself sat in the front row. The applause after Churchill's jingoistic speech was deafening, and I joined in it wholeheartedly. The support for his call to arms was in blatant contradiction to my pacifist convictions, but then in general our pacifism was hardly in tune with our militant antifascism. Cambridge welcomed those returned from the war in Spain much as the volunteers were welcomed during the Great War, and yet our wreath on Armistice Day proclaimed "against war and fascism." Perhaps we wanted to have the best of both worlds; at any rate I never saw the contradiction in our attitudes.

My applause for Churchill's speech may have been partly due to the fact that in these prewar years I rarely failed to respond to the enthusiasm of crowds. To be sure, the crowd in Paris left me no choice, but earlier, at a rally of the British Union of Fascists just outside Bootham Gate, I had the same experience. I was opposed to what was happening with every fiber of my body, and yet joined in the rhythmic shouts and movements.

Many decades later when I came to write about right-wing political mass movements, I felt that I could empathize with crowds whose actions had been choreographed so that they obtained a feeling of participation. The fascist events I had witnessed close-up—and they included some not mentioned here—made such empathy easier. We must understand the actions and commitments of people as they themselves saw them and not project ourselves back into history.

I remember traveling to Italy in 1936 with my mother and witnessing what today would be called an exercise of popular participation. The journey itself, my first visit to Italy and to Florence, almost did not take place at all. That same year Hitler and Mussolini signed the agreement for the Rome-Berlin Axis, and one clause required the expulsion to Germany of all those wanted by the regime. There was no doubt that we were on this list.

But now one of those events occurred which seem incredible but are nevertheless fact. Before he became prime minister, Benito Mussolini, the ex-journalist, toured the principal newspaper offices of European countries in order to gain support for a fascist government. My father, a good liberal, gave him that support, for Mussolini would clean up Italy ("make trains run on time") and bring order out of chaos. There was, I am sure, at that time, no talk yet about a fascist dictatorship; moreover, many reforms were proposed, which must have appealed to my father, as ever interested in all that was new.

Mussolini had not forgotten this support fourteen years later, and had a message sent to my mother that we would not be touched and that we could stay as long as we liked. (I even seem to remember that he telephoned her in Florence to quiet our fears, but this may not be true.) Perhaps this episode throws light on Mussolini's character, at least upon his sense of gratitude. There was no need for him to have intervened on behalf of powerless Jewish refugees.

But the principal episode whose memory has remained with me from the visit itself drove home the lesson I had already learned from the mass meetings I had attended, if in a different guise. A division, or a regiment perhaps—I do not remember which—had returned to Florence from fighting in the Ethiopian war. How were they welcomed? The soldiers were allowed to take over the city: they regulated the traffic and in their bright uniforms even drove streetcars. These very young men were rewarded by being given the chance to participate in actions which have always been tempting to youth (I myself remember how I would have liked to regulate traffic and drive a streetcar).

This was a different sort of participatory action from following a set choreography in mass meetings, yet it was basically the same. Even then I realized, however inchoately, that fascism controlled crowds—men and women—through institutionalizing their desires and their urge for action in the symbols of its political liturgy. How typical that some English schoolteachers with whom we had become friendly in Italy locked themselves in their rooms the day the soldiers were given the run of the city, fearing chaos and rape, a fear that would have been justified if these had been simply soldiers on a rampage permitted by the government. But instead this was highly disciplined and controlled chaos, even though those who took part could have seen it as individualism in action.

At Cambridge, even though my part in the antifascist movement—in its discussions and demonstrations—consumed so much of my energy and attention, I nevertheless was concerned with my commitment as a Jew,

109

which even led to some action while I was a student there. Until that point, it was fear of the consequences such an involvement would bring—that it would single me out as a Jew—which kept me from showing any solidarity, and at Bootham I had even declined to go to Leeds with a few of the Jewish students for the Jewish High Holidays (perhaps I remembered being singled out as a Jew for just such services at the Hermannsberg). Looking back, there was nothing very singular about my attitude. During the war, as I have mentioned already, quite a few of my Cambridge refugee friends vanished under their new English and Christian identities.

The plight of my fellow refugees finally encouraged me to work for a Jewish organization. The year was 1938, and Jewish refugees from Austria were streaming into England, fleeing from *Anschluss*—the annexation of Austria by Nazi Germany. Two organizations, one Zionist and the other non-Zionist, were set up in London to help them. I worked during the long summer vacation that year for the Lord Baldwin Fund for Refugees (named after the former prime minister), the non-Zionist organization; my interest in Zionism lay far in the future. Here I became the receptionist who directed the refugees crowding my desk to the relevant official on a first-come, first-served, basis.

Through this work I came once again into contact with the so-called native aristocracy of English Jews. When I had first arrived in England, I had been invited to the home of the Frankels, whose hostess was the daughter of Lord Bearsted. I was immediately struck by the fact that the refugees who were guests in this house were treated as absolute equals (a far cry from what I had witnessed among some French Jews). But the crowning experience of such equality came during my work at the Lord Baldwin Fund. One day, when a long queue of refugees sought my attention, the turn finally came to a rather small man; I inquired in routine fashion whom he wanted to see and then asked for his name, so as to pass it on to the relevant official. "Herbert Samuel" was the answer, and to my utter astonishment I realized that I was facing Viscount Samuel, a former member of the British cabinet and high commissioner for Palestine. It apparently never occurred to him to pull rank and to jump the queue of supplicants. I am pausing to tell this story because it seems to me to illustrate how the members of a true aristocracy should behave, and, I might say, it helped make me an Anglophile for life. Just so, the Frankels had taken in the former vice president of police of Berlin, Bernhard Weiss, who was a Jew, and who had been driven to near-insanity by the relentless attacks of the Nazis.

Many in these native Jewish circles were leaders in the Reform Congregation; thus the connection to my family. My father had met them through the World Union for Progressive Judaism. I was supposed to be confirmed in their synagogue in St. John's Wood, where Lady Montagu (the daughter of another former Jewish cabinet member) volunteered to arrange it. But nothing came of it: I was still in school and managed to get many postponements, and my father himself did not seem heavily committed to this ceremony. I can no longer remember why I objected; perhaps it was rebellion against a tradition with which I had little contact and about which I was ignorant. My commitment as a Jew was never based upon religion but was secular in nature, even when I overcame my hesitation and gave my Jewishness a more prominent place in my life.

The Cambridge period of my youth meant finally being largely on my own, responsible for freely chosen actions. I did sow my wild oats, but not unduly so. The ideals which I took away from boarding school—self-control and control over the passions—acted as a constraint, and so did an ingrained fear of authority, which was also the fruit of my earlier education. To this day I become humble when face-to-face with a representative of the powers that be, whether a policeman or a tax auditor—not to speak of the many governors, representatives, and senators I have met in my life. I consider this fear of authority the worst legacy of my German education, because although I did by and large overcome my early attraction to nationalism, I never quite overcame this handicap. The experience of being a refugee, an essentially stateless person, when confronting passport officials or applying for residence permits, no doubt encouraged such an attitude. I have always realized my own failing, however, and perhaps sought to compensate by becoming a kind of agent provocateur. But even this has not broken my inherent fear of those who are supposed to watch and rule over us.

Cambridge, then, set the course of much of my future life. I even became interested in historical scholarship, despite all the distractions, and must have been attracted to the profession of writing and teaching history at that time. This was not yet a firm commitment, however, for at Haverford, my American college, I at first majored in English literature, not in history.

I fully planned to graduate from Cambridge and live the rest of my life in England, where I felt thoroughly at home. My sister had already immigrated to the United States in 1938, believing that the march of National Socialism in Europe could not be stopped, and, as my mother said at the time, leaving the rest of us to the bombs which were bound to fall sooner or later. She had taken her medical degree in Basel and was now interning in

Schenectady, New York. When the Second World War broke out, my mother and brother were still in Switzerland, and my father and step-brother were caught by the conflict in France. But my father had previously gone to the United States, not just as a visitor—he had immigrated as a precautionary measure against whatever might happen in Europe. He got a special visa, out of turn, I believe, but I cannot say why he should have been granted such a privilege. Now, in 1939, I was about to turn twenty-one and therefore had to go to America on my father's visa before I came of age if I wished to emigrate; otherwise as an adult I would have to wait in an endless queue.

I was not keen on going to the United States. I had scarcely even met an American, except in passing at Cambridge, and this in itself says something about the isolation of that nation in the interwar years. European journalists and statesmen frequented our house in Berlin, but despite my father's position as the proprietor of renowned newspapers, only one American I can remember was a valued guest, and he was a Jewish philanthropist from St. Louis who was interested in music. None of us knew much at the time about the country which was destined to be our home, and what we knew was filtered through the sensational press. I did know that a relative of my Mosse grandmother's who had had an affair with a truck driver in Germany was promptly shipped out of sight over to the New World.

I vividly remember my last haircut just before I embarked for the United States, which took place in Chamonix. The barber on hearing my destination said: "Vous allez chez les fous"—you are going to a place inhabited by lunatics. From what I knew, I heartily agreed. It had taken threats of stopping my allowance to persuade me to go in the first place. But not all was lost: I possessed a British reentry permit, and after several weeks in New York and Schenectady, I would resume my studies at Cambridge and settle down as an Englishman, or so I thought.

7

Gaining a Foothold

Y FIRST month in the New World, instead of being the brief visit of discovery which I had planned, turned into a veritable adventure story. It all began normally enough with the kind of experience millions of immigrants had encountered as they arrived in the United States. I had crossed the Atlantic in August 1939 from Southampton to New York in some luxury aboard the *Statendam* of the Holland-America line, for it was said that first-class passengers received much better treatment from the United States immigration officers. This was surely one of the many rumors about crossing borders which circulated among refugees, for whom such passages from nation to nation were often a lifeline.

I remember that indeed I received preferential treatment, as the immigration formalities were handled aboard ship and not at Ellis Island, where passengers in steerage entered the United States. But I recall much better being on deck in the early morning as we entered New York harbor, facing the Statue of Liberty. Sometimes, even though you are aware of the myths which surround such a well-worn symbol, and are determined not to be affected, your emotions are nevertheless aroused, and so it was on this occasion. I was met by my cousin Manni, who, like my sister, had already immigrated. Though I gratefully remember her many kindnesses, I also remember that she at once remarked upon my dirty fingernails, which had become my own particular symbol among some members of my family, following me even to the New World. I had to find an apartment where my stepmother, who was soon to arrive, and I could live during our visit. I rented one on the upper West Side; it was cheap and its windows looked out upon a brick wall. That made my stepmother dislike New York from the beginning.

I bought a second-, or, better, third-hand car, an old Plymouth, so that I could visit my siter in Schenectady. There, I was fast asleep in a nearby hotel when she called me in the middle of the night on the first of September to tell me that Hitler had just invaded Poland. I berated her for awakening me with news that could have waited until the morning. Little did I know that my life would be thrown once more out of joint, and that I would again be propelled into an unknown future. Now my account of the past, for a short while, will resemble a journey into the blue yonder, and this is precisely how I experienced this turn in my new and unwelcome fate.

The outbreak of the war in Europe made it extremely risky to take advantage of my reentry permit into England because, as a former German citizen, I could now be considered an enemy alien. My provisional English residence permit, on which I had traveled to the United States, was of little use (and the Luxembourg passport, as a forgery, was perhaps of no use in the long run). The only sensible course of action was to stay in America and to try to finish my studies here. Just how well I had chosen soon became clear when German Jewish refugees living in England were interned as Germans and had to spend much of the war in camps in Canada, Australia, and the Isle of Man.

But time was pressing, and where was I to continue my studies? The fall term was about to open at American colleges and universities, and I had to find academic shelter—not just academic, for at that precise moment the money supplied by the family also threatened to dry up, and though this proved to be temporary, a solution to this had to be found as well.

At that point Miss Squire again entered my life, if indirectly, as the good fairy. I knew absolutely nothing about the United States, but I did know that there was a Quaker city called Philadelphia; as a former Bootham boy I might find help there. To take a train from New York to Philadelphia was simple enough, but it was not so easy to think of a way to approach Quakers who might help, as I knew literally no one and no institution in that city. At that point luck intervened, an absolutely essential factor in such an adventure if it is to be concluded successfully. Once I had arrived at Philadelphia's Thirtieth Street Station, I got a taxi and asked the driver to take me to the nearest Quaker institution. He took me to Friends Select School (perhaps I still looked like a schoolboy). There I immediately asked to speak to the headmaster, and, as an old Bootham boy, got in to see him at once. He explained the American system of higher education, so very different from that of England, and told me I had to get myself admitted to a college. At the same time he mentioned that the Quakers had two colleges nearby, Haverford and Swarthmore. I had never heard of either of them. A quick decision seemed imperative because of the late date (by now college had begun), and my own impatience to pass from an unknown future to a more settled existence.

I looked up train schedules and found that the Ardmore Local, which went to Haverford, departed before the train which would have taken me to Swarthmore. I took that train and walked from the station to the college (my money supply was nearly exhausted by that time). I immediately got in to see the president, once again thanks to my Bootham credentials. I have always had a great deal of affection for William Wistar Comfort, the president, who in his plainspoken Quaker manner soon uttered the magical words: "We will take thee." I stayed there, my most pressing problems solved, and, hungry as I was by then, sat down to my first Haverford meal. I had no way of knowing that Haverford was very difficult indeed to get into and that the college had a tiny Jewish quota; both factors would have kept me out had I applied in the regular manner. There were only two or three Jews at Haverford in my time. (Indeed, many years later when I was asked back to give a lecture and a Jewish student was assigned as my guide, I burst out, "What are you doing here?" By that time such quotas were, happily, a thing of the past.) I was incredibly lucky to be entering a college with an enrollment of only five hundred students, who were taught by many distinguished and widely published scholars. It was here that I was truly initiated into scholarship as a lifelong preoccupation.

I entered Haverford as a junior and therefore had to choose a major subject at once. I chose English, another lucky decision, for Leslie Hotson, who became my mentor, was one of the great literary detectives of his time. Exploiting all possible primary sources, he found out, for example, who had killed the English poet Christopher Marlowe in the sixteenth century, and also discovered some manuscripts presumably written by Shakespeare. He taught me how to do research, though I could never follow in his footsteps; I had too little patience for that kind of scholarship and was always keen to see the bigger picture. Soon I found my way back to history, though professors of English like Hotson were in reality historians, trying to reconstruct the past as the context not for kings or generals, but for famous writers instead. The only distinction between them and historians was that they dealt with a much smaller segment of the past, and in those days mostly focused on details—however small—which might place a literary passage in context.

In the history department I encountered William Lunt, an austere figure who was a historian's historian. His chief work on England's relations with the papacy in the Middle Ages has stood the test of time; he also wrote a textbook on the history of England which was used in many colleges and universities. He became my supervisor in my second year, and it was under his direction that I wrote an honors thesis, which was my very first venture in serious scholarship—for good measure, I changed my major to history. The senior honors thesis at Haverford was, for those who wrote it under Lunt's direction, the equivalent of a master's thesis elsewhere. I myself, for example, was able to use my thesis on the beginning of the English constitutional conflict in the seventeenth century as a chapter in my Harvard doctoral dissertation.

The subject which would determine my scholarship for the next sixteen years I started to study under Lunt's direction, though I had been prepared for it during my studies at Cambridge. Both at Cambridge and at Haverford, medieval and early modern history were the periods devoted to serious study. I was caught up in the study of Tudor and Stuart England in particular, but also in the age of the Protestant Reformation.

At the time I did not give any thought to why this should have been so, nor did I find it strange that someone with my background and experience should take just these subjects to heart. Was I merely following the example of my teachers in England and America (perhaps the most obvious explanation), or was it as a desperate attempt at assimilation, at conformity, that I set out to become an expert in English constitutional and Reformation history? Certainly, this was a subject strange to the German Jewish experience. That my distant relative Felix Liebermann had indeed been a famed English constitutional historian did not enter my mind at the time.

Just as I had drifted into history as a subject at Cambridge, I now drifted into early modern English history at Haverford simply because it was there. Moreover, I had acquired a good background in it already, and once I started to look into it further, I became interested. The difference between myself as a person and what I was studying and writing about was brought home to me much later by a friend and fellow historian who said, "How come that you yourself are so interesting and your books are so dull?" But I did not find my books dull, and, indeed, from the beginning tried to apply to sixteenth- and seventeenth-century English history theoretical concepts which came from my German background and my quite un-English interest in theory.

Though I was increasingly preoccupied with history, Haverford was not Cambridge, where one could immediately specialize in one's interest. As was common in America, I first had to obtain a general education. I had vaguely heard about this when I decided to stay in America, but when, in my first meeting with him, William Wistar Comfort had mentioned the science requirement, I became desperate, and with what might be called singular chutzpah—badly translated as cheek—said that I could come only if I were freed from such a requirement. Even without forcing me to explain my failure to grasp scientific subjects, he exempted me forthwith. Once again I was lucky; perhaps it was wrongly assumed that someone who had been admitted to Cambridge would have had much of his general education behind him.

If I wanted a B.A., however, rather than a B.S., which was not deemed suitable for a historian, I would have to take classics; thus another one of my academic traumas would catch up with me, though, I felt sure, no longer in the shape of having to memorize Latin irregular verbs. Haverford had a very distinguished classics department, and one of its leading scholars now took it upon himself to instruct me. For that purpose he came to my dormitory room, the kind of personalized instruction which today seems like an excursion into utopia. But it did no good—I could not do justice to Latin, and the instruction was soon stopped. I graduated as a bachelor of science and not of arts. Ten years later I was aggressively to champion general education at the University of Iowa without ever admitting that I myself had either failed or avoided such a curriculum.

Haverford was a Quaker college, and though we did not have a compulsory meeting on Sundays, as at Bootham, we did have a Fifth-day Meeting of students and faculty which took place every Thursday morning in the meetinghouse a short walk from the college. During my first year this was a regular meeting with refreshingly long silences and short messages, usually from the faculty. But during my second year the character of the meeting began to change as some students took it upon themselves to give a message, not describing some moral problem, but criticizing individual professors—castigating them for supposedly dull lectures, unfair grading, and ignoring students' needs. I remember that William Lunt came in for much of this criticism. By the time I left the college, Fifth-day Meeting was no longer a place of shared spiritual experience but a student forum which the faculty were compelled to attend. Today, I would regard such a development as almost inevitable, given the nature of a Quaker meeting, where everyone could talk (even at Bootham problems had arisen when some patients from The Retreat, the Quaker-run insane asylum, attended and sometimes spoke). I myself also aired criticisms once or twice at the Haverford meeting, though I can no longer remember the specific occasions. This meeting was eventually abolished, presumably as it no longer fulfilled its spiritual task, though as a student-faculty forum it could have continued to serve a useful and innovative purpose.

I have stressed my time at Haverford College as a learning experience, for I remember it as such, and it is as such that I have integrated it into the course of my life. But social life was of some importance as well, and it was lively, especially as some friends and I occupied a dormitory which stood apart from the rest of the campus. Excursions to Ardmore were frequent (and to Philadelphia rare—it was supposed to be too dangerous, even then). Friendships formed at Haverford did not prove lasting, however, and I do not remember many details of my social life. I do not know why both here, and later at Harvard, few lasting and continuous friendships developed, or why I stayed in touch with hardly any of my friends from school.

Here also, personal preoccupations might have contributed to making friendships more transitory. My sexual orientation has not intruded much into this account up to now, partly because I never experienced the trauma of despair which has driven other homosexual young people close to suicide because of the discrimination and the insults directed against them. Perhaps being a double outsider, both Jewish and gay, made the latter an easier burden to bear, as I became accustomed to my outsiderdom. Moreover, it is important to remember that there was no pressure or temptation to come out of the closet, unlike today, when an open, public, gay subculture exists in which one can join. It was a little like the reason for the low rate of desertion of German soldiers on the Russian front during the Second World War: where were they going to desert to? I knew nothing about gay newspapers or a gay literature, which is hardly astonishing, for the gay subculture came into its own only after the 1950s, and I discovered its existence only in the late 1960s when I was already in middle age. This could have made being gay more difficult during the first half of my life, but actually made it somewhat easier to accept a silence which seemed inevitable and for which I could compensate through a rich and very private fantasy life.

A lively fantasy life helps to come to terms with deviancy, as well as helping to keep one's feelings under control. And yet I was very often in love, unrequited love, of course, as I could not express it, and those I loved were at this time always heterosexuals. Indeed, I found their very normality attractive. Where, in any case, would I have met fellow gays at such a small college where they themselves had to be closeted? It never occurred to me at Cambridge or at Haverford to search for gay bars or similar establishments, which surely must have existed. I was so deep in the closet, to use a contemporary term unknown at the time, that it seemed to become part of my very nature, something taken for granted. But being in love did

118

direct my attention away from other, perhaps more stimulating or challenging, friends.

Immigration to the United States brought to the fore my awareness of being Jewish, something that had been partly obscured at Cambridge by the commitment to antifascism. It is difficult now to recall the depth of our shock as German Jewish refugees, when, shortly after our arrival, my mother and I were told by a travel agent that we could not have the vacation we wanted because the place we had chosen was "restricted" for Jews. As I mentioned, Haverford itself had a Jewish quota, and though this did not affect me, it was different when my application to the graduate school at Columbia University was rejected quite overtly because the Jewish quota was full.

History, like English, was a risky subject to choose for a Jew trying to make a career teaching. Indeed, as I mentioned, I had already come across this professional prejudice at Cambridge. The profession of history may well have shed its strong nationalist prejudice by this time, but those not belonging to the national mainstream were, nevertheless, considered foreigners, not to be trusted with the sacred past. This is a part of the history of my profession which has not yet been properly analyzed.

At Haverford as at Cambridge, however, I myself felt no prejudice. Here, as at Bootham, it was different for those Jewish students who, unlike me, were not exotic, but native born; in this case, though, the prejudice was even milder, and in no way consistent. Once more I was protected because of my respectable, indeed snobbish, background, which later would help me to obtain my first academic position as well.

At Haverford the fact that I was quite good at cricket no doubt aided my popularity. Haverford was perhaps the only American college at which this game was played, and while I had done my best to avoid it at Bootham, knowing the game now became a distinct asset. Teams to play against were difficult to find, apart from one other Philadelphia team; but this was wartime, and the crews of British battleships docking in Philadelphia were always ready for a game. While I was quite good at bat, I was not so good that I was in constant demand, and played only occasionally.

During my second year at Haverford, public life once again overshadowed private life. The war in Europe precipitated political activism even on this sheltered campus deep in the heart of one of Philadelphia's most prosperous suburbs. The occasion was the election of Felix Morley, a supporter of the America First movement, as president of Haverford. That movement wanted the United States to stay neutral in the war, and it opposed any aid to Britain. Such an attitude awakened in me the antifascism which had lain dormant since my arrival in the United States, and together with many other students I staged protests against the college president. Many faculty gave their support as well. As far as I remember, Felix Morley is the only human being I ever helped burn in effigy. This unrest took place shortly before commencement, when I was supposed to receive my degree, and we discussed at some length whether to disrupt that ceremony or, in my case, refuse to attend it. Nothing was done, and the protests petered out with the advent of the summer vacation. When college resumed I had left it, and the United States was shortly to enter the war.

I received my B.S. diploma in 1941 from the hands of the commencement speaker, former President Herbert Hoover. Just as I was passing the platform the procession had to stop for a moment; I thought that I had never seen such cold eyes as those of the former American president, although I had no particular dislike of his presidency, of which I knew little.

At this point I found myself facing a dilemma similar to that which had haunted my education thus far: no longer what to study, but where to take my Ph.D. in history, an aim I now had firmly in view. Yale was considered the best place for English constitutional history, where Wallace Notestein would be the major professor. But before I made up my mind I went to New Haven to consult Theodor Mommsen, whose name had been given to me by a cousin who knew him well. A historian of the Renaissance and a grandson of the famed historian of ancient Rome, he was then teaching at Yale. Theodor Mommsen advised me to take my master's at Harvard and then come to Yale for the doctorate, thus combining the two most prestigious American universities and possibly improving my prospects for obtaining an academic position. I followed his advice halfway: I never returned to Yale from Harvard, which was perhaps just as well, for Notestein's students were apt to edit English parliamentary diaries of the Tudor and Stuart period for their doctoral theses, and that would not have suited my more theoretical and adventurous bent of mind. I continued to see Theodor Mommsen from time to time, until he committed suicide after a visit to postwar Germany. Notestein himself told me about Mommsen's death when we met during a respite from work in the British Museum and were having a drink at the pub opposite. I was deeply shocked; it was the first violent death, outside of war, of someone whom I had known and who had been of great help to me.

Cambridge, Massachusetts, was not like the older Cambridge; the political and intellectual excitement which came with the kind of commitment that the antifascist movement had brought was missing, and its place was taken by deeper involvement with academic work—living in the past centuries which I was studying. And yet, this was not entirely true, since as time went on I attempted, once again, to take part in political discussions, even if no very concrete political action followed. To be sure, in the United States the Left still made an effort to maintain a united antifascist front, but I was no longer interested. The fight against fascism was now in the hands of powerful nations, and the former antifascist struggle once waged against great odds seemed irrelevant. Moreover, antifascism in America was emphasizing "against war" rather than "against fascism," and even justified the Hitler-Stalin pact. I suppose that I had never really focused on a specific program of social change, even in the old Cambridge days, but had been interested in social change in general, in the romanticism of "the people" taking charge in place of a reactionary establishment.

Marxism had interested me, but I had never really studied it as a theory of history and therefore as a blueprint for the future. Courses or seminars on Marxism (such as I was to teach much later) were unknown on both sides of the Atlantic and had no place in my official curriculum of studies. But I found out from my closest friend, who was a Communist at that time, that the eminent mathematician Dirk Struik was giving an informal seminar on Marxism at the neighboring Massachusetts Institute of Technology, and I decided to join it.

I followed in the footsteps of many young intellectuals—some later prominent—who also wanted to know more about Marxism, which was, after all, close to the center of most of our discussions on contemporary politics. When times changed and, at the beginning of the Cold War, anti-communism became an article of faith, one former participant denounced the members of this seminar, as he remembered them, to the notorious Un-American Activities Committee of the House of Representatives. I myself was endangered by this denunciation and lived through some anxious months, for I was not yet an American citizen, and my position at the University of Iowa, where I was then teaching, was far from secure. Some colleagues in the eastern United States did lose their academic jobs, but Iowa was a conservative state, whose conservatism was closer to an old-fashioned liberalism than to modern populism; the activities of this congressional committee (and later Senator McCarthy's) were regarded as an invasion of people's privacy.

My interest in Marxism took another and more original turn, however, through a combination with Christian theology, which I was busy studying as part of my work on the sixteenth and seventeenth centuries. The Oratory of St. Mary and St. Michael in Cambridge had been founded by Frederic Hastings Smyth, based upon a movement in the Anglican Church originating in the industrial city of Coventry. Its basic document was a pamphlet on the church and the working class, and this, in turn, was based on the doctrine of incarnation: that Christ is part of every human being. This meant a commitment to an essential equality which only socialism would help bring about. The church service was filled with symbols of equality and social justice, such as, for example, the blessing of the bread as the staff of daily life, or the agape, the communal meal, after the mass.

In practical terms this interest meant joining picket lines and seeing some radical Boston labor leaders attend Sunday mass in the simple chapel, which was part of an unpretentious house. Several of my friends and I became active in the Oratory, joining in such ceremonies as marking ourselves on Ash Wednesday or carrying palm leaves on Palm Sunday (much to the astonishment of our professors). But, most important, I helped to serve mass; at my request Father Smyth served mass each Sunday from different Anglican rituals. I thus became acquainted with the central Catholic rite, much to the benefit of my scholarship.

At the time I was much taken with this combination of theology and a socialist commitment which was not vague but included the Marxist drive for equality on the basis of the Marxist analysis of society, sanctified through the symbolism of the mass. But I never took the final step of conversion, and when I declined Father Smyth's request to sponsor an Oratory in Iowa City, I left this experience behind me. It had never been motivated by a true spiritual quest, but rather by curiosity and the attempt to enter Christian theology on a more profound level of understanding. There is, however, no doubt that I felt myself intellectually stimulated by this experience. Judaism, as I mentioned, had never played any role in my life, and this was the only time that I departed even slightly from my usual and accustomed agnosticism.

While studying at Cambridge and at Haverford I had learned valuable lessons about research and about lecturing; at Harvard I attained maturity as a scholar. My major professor, the medievalist Charles Howard McIlwain, impressed me with his learning, but he was a concerned human being as well. He lectured without a single note and, as he asked at the beginning of each lecture where we had ended last time, those who had missed a lecture, if they were quick enough to call out, could get a repeat of the one they had missed. Yet I never missed a lecture—they were true learning experiences.

The other lectures I attended regularly were those of Roger Bigelow Merriman, the historian of Spain and the Spanish Empire. He was an accomplished lecturer and a great narrator. Though his multivolume history of Spain is now mostly forgotten, I still think it a wonderful read, the kind of old-fashioned political history which focuses upon the story itself. Personally, Merriman was often outrageous, full of prejudice; but he seemed to like me and told me more than once that I should do my doctorate with him and not "with that fool McIlwain." The ethics of that remark made to a graduate student is questionable, but then, Merriman, as a genuine Boston Brahmin, looked down on most of his colleagues. When time came to register for the draft at the beginning of the war, he asserted that I was too good to serve simply as a private (to which I could only assent), and that he would see what could be done about it. And indeed my place later in the Army Specialized Training Program may have been due to his intervention, for he was very well connected in the Roosevelt administration.

But my real learning experience at Harvard was in David Owen's seminar in modern English history. This was far from my real academic interests, but at the time his was the only seminar in European history which I could enter. Here I was lucky, once again. David Owen was one of the rare members of the European history faculty who took a personal interest in graduate students, and who would even help them in getting positions (he was instrumental in placing me in my first academic job). He was also an excellent teacher of seminars and attracted an interesting and lively group of students. The emphasis in the seminar was on doing a research paper. I finally came into my own, producing a paper which was accepted for publication in the prestigious *English Economic History Review,* thus greatly enhancing my self-confidence. I shall say more about the "Anti-League," the subject of the paper, in a later chapter devoted to my own view of my work as a historian. At this point the paper deserves mention as my true start as a publishing scholar.

But this performance in David Owen's seminar gave no intimation of the difficulty I would have in passing my preliminary examination for the doctorate. I had never been good at passing examinations; I lacked the patience to study subjects which did not interest me, even though, in this case, they might have been required to earn the doctorate. (Such impatience was to persist. Much later, I failed the written test for the driver's license seven times because I could not be bothered to study the handbook.) Now, however, all my subjects were located within my special interest, European history before 1800—a specialization which was no longer possible after my time, as it was considered much too narrow. But I nearly failed the examination, partly because of lack of knowledge, but also because of the clash of personalities among my examiners. The preliminary examination, as it was called in my time, was an oral examination, and in

my case the committee was composed of some of Harvard's most distinguished senior historians, whose combined ages totalled something over
two hundred and twenty years.

The auguries were bad from the very beginning. As I was about to enter
the examination room, Merriman asked me to come in, but Giorgio La
Piana, another medievalist, told me to wait until I was summoned. I knew
that these two professors hated each other, but even so made the wrong
choice. I obeyed Merriman, who would have been kind to me in any case,
and not La Piana, who could and did ask impossible questions. McIlwain
and Merriman were on my side, but Sidney B. Fay, the aged German historian, had some vague idea that I had been connected with printing, and
meaning no doubt to be kind, asked questions only about that recondite
subject. Giorgio La Piana nearly ended my career as a historian. He had
been an abbot in Sicily, and his picture in full regalia had greeted me when I
went to introduce myself before the examination. I no longer remember
how the interview went, but in the oral examination he not only insisted on
asking some questions in Latin (never my strong point), but also posed
others which I was not able to answer. After the examination one had to
wait in the hallway until the results were announced (a torture since abolished). These were probably the worst minutes in my young life. When
Merriman came out he told me that I had passed "by the skin of your
teeth."

I was now free to pursue my thesis on the struggle for sovereignty between king and parliament in the early seventeenth century, and once I had
given my topic to Charles Howard McIlwain, he asked me to come back
when I had finished the book. There was no coddling of graduate students,
no holding of hands (which was to become the rule); instead, I was completely on my own. This, as far as I was concerned, was just right, excellent
training; and eventually the thesis did become a book.

Meanwhile, I was involved in a deep friendship with a fellow graduate
student which was to dominate much of my life at Harvard. Allan was
somewhat of a womanizer, resolutely heterosexual, and I do not know if he
ever realized how deeply I was in love. He was a new kind of phenomenon
for a Jewish refugee from Europe—a good-looking, very manly Jew, who
was proud of his heritage without being unduly self-conscious about it: he
accepted as natural an identity which had caused me suffering and embarrassment. Here, indeed, was the "new Jew" of my imagination, a departure
from the Jewish stereotype I had accepted as normal. As I see it now,
through the prism of my historical studies, I and so many others I knew
were prime and unwitting victims of anti-Semitic propaganda. Minorities

believing in their own stereotypes as created by the majority are a common enough phenomenon, but no less degrading for all that. I was to retain this prejudice as an important part of my life, for it had been ingrained; I will have occasion to return to this subject later, when I describe my experience living and teaching in Jerusalem.

Allan at that time was a Communist, and did not see any contradiction between this belief and his proud Jewish heritage. But it was the Party which ended a very promising graduate career when, quite arbitrarily, it ordered him to leave Harvard in order to organize factory workers on the West Coast. We were inseparable while we were both in Cambridge—"the twins," as we were called by our friend the philosopher Gurevitch and his wife, in whose house we were always welcome, and where we endlessly debated questions of Marxism and the American future. One summer I helped Allan organize the UAW bookshop in Detroit. I also went home with him on several occasions and got to know the lower-middle-class Jewish quarter of Detroit where his parents lived. I must count this friendship as another important experience of my integration into American life.

Allan was my closest but by no means my only friend. Graduate student life was very sociable in both Divinity Hall and then Perkins Hall, where I lived, and especially in the Anglican Theological Seminary, where, because it was cheap, we took our meals. All this was the normal graduate school experience. But like so many others I was listening to the broadcast of the New York Philharmonic concert when it was interrupted by the news of the Japanese attack on Pearl Harbor. I rushed to the rooms of a very good friend of mine who lived next door and shouted, "Your country is at war," whereupon he shouted back, "Say 'our' country." Obviously I was not yet fully American and, as a matter of fact, still often thought of the United States as "they," however much I continued to admire some American characteristics. What was so refreshing at the time was precisely the absence of the stifling nationalism which I had found in Europe, not necessarily aggressive but always characterized by an unspoken division between "us" and "them."

Here the contrast with an experience which occurred when I was a student in the older Cambridge seemed striking. With a friend I used to go to listen to trials at the Old Bailey, London's criminal court, and whenever someone with a Jewish name testified, the judge invariably asked, "Is he English? Can he understand the English language?" And this in a country priding itself on its toleration and muted nationalism.

America's entry into the war first began to intrude into my life in a bizarre way. The Chaplains Corps trained at Harvard, and as part of this training practiced the digging of graves all around Divinity Hall, where I lived. For me, a broken leg was the consequence, but it did not prevent me from presenting myself at the Cambridge draft board early in 1942 as a volunteer before my turn in the draft had arrived. However, this was not only in vain but proved counterproductive. I passed the physical, answered all questions, and finally appeared before the colonel in charge, ready for induction—or so I thought. He was Jewish, at least so it appeared, and after taking one look at my German passport, the only relevant document for this occasion which I possessed, asserted that the United States did not need Prussians in its army. It could surely not have been my appearance or even the German passport itself (with a "J") which were at issue, but that such passports listed in a prominent place the German state to which their holders belonged, and in my case this had been Prussia. I had been discriminated against because I was Jewish, but now to be discriminated against because I was a Prussian, that was new and unexpected. I was now 4F, that is to say, unfit to serve, and until I later obtained a position with the Army Specialized Training Program I was not able to contribute to a war effort which I regarded as the climax of our antifascist engagement.

I have never quite understood why I should have been given this particular classification. Surely, on reflection, being born in Prussia could not be reason enough. Was my loyalty suspect as "a premature antifascist," to cite a United States Army classification? That could hardly have been the case; I was not a recognized leader of the antifascist movement, nor had I fought in Spain. Was my homosexuality, which was supposed to be a secret, the reason? If so, how could this have been known, as I had no contact with gay society or its organizations and, moreover, had been totally chaste? My secret longings or my fantasy life could not have been known to the United States government, and if by any chance they had been discovered, then hundreds of thousands must have shared my fate. The mystery remains.

Yet, I was not immediately concerned, for life at Harvard went on much as usual. To be sure, there were interruptions—one of them when I was asked to act as guide to a rather formidable Russian female soldier who had been invited to the United States as a reward for her effectiveness as a partisan and sniper behind the German front. But I was now involved with the approaching preliminary examination and the problem of then finding a job. The latter was going to be no easy task. Somewhat earlier Arthur Schlesinger, Sr., the famed historian, had told the assembled graduate students that Harvard was not obliged to help them find positions but was concerned only with their education. I know many of my fellow graduates whose bitterness toward Harvard was long lasting as a result of such arrogance and contempt. Even then many professors individually would try to find places for their students, and some departments in other universities—like, for example, the University of Wisconsin—took pride in their placements. I never felt such bitterness toward Harvard, for I was rescued by David Owen, if in the short and not in the long term. He got me a temporary position for the summer session of 1944 teaching Tudor and Stuart England at the University of Michigan. That was certainly an excellent start. My graduate days seemed past, though I was not yet far advanced with my thesis.

There was, as a matter of fact, no pressing reason for me to leave Harvard, for I was well taken care of. When I entered graduate school it was clear that with my spotty academic record no scholarship would be waiting for me. My parents paid for the initial years, but then I miraculously found in the Harvard catalogue a scholarship reserved specifically for those born in Berlin-Charlottenburg. I guessed correctly that the competition could not be great, and that all I had to do was prove that the side of the Berlin street on which I was born was indeed Berlin-Charlottenburg, for it happened that the borderline between Berlin proper and this suburb ran down the center of the Maassenstrasse. I became a Holzer Fellow, which gave me some money and looked very good on my professional résumé, especially as no one knew the terms of that fellowship. Even so, my mother continued to provide me with a small subsidy. It came from the sale in 1939 of the Rudolf Mosse advertising agency in Zurich, which the Nazis could not touch; for the time being that gave the family enough money to live on, if in nowhere near the old splendor.

Nevertheless, I wanted to get out and start a career, not out of love for hard work (that came later), or even an adventurous spirit, but out of fear of being caught up in Harvard life without being able to cut loose, as well as to disprove the contention of those (not only in my family) who said that I would never earn a living as a historian and, in any case, was too spoiled to face the adjustments and hardships needed to make good in the real world. I was vividly reminded of what being stuck at Harvard might lead to when I came back for a visit from my first teaching post at the University of Iowa. The steps of Widener Library had been the place where graduate students gathered when they wanted to take a break from their work. One history graduate student in particular was a fixture on the steps, and when I returned after more than a year he stood on the spot where he had always stood and asked me, "Where have you been lately?" assuming that I too had never left. And here I was, a visitor from a different planet, filled with new experiences. This particular student got a position at a neighboring university and was to spend his whole life on one minor scholarly project. Clearly no one could have been more different from my own impatient and restless self.

As for disproving the reputation gained from my mischievous and flighty persona, as I have described it from my life in Berlin and even later, my first paycheck and the fact that I lasted at my first real position sufficed (even if few I knew had ever heard of the University of Iowa). I was and still am satisfied that I left Harvard as soon as I could, without having finished my thesis, even if it was to prove daunting to write a book while spending sixteen hours a week in the classroom.

My academic education, properly speaking, had come to a close. Through it I had, almost by accident, found my profession and had accumulated a store of historical knowledge, which, though not in modern history, would prove an excellent background for all my work. And I had even experienced some intellectual excitement along the way.

I was now about to enter the Iowa period of my life, which I regard as one of my chief defining moments. This could not have been foreseen when I arrived early one morning in the autumn of 1944 at the Rock Island Railroad Station in Iowa City. The taxi took me to a hotel on the main street of town. As I looked up and down the street, the row of houses seemed to begin nowhere and to taper off into nowhere, a speck in what I thought of as the great steppe. And though I had already freed myself from the many constraints imposed at home and at school, had, as it were, left the broom closet where as a child I had to do penance, I was unprepared to face such unlimited spaces. I felt lost, and indeed began to cry, perhaps out of fright or out of despair that my academic journey seemed to have ended in another exile, this time perhaps from civilization as I had known it.

I could not have been more mistaken. Iowa City may have been an academic and artistic oasis in that predominantly rural setting, but it was one brimming with creativity and intellectual excitement. I would never again experience quite such intense stimulation as in those years in the heart of the American Middle West.

8

The Iowa Years

THE UNIVERSITY of Iowa, as I saw it in 1944, was a strange mixture of avant-garde, sharp young faculty and elderly men gone to seed. The avant-garde aspect was the most striking, especially for one concerned with cultural history. The departments of art history, fine arts, creative writing, and theater were then at the height of their creativity and power, and it would have been difficult to find their equal anywhere else. They formed a contrast with the relative remoteness of Iowa City, the absence of an urban hinterland, and the seemingly endless cornfields which surrounded the small town (the population at the time was roughly 25,000). To be sure, Cedar Rapids, a city of some 60,000 inhabitants, was nearby, connected to Iowa City by an old-fashioned tramway, but in that town there was apparently no notable cultural life which could attract those living in Iowa City, and I remember visiting Cedar Rapids only a few times during my years at the university.

Why then this flowering of the arts at this place and at this time? It was due largely to an inspired dean of liberal arts, Carl Seashore, an old Norwegian, who in the 1930s wanted the University of Iowa to excel in something that was new and affordable, and that other universities lacked. The School of Fine Arts was his creation. I drifted at once into the orbit of its faculty—painters like Philip Guston and poets like Robert Lowell, among others—and in such company I completed my education which, in a serious manner, had begun at Cambridge University.

This education had bypassed the modern in the fine arts. As a historian I did have some sense of historical background in the arts, but this was confined to the classics. And even in Berlin, in a household dedicated to the appreciation of music and art, where the moderns in music were discussed, modern painting was hardly mentioned. Here, as elsewhere, bourgeois taste ended with the French Impressionists, joined by a very few Expressionist painters and composers of the 1920s. As far as music was concerned my own rejection of the moderns would not change; even today I have no ear for the new musical vocabulary.

The theater was different, and the newest plays, such as Bertholt Brecht's *Threepenny Opera,* were eagerly awaited. Thus I did not need much reeducation about the modern theater. Not only was its avant-garde accepted in my family, but my brother showed a special interest in the new and experimental, and I was allowed to share something of this interest. He had a genuine commitment to theater and film, but one that he was never allowed to translate into a chosen profession. Just as preoccupation with history was not considered fit for earning a living, so theater and film were not considered serious professions which one could enter for a lifetime of productive and remunerative work. My brother was by no means the only son of a successful bourgeois family whose life was blighted by the forced rejection of his real interests for a so-called respectable profession. Much later, from the 1950s onwards, when I advised students, parents would come in to my office complaining that their sons wanted to major in history whereas they should become doctors or lawyers.

The lessons I was taught in Iowa City were in the fine arts and in literature: those were the departments where I had the most friends and from which many of my students came as well. Especially when I learned about modern art my eyes were opened to a new world, one I had not even considered before. In 1946 and 1947 I attended lectures given by Mary Anne Holmes, a professor of art history whose explanation of what was then contemporary art I have never seen equalled. Indeed, members from a variety of faculties attended these lectures, which were not simply another academic course, but cultural events. She never wrote much, but she is a good example of the kind of teacher who enriches lives. She left Iowa City for a post at Ohio State University only two years after I had arrived, but by then her lectures and my friendships with artists who were actively engaged with their craft had done their work.

My further education illustrates one important dimension of university and intellectual life which was present then, but seemed often to be missing in later years. At Iowa one had the feeling of being part of a group characterized by a camaraderie of shared interests in which it mattered little to which department one might belong, even though it was confined, for the most part, to the humanities. Because of the variety of people who belonged to this purely informal group, many from strong departments, like the English department, this in itself was a learning experience. Conversation tended to be serious: we were all young together, all deeply engaged in research and analysis, wanting to make our way in the academic world. We were committed and ambitious; life lay before us. I do not think I am glorifying my Iowa years; they were crucial in broadening my outlook not just in the arts, but also, as we shall see, in public service and even politics. However, my feeling that such a camaraderie was absent in later years may well be due to the recollection of youth and what it meant, for I was to encounter academic friendships throughout my career, some of them deep and decisive.

The rapid increase in size of the state universities where my academic career was spent made such an ecumenical camaraderie ever more difficult. But the liquidation of so-called core programs for undergraduates, courses which were compulsory and offered only a very limited choice for students, also aided in the fragmentation of the faculty. At Iowa, such courses had provided a constant forum for debate and discussion, not just for all of those like myself who taught them, but for the whole faculty, which had to approve such programs. The fact that lively departments sponsored events in which faculty from different departments took part was also important. I have mentioned the art history lectures, but readings and discussions in the Writers' Workshop must be mentioned as well. Moreover, certain "salons," almost in the European meaning of the term, were centers of social and intellectual life. Thus my friends Jean and Alex Kern, both specialists in American and English literature, had just such a hospitable house. There one could often meet the kind of interesting visitors from out of town who today are apt to pass through university towns known only to their host department. The very isolation of Iowa City made for an intense intellectual life, even if it also encouraged deep enmities and an undue emphasis upon quirky personality traits.

The Humanities Society deserves special mention: it was a membership society which encompassed all of the humanities and brought most of the distinguished academic visitors to the campus. To give only one example, during the year 1947–48, when I was secretary-treasurer and later president of the society, we invited the poet Stephen Spender, the sociologist Louis Wirth, the philosopher Raphael Demos, and J. E. Morpurgo, the English literary critic. They were paired with our own faculty as discussants and commentators. I vividly remember the time, when I was presiding over the society, that the English medievalist Sir F. M. Powicke, reading from his own autobiography, was moved to tears. The beautiful room in which the society met added to its attraction: the centerpiece of

131

the campus was the old state capitol, and the society met in the senate chamber.

The Humanities Society is one more illustration of the relative coherence of the faculty, which meant a speedy integration into university life, and furthered a broadening of one's outlook. The Humanities Society was a forum where one could meet colleagues from departments other than one's own, but faculty meetings also served as a vehicle for acculturation, this time across the entire university spectrum. Eventually meetings of the whole faculty, presided over by the university president, would no longer prove feasible in rapidly growing state universities, and would be replaced by an elected representative faculty body. And indeed, at the University of Wisconsin, where I taught next, they were discontinued with the large influx of new faculty members in the 1960s. But at Iowa at this time the whole faculty still met regularly, and the debates were lively.

I took part in these debates, especially in matters concerning the core curriculum. But perhaps my greatest triumph came with a motion I introduced after I had been in charge of the large Western Civilization core course and was subjected for several years to pressure from the athletic department to pass football stars who were either incompetent or too short of time to do justice to their studies. I proposed that football as a part of the university program be abolished, and that instead the Chicago Bears be hired as artists-in-residence, following the model of the artist-in-residence program in the art and music departments. The motion passed, and I got some satisfaction in seeing the usually unflappable president, Virgil Hancher, turn white. Though my motion made the local and national press, it was stillborn. The president managed to circumvent it, and the only lasting result was that I got the reputation of being the scourge of the athletic department. Some five years later when I was interviewed for a position at the University of Wisconsin, sitting at lunch in the University Club with members of the history department, a gentleman came up to the table, shook my hand, and said that he hoped we would get on together. That I was such an important person in the eyes of the head football coach no doubt increased my reputation and caused much amusement among my future colleagues. However, had my motion been enforced, it would have ended, in one place at least, one of the largest sources of academic corruption at football-conscious universities.

Academic involvement and dialogue were helpful not only in my continuing education, but also in further acclimatizing me to the new surroundings, in fostering the feeling that here I might be at home. Social life was not neglected. The social event of the academic year in my first years on the faculty was the Beaux Arts Ball, sponsored by the art department, a costume ball which seemed quite daring for its time. But the university president, who was never comfortable with anything outside the traditional, saw to the dance's respectability. An order was passed down as to how long a woman's skirt must be for her to be admitted to the ball, and many of us, as a protest, amidst great hilarity, took out a measuring tape and proceeded to measure the skirt of every woman who entered the hall. Other dress codes soon followed, and a few years later the dance was discontinued by the conservative director of the School of Fine Arts, who was afraid of offending the regents and the university administration. He was not himself an artist or art historian, but had been appointed by the president for the sake of public relations. There was bound to be tension between the avant-garde in the School of Fine Arts and the Iowa public. I remember the painter James Lechay telling me that people from the hinterland often asked why he painted green fishes, if in reality this was a color no fish possessed.

But Iowa City itself was much more tolerant. The poet John Berryman, for example, who was visiting the Writers' Workshop, decided one day, dressed in nothing at all, to lead an ostrich down the main street, and no one seemed to take special interest. Just so, Iowa City seemed to mimic Montmartre when the same poet, in a dispute over a sonnet, smashed a beer tankard over a student's head. Of course, not all visitors were this colorful, but many had something to say, or presented attitudes toward life which were quite foreign to the academy, the kind of environment which I knew best.

For several years the poet Robert Lowell and his wife Elizabeth Hardwick were my colleagues. One year, as I remember it, Robert Lowell and I decided to visit some of the forty-nine fundamentalist evangelical congregations active in and around Iowa City. Many were tiny, and when we as guests were called upon to give witness, I used to say to Robert Lowell, "You do it, you are a poet." And he did it very well indeed. But afterwards the poet's and the historian's views would compete in a fruitful discussion.

But what about my own field of history? When I arrived, that department was much less interesting than the others which I have mentioned. Most of my colleagues had been at Iowa for a long time, and their earlier scholarly promise had faded. They disguised this failure through their pompousness or the poses they took. To be sure, the head of the department, Winfred T. Root, appreciated scholarship and had appointed one rather scholarly older, if dry, European historian. Chester Clark was very friendly, but at one point berated me for having put a red cover on my

133

sourcebook for the Western Civilization course, which can tell us something about the atmosphere even before the Cold War had properly begun. He left to join the CIA only a semester after I had arrived. I myself had been instrumental in persuading Root to hire a friend of mine from graduate school as the medievalist. He was an excellent scholar, but, as it turned out, driven by ambition, which increased markedly the competition for a place in the sun, that is, in the grace and attention of the department head, who was an absolute monarch in his realm.

Winfred Root had once been a very promising scholar and was a decent man, but easily swayed. The head of department system no longer exists today—certainly an advance over previous times. Although Root himself was a benevolent dictator there were others who were vest-pocket tyrants. As soon as Root came in to his office he went to a nearby coffee shop, and it was there that one had to visit him if one wanted to get anything done. His two principal senior colleagues were very different. One was a distinguished scholar of the Middle West, Louis Pelzer, editor of the *Mississippi Valley Historical Review* (my very first publication [a book review] was placed in this unlikely journal). His relationship with Root was rocky, going back to almost prehistoric times, and he played no role in the department itself. But the other senior colleague, an American historian, born in England (which he kept rather secret), was the sort of figure who seems to have vanished from academic life, and were he alive today, would not be taken seriously. Harrison John Thornton had written one book (a company history) in the past and was engaged in writing the university's history, but in reality his scholarly activity lay behind him. Instead, he was an old-fashioned orator of the kind once popular in the Middle West, not unlike the itinerant preachers who had toured the country providing motivational and uplifting speeches. He still gave such speeches all over the state. However, his oratory carried over into his private life, where it was transformed into a certain pomposity. He took on a weighty demeanor and used many big words where one simple word would have sufficed.

I do not mean to denigrate this kind of oratory, which served a function as a means of communication at a time when as yet few other media distracted men and women from paying attention. I myself perhaps benefited from the afterglow of this tradition, once I had discovered my talent for public speaking. I began to speak to a wide variety of audiences, from Lions Clubs to Red Cross meetings and high school commencements. The topics also covered a wide spectrum: some, for example, "The Future of Liberalism," were still related to my profession, if not to my immediate scholarly interests at the time, while others, such as "What Price Freedom?" or "Freedom For What?" were mostly inspirational. I shall return to such activities later.

Even aside from these colleagues, there was one other of that older generation whom Winfred Root had brought to Iowa when he became head of the department not long after the First World War. This professor had given up on scholarship and teaching long ago; all that was left of the former promise was, again, a certain pomposity in comportment and language. He was not alone—there was, for example, one professor from another department who must also have given up, and who dressed like an elderly Shakespearean actor, sporting a white mane and a flowing cape. These men may have been eccentrics, but in contrast to the vigorous and active younger faculty they represented a difference that was stark and startling, a warning never to let go (and therefore partly responsible for my writing these memoirs as I am about to enter the ninth decade of my life).

This academic landscape changed drastically in 1947, not many years after I had arrived, when Winfred Root died suddenly of a heart attack. Harrison John Thornton was poised to take his place, but we Young Turks organized to prevent this, aided by a new colleague who was the son of the president of Princeton's Institute for Advanced Study and who had excellent ties to our snobbish president. William Aydelotte persuaded the president to allow an election to take place for the first time in history. It was organized on the spur of the moment, with ballots gathered in an old hat of mine. Bill Aydelotte was elected chairman (no longer head), not just to make it easy for the president to accept this election, but because he was generally respected. Our choice was fully warranted, for now a new and distinguished chapter in the history of the department began.

Soon new faculty were added, always after a most thorough selection process, and nearly all of them became distinguished scholars and eventually moved on to major research institutions. I used to say that any historian who had not passed through Iowa was not worth his salt. New kinds of history were pioneered, such as the use of statistics in historical research, and an attempt was made to build bridges between history and other social sciences. The old order was definitely dead.

Yet I was once again the insider as outsider: I took part in departmental business and made close friends with many of the new arrivals, but once Bill Aydelotte had pioneered the statistical approach to history, I stood aside from the scholarly discussions. I had no training in mathematics and was not enthusiastic about the nature of this research, especially as its practitioners seemed to find it difficult to arrive at coherent, publishable, analyses. But then, I was at the time leaving the constitutional and legal history in which I had been trained for what is sometimes called the history of mentalities, or, rather, for a kind of cultural history which I tried to make my own, dealing with perceptions, myths, and symbols and their popular appeal. When I talked about my research I had as partners philosophers, literary scholars, and art historians, rather than historians as social scientists. I very rarely joined the almost daily lunches at the Mad Hatter Restaurant, just off campus, where my colleagues discussed problems of historical research.

But I was also put off by their very seriousness. Bill Aydelotte did have a private sense of humor, but in public he was always deadly earnest and I think hardly appreciated it when I made fun of him, or seemed to take research too lightly. His disapproval was often justified, as, for example, when I started playing merry tunes on the complicated calculator the department had acquired for its statistical work. But then, as I have said, I have never been able to take myself too seriously, perhaps as a result of not having been taken seriously as an individual during most of my youth. Yet this attitude has stood me in good stead during crises and kept me from undue arrogance when, in my seventies, quite a few honors came my way. When the *laudatios* were read I always felt like laughing, "What? me?" Perhaps this view of myself has even helped me look at history more impartially. But at Iowa it kept me from truly entering a community of scholars such as I have not found, at least among historians, anywhere else.

Nevertheless, within this professional context I made my way rapidly, and this without having to spend overly much time in the coffee shop. When I arrived in Iowa City toward the end of the war most of my time was taken up with the Army Specialized Training Program, training soldiers for occupation duty in Europe. These soldiers were divided into two groups, one to occupy part of Czechoslovakia, and the other to be stationed in France. Oddly enough, the groups, though made up of conscripts, were quite coherent: those who were to occupy Czechoslovakia were nice and polite midwestern boys, and those destined for France were for the most part rather aggressive and contentious eastern Marxists. The latter presented a formidable challenge to what was, after all, my own first real teaching assignment. No statement about French history or ethnography was left unchallenged, and I only wished I had spent much more time in Dirk Struik's seminar on Marxism. But this was certainly an excellent baptism by fire, and I never regretted it (except at the time).

Meanwhile, the College of Liberal Arts had instituted a course on the history of Western civilization as part of the core curriculum. I was assigned to this course, at first teaching discussion sections. This was another piece of luck in what seemed like a string of fortunate occurrences. The war ended after I had been at Iowa nearly a full year, and the army program of which I had been a part was discontinued. As a matter of fact, all those soldiers whom I had drilled in French or Czech history so that they might be better occupiers were speedily sent to Japan. So ended what must have been one of the more useless war services; but it was not an unusual fate for many of those engaged in warfare, which often does not live up to its customary billing of performing useful service for one's country, let alone saving the country and showing so-called manly courage.

But I was now out of a job. I had been hired for the Army Special Services, and my assignment in the history department had been considered secondary. I was saved by the GI Bill, through which the nation paid for education for war veterans, who now streamed into the universities. This meant in practice lecturing to crowded classes and to an audience which was mature and critical. The Western Civilization course mushroomed rapidly from an enrollment of barely one hundred to over eight hundred by the fall semester of 1949–50. These numbers seem unreal as I write this nearly fifty years later, and yet it was true, and there were many sections taken by teaching assistants. I had in the meantime been enlisted to lecture as well as to teach sections, which meant becoming a full-fledged member of the history department. I never went through a formal appointment procedure at Iowa but simply slid into my new position, at first tentative and scandalously low-paying. But this changed when I proved my effectiveness in the Western Civilization course.

I was now in charge of the teaching assistants, who were at the same time graduate students. Soon I made an arrangement with a colleague at Brooklyn College, then home of some of the brightest students anywhere, but lacking a graduate school, to send students to Iowa for graduate study supported by assistantships in the Western Civilization course. This core course became both my in-house training in lecturing and my vehicle to academic success within the College of Liberal Arts.

Lecturing over a period of years to so many students and at the same time building a reputation as an exciting lecturer meant acquiring skills which stood me in good stead at Iowa, and then later at the University of Wisconsin, though there my classes were never as large. Still, in both universities I managed to build up the freshman course to undreamt-of enrollments. I cannot say with certainty what it was that made my lectures so successful; perhaps teaching is a gift one has or does not have, one that is difficult to teach. But even if this should be so, there are methods and ways of teaching which can be taught and which are of help when standing

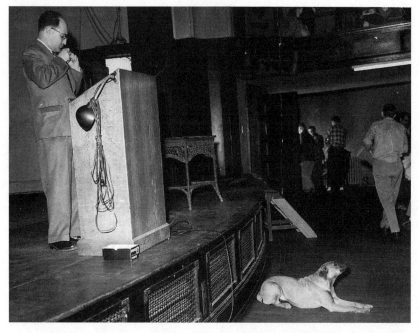

The University of Iowa, 1951, after a lecture to a large postwar class

before a class. I was never taught how to teach, nor was I given any advice. Yet I had learned by sitting through lectures at Cambridge and Harvard that boredom is one of the greatest enemies of education. I had to find my own way, and somehow it worked.

Certainly, personality is involved: the more forcible your personality, the easier it is to keep the students' attention. But a sense of mission is also vital—it will communicate itself to the students. Speaking clearly and having a definite structure to your lectures are necessities. I have been appalled, for example, at how many academics believe that the letter *e* or the sound "ah" is meant to link words or sentences. I also soon learned to single out a few selected students with my gaze, which seemed to bring all of them nearer. Moreover, it never occurred to me to read my lectures, though I have always written them out in order to have them firmly in mind. There is nothing more apt to be boring, to my mind, then a lecture read before a considerable (and often somnolent) audience. German professors especially seem to read their lectures in an even, unmodulated voice, perhaps because in German the words for lecturing and reading are identical. To give an extreme example: I was presiding over a lecture by a very fine German scholar when I was teaching in Jerusalem. The thick sheaf of paper he brought to the podium heralded no good, and indeed he went on and on in his monotonous voice. Soon people began to leave until only two or three of the audience remained, but he went on reading until the bitter end.

You might as well not lecture at all, and save yourself the trouble, if you cannot hold your audience and interest them in what you have to say. Some of my colleagues have been shocked when I have likened lecturing before good-sized undergraduate audiences to a show; you must communicate knowledge, but not in the manner in which I was taught at the Gymnasium: dry facts are soon forgotten. You have to use your voice, even body language, to focus attention and communicate what I like to call the rhythm of history. This means a certain simplification, but once the students have been given a structure, a way to approach and to make some sense out of events, they can fill in or even reject viewpoints and find a structure on their own.

I have found it most effective to teach history within clearly defined parameters of geography and chronology so that the subject matter can have a certain natural coherence. The course entitled "The History of Western Civilization" was in reality a modern European history course with a bent toward cultural history. At first it was supposed to combine U.S. and European history, but this did not work well, not because I myself knew little about U.S. history, but rather because the subject matter was too diffuse and lacked the necessary coherence.

My curricular battles with colleagues centered upon my realization of this, as there was constant pressure to change the core program into one of "Great Books" or into a smorgasbord of academic fields and cultures. What is called multiculturalism today is fine in theory, but in practice it is apt to leave the student without any one solid foundation from which he can extend his knowledge. At that time I won my battles, largely owing to the success of the course. Today I would be sure to lose in the name of multiculturalism. Students should learn about cultures other than their own, but they will do it better if they have a firm basis from which to proceed.

At first my senior colleagues took turns lecturing in the course, but they soon preferred that I cope with the ever larger audience. Through the way in which I ran the course I got into the good graces of the dean as well, and about three years into my stay at Iowa I decided to take my fate into my own hands in a rather daring move in order to obtain tenure. I was afraid of the jealousies that had begun to build up among my colleagues, but, above all, I was tired of waiting to take this hurdle and decided to face it at once.

(Impatience, as I said earlier, has always been a characteristic of mine.) I knew that Earl McGrath, the dean at the time, was very keen on the success of the core program, and therefore I decided to risk a bluff. One day when I met him on the stairway of the hall where both his and my offices were located, I mentioned that I was seriously thinking of leaving Iowa and moving east. I said nothing about an offer, which would have been an outright lie; nevertheless my little bombshell worked, and I was immediately assured of promotion to tenure.

The success of the course had another far-reaching effect, however, aside from my promotion or even my friendship with this remarkable dean. It proved important for the offer I was to receive from the University of Wisconsin in 1955, by way of an episode having to do with athletics. When the new football coach was given a Cadillac by alumni as a welcoming present, students and some faculty decided to protest this overvaluation of athletics at the university. One day as I climbed onto the platform in order to lecture to my class, by then numbering more than five hundred students, some students and fellow faculty members surprised me with a mock ceremony, presenting me with keys to my old, beaten-up Dodge. This immediately became a media event, as we would say today (the *Des Moines Register* even ran a front-page cartoon about it), and persuaded my future colleagues in Madison that I must be a good teacher, and the right person to build up their own freshman history course.

I taught not only the Western Civilization course but also early modern European history, and began to have graduate students besides. When I began at Iowa I had sixteen hours of classroom contact, much of it in discussion sections (at a salary of $1,800), and while this load did diminish later, I remember it with awe. Not only was I expected to publish, but I was still writing my doctoral thesis. With energy that today I can barely imagine, between 1944 and 1946 (when I received my doctorate) I worked nights to finish my thesis and managed to do so in a year and a half (without that no tenure would have been possible), and what is more, to publish my first two articles.

I suppose being focused helped, and I was totally devoted to my academic tasks; that was my little world, and my fantasy life had to make up for the rest. Ambition was crucial here as well; I was determined to make a mark in my profession, to make good, as it were, and this ambition never left me. Was it due to a very differently oriented youth? Or to belonging to a minority group where it was always emphasized that Jews had to do better than everyone else? (Being gay was of no concern as yet—the idea that homosexuals could constitute a legitimate minority was still far in the fu-

140

Posing with car keys presented by the students and faculty friends, Iowa City, 1954

ture.) I do not want to go in for self-analysis here; perhaps such ambition was just part of my character, like my drive to accomplish the tasks put before me, or my impatience with anything that moves slowly, from people to objects. Standing in line is torture, and I have never willingly waited for a table in a restaurant. Fortunately, however, I have been able to subdue such personality traits when it came to teaching or research, though somewhat less as the years wore on.

My research certainly required patience and concentration, for it was based on a close reading of the sources. That held for my doctoral thesis as well as for other books which I managed to write during my Iowa years. All those books dealt with English constitutional history or political thought in the sixteenth and seventeenth centuries. These were certainly respectable, indeed core subjects at the time, and subjects in which I had been trained at Cambridge, Haverford, and Harvard. That they were also far removed from my own origins may have played an unconscious role as I tried to dive into my new Anglo-Saxon environment.

But even at that time I was already looking ahead and starting to investigate National Socialism, a subject which I had avoided, perhaps because it touched me so closely. Nearly two decades had now passed since I had arrived in the United States and there was no more need to immerse myself in a respectable Anglo-Saxon subject in order to distance myself from my past as an outsider. I have no good explanation for my switch to modern history, which occurred even before my position at Wisconsin locked me in place as a modern historian. Surely my interest in the more recent period had always existed, but my graduate training had been entirely in the earlier periods of European history. History was divided into clearly marked fields of study, and one was not allowed to trespass. I was the early modernist and at Iowa there was no way to break out (except in the course on Western Civilization, where I already began to emphasize the fascist experience).

If at Cambridge I experienced my political awakening, at Iowa I completed a vital step in my self-formation; I became truly mature and my life took on the direction which it was destined to keep. My own family receded still further into the background. I was now largely self-sufficient, earning a living and doing what I liked thousands of miles from the Eastern Seaboard where all of them lived.

And yet the last reunion of the immediate family, my mother and us three siblings, took place in Iowa City, in 1948, on the occasion of my mother's sixtieth birthday. I was now a homeowner and could show off this sign of independence as well. I will not say a "proud" homeowner, for the house itself was rickety, though it possessed a flowering cherry tree, and the "easterners" did not have to know that I had to get up twice in the middle of the night to stoke the furnace. They seemed duly impressed at the time (making no comparisons to Berlin or Schenkendorf). This was the first and the last time my mother penetrated so deeply into America. I remember this as a successful gathering, but from now on the four of us

The family celebrating Felicia Mosse's sixtieth birthday, Iowa City, 1948

would never again get together for an uninterrupted happy period of time. Here too Iowa City was both an end and a beginning.

Iowa City was also a vital step in my Americanization, in a manner which few refugees even of my generation have experienced. It helped that there were relatively few refugees on the faculty. Kurt Lewin, the well-known psychologist, was still teaching during my first year, but our acquaintance was fleeting. Gustav Bergmann in philosophy was the most visible refugee on campus, a distinguished logical positivist, yet a difficult person, opinionated and combative. He might have said the same about me, but, as a matter of fact, hardly any of his colleagues managed to get along with him. We clashed straight away about the Western Civilization course and much else besides. Kurt Schäfer was a largely self-taught geographer with connections to the Ullstein publishing house in Berlin before his emigration. The refugees to whom I was closest were at Iowa for only a few years. René Wellek, the literary critic, was, like so many literary scholars of the time, also a historian, but one with a broad outlook, unlike Leslie Hotson, who had helped train me. Hans von Hentig I knew best, perhaps because I have always been attracted to willful but learned and intelligent outsiders, endowed with a fertile imagination. He fitted all these categories. Hans von Hentig was a political refugee from a distinguished family, whose military bearing belied his often quite radical views. He could have served as a caricature of the Prussian officer in the cornfields. Nothing would have been more mistaken. He was a criminologist by profession, but he had also written books on such topics as how nations go about making peace. His political views in the two years I knew him tended toward the Left, even toward anarchism. After the war he and his wife returned to Germany, and I unfortunately lost sight of them.

Clearly, I lived apart from the small circle of refugees who had formed the cohort of my parents' generation. But that was not all: thanks to my ability as a speaker, I was drawn into the wider world outside the university environment. The university encouraged some faculty members to speak to groups in the state, such as Rotary Clubs, Lions Clubs, and other civic associations, as well as to give commencement addresses at high schools. For this purpose it issued lists of possible speakers and their subjects: thus, for example, in 1949, my subject for commencement speeches was "The Citizen and World Peace," while my more usual topic was simply "What Price Freedom?" Invitations came mostly from rural areas or very small towns. The graduation classes were small, sometimes a mere dozen students. As this was supposed to be part of university relations, you got some instructions; thus, for example, you should be the first to shake the new graduates' hands. I improved on that by reading the names of the small graduating class ahead of time, and then remarking that what I had to say was meant for John, LaVonne, or David. The ceremony itself was standard: the processional, a song (usually "Ah Sweet Mystery of Life"), my speech, a valedictory, and a blessing either before or after the speech ("Bless the speaker and his message"). The class flower usually graced your lapel. I remember being shocked only once by a rapid change of pace, when in Oskaloosa a band appeared beneath the platform, nearly blasting me out of my seat with "Jazz at the Philharmonic."

I could fill many pages with my adventures on this commencement circuit. Sometimes I had to go search out the superintendent of schools or the principal from a local bar or diner and bring him to the ceremony. On one memorable occasion, when the priest rose to say his blessing, an unmistakable odor of whiskey wafted across the podium, and indeed a few seconds later the priest collapsed on the stage. A heart attack, the president of the school board told the alarmed students and parents. Nor did all the audiences listen to the speaker's message with rapt attention. A graduate assistant who drove me around one year as I gave these speeches told me that while, in that McCarthy era, I was extolling freedom, the talk in the auditorium was all about hog prices. Still, I got to know a part of Iowa and some of its people, an experience which few German Jewish refugees would have known.

During the academic year I spoke before many other groups as well, most of them voluntary associations that needed a speaker. Women's clubs were among the most active of such groups. Many were reading circles that invited so-called experts to fill in the background of the books under discussion. There was a definite social hierarchy among such clubs in Iowa City, dependent upon the social status of their members. I remember that the Nineteenth Century Club was considered the pinnacle in Iowa City because the university president's wife was a member. It was an honor to be invited to speak. Alas, I confused the name of the club with the talk I was supposed to give about their reading and made a fool of myself by talking about the nineteenth century in general. That kind of woman's network seems archaic at best, but the role which it played in such small towns is worth recalling.

However, I became better known in the state through a Sunday radio program which I was asked to moderate. Sponsored by the Iowa Bar Association, it was broadcast from Des Moines, the capital of the state, which at that time, for someone driving on narrow Iowa roads, was several hours

145

from Iowa City. I drove back and forth one evening a week for about a year, not without mishaps; once my old car broke down and I had to spend the night in a barn, in closer association with the Iowa countryside than I ever desired. The program itself was an interview program, mostly of politicians—for example, present and past Iowa governors.

The U.S. senators were interviewed as well, and here I once had to handle a situation not so different from that which the priest had brought about at commencement, except that the program had a very large audience. During the interview the junior senator from the state suddenly slipped off his seat and under the table. The smell which he had given off was familiar, but I could hardly say publicly that the senator had passed out in a drunken stupor. That would have been construed as a partisan remark. So, on the spur of the moment, I took a leaf out of the earlier experience and said that I was very sorry, the senator had just suffered a light heart attack. I thought that such presence of mind deserved praise, but instead the president of the university, a former corporate lawyer not noted for his courage, saw to it that the bar association ended my part in the program. Perhaps there was even some justification for this action—the fear that a junior, and, from his point of view, radical, faculty member interviewing all manner of state officials might become a loose cannon.

I was grateful for all these experiences, though they were frowned upon as unscholarly by several of my colleagues: one so involved in public speaking must be neglecting research. To be sure, the events at which I appeared required what was called motivational speaking, which made reputations in America earlier in this century and is today once again a lucrative industry. Such speeches were not especially lucrative at the time, but they were an excellent exercise in effective lecturing, in capturing rather than boring audiences. The critics failed to understand that this speaking included a style, a way of doing things, which in my case contained a serious, often scholarly core. The motivational speeches about freedom, after all, were given against the background of McCarthyism, which was then at its height; thus they also had a didactic purpose.

All this activity outside the university fed my dream of attaining some public office, of being elected to, or at least running for, a political position. But first I had to become an American citizen, and this was accomplished in April 1946 at the Johnson County Courthouse. I had been without proper nationality ever since I had been stripped of German citizenship thirteen years earlier. We used to say half jokingly that only those naturalized west of the Mississippi could claim to be true red-blooded American citizens, and I just managed to make it, the Mississippi being an hour's drive to the

146

east of Iowa City. The dream of holding elected office might be a final act of integration, of acceptance, but I was certain that I would enjoy the campaigning as well.

Meanwhile, I addressed political groups on campus. But I also took an active part in the 1948 presidential campaign of Henry Wallace. Wallace, a native of Iowa, ran as a third-party candidate against Harry Truman and Thomas Dewey, and I made quite a few stump speeches for Wallace and his running mate, the "Singing Cowboy," Senator Taylor from Idaho, who also visited Iowa City. The result was a complete fiasco; as I remember it, Wallace got some 12,000 votes in his own home state. Why did I actively support him instead of Truman or Dewey? I still believed in the possibility of avoiding the Cold War; one did not have to be a fellow traveler to fear what a new war might bring. But it also took time to shake a pro-Soviet stance that had begun with the antifascist movement and continued during the war with appeals to aid Russia. Today I know that Truman's policies were correct, that a line had to be drawn in the sand, but then he seemed aggressive and belligerent. I must also mention my delight in being an agent provocateur, constantly provoking the establishment, breaking taboos in order to arrive at answers to problems. This posture was a crucial part of my teaching as well: history was supposed to demystify reality, to probe and penetrate the myths people live by. Here I was taking advantage of my outsider position rather than attempting to assimilate. I was always torn between these two attitudes, a dilemma to which I will return.

Did I make up for the Wallace campaign when four years later I was listed as speaking for the Republican Party? I was impressed by Senator Taft, then a candidate for president in the primary—by his stand for civil liberties, by his kind of conservatism. I had reason to be impressed, for conservatives like Taft seemed to approve of my repeated attacks on the House Un-American Activities Committee. Indeed, at the high noon of McCarthyism, when, in my capacity as president of the Iowa Association of University Professors I organized a public meeting opposing the congressional witch hunts, the main speaker at this anti-McCarthy meeting was no radical or even a liberal, but the finance chairman of the Iowa Republican Party! Here the radicalism of the Right was as abhorrent as that of the Left. While I myself was much more radical in social and economic matters than the speaker, I did hold fast to a left-liberal position, not unlike that for which the Mosse publishing house had stood in Germany.

There was one time, in 1948, when I had a tiny and fleeting taste of being a candidate for public office. I had come home from some speaking engagement out of town and was lying in bed on election night, listening to the results on the radio. Truman was winning, and then suddenly I heard that Mosse had gotten so-and-so many votes for Johnson County coroner. I nearly fell out of bed. What had happened? While I was out of town, colleagues, led by a close philosopher friend of mine, an expert in the history of skepticism, had hired a van with a loudspeaker to proclaim my candidacy, and as a hoax had started a write-in campaign. It was more successful than they had expected, and, being unfamiliar with Iowa law, they were ignorant of the possible consequences. If I had won, it would have cost me several thousand dollars to hire a doctor to do the examinations, and if I had refused to take office, the same sum would have had to be paid as a fine. As it was, I lost, but while the election was being decided, the annual faculty reception given by the president took place, and amidst general hilarity I was "Mr. Coroner" at least for that occasion.

All this while I was living in the somewhat ramshackle house I had acquired, renting out the lower floor. Here the spirit of the frontier, which had frightened me so much when I first encountered the main street of Iowa City, seemed alive. The furnace of the house was fueled by coal, and there was no automatic stoker. So even in the severe Iowa winters, if one wanted heat, one had to get up twice in the middle of the night and shovel coal into the big furnace. I had, of course, been totally unfamiliar with such heating arrangements. This was hot-air heat, and so when a colleague once told me that one must put water into the furnace to prevent dryness, I happily poured water down the heating duct. The consequences and subsequent discomfort can be imagined.

As a householder I had to learn all sorts of new facts of life, from dealing with plumbers to hiring carpenters (the house was an old wooden structure). When I discovered that a squirrel had penetrated into my attic through defective eaves, I was at a loss what to do about it. I borrowed a hunting rifle and for the first and last time in my life fired some shots. I hit the attic, but in doing so also shot a hole in the floor through which the squirrel escaped into the house.

The house itself stood on a rather steep incline on a street which was part of a much-traveled cross-continental highway. I used to say that I lived where the trucks changed gears, and in winter I was often awakened in the middle of the night by some trucker who had gotten stuck on the ice and wanted to use the telephone. Still, in the end I sold the house for as much as I had paid for it ($8,000), which, given its rather dilapidated state, was satisfactory.

Iowa made a valiant effort to keep me when the University of Wisconsin made its offer in the autumn of 1955, but I was ready to move on. I had behind me a journey which had begun a little over twenty years earlier on the deck of the ferry across Lake Constance between Germany and Switzerland, and which had now reached a conclusion. The sense of liberation I felt then had been fully justified; I had done what I wanted to do and it had turned out well. Luck had played a part throughout—in the excellent teaching at Bootham, in my political awakening at Cambridge, and finally in finding Haverford College. Nevertheless, while it seemed to me that luck had played a great part in helping me settle down in a profession, still I had reinvented myself from an uncontrollable child into a respectable person. Character traits such as a driving ambition asserted themselves, helped along by the discipline learned from boarding-school life and the self-reliance necessitated by exile. Moreover, I now believed that I had a feel for America—a kind of relationship I had been too young and not self-conscious enough to experience in Germany, while it had been difficult for me, as a foreigner, to truly understand England in spite of my love for that country. But in America, even though there was racism and discrimination, one was not treated as a stranger and could even enter into politics as an equal.

The Iowa experience ended a long period of searching and lack of security. I had found a home and, just as important, had discovered what I was good at—as one who in the past had done badly academically and had entered his chosen profession only for want of anything better. I could teach and I could write books, skills for which no one who had met me in Germany or in England would have given me credit. As my former headmistress put it when I visited her in Germany after the war, "How come you are a professor when you were such a dreadful student?" This does not mean that my intellectual growth had ended, or that I would not discover many more aspects of America after I left Iowa, though my roots in the Middle West would remain in place. My chief contributions to an understanding of the past and my chief effectiveness as a teacher were still to come, but they would be elaborations upon an already present foundation.

9

Finally Home

WHEN I arrived in Madison, Wisconsin, in the autumn of 1956 I had no real sense that a whole epoch of my life had ended, that the years of apprenticeship were over. While my time in Iowa brought an end to a long period of searching and gave me a feeling of self-confidence and belonging, the years in Madison had no such far-reaching consequences. I now had a foundation upon which I could build; there was no real rupture with the past, and themes like Americanization or the road to respectability no longer applied. In Madison I started on an intense academic involvement which at the same time led to a new intellectual understanding of my environment. The broadness of experience which in Iowa came with involvement in modern art or creative writing no longer existed. Moreover, I was no longer a novice in the American Middle West, and even here I could build on existing foundations. The story now becomes one chiefly of intellectual growth, and not of an attempted adjustment or the need to reinvent myself as teacher, scholar, and member of an academic community.

At the time the distance between Iowa City and Madison seemed to me much greater than the six-hour drive which separated the two towns. That I would have to live on a lower salary than I had been offered at Iowa did not weigh heavily. My indifference to money, because it had always been there when I needed it—even when the family's earnings were low—paid off, and so did the fact that while I certainly liked luxury, thanks to Salem and Bootham I could do without it as well. I was excited to be joining such a lively and famous history department, and a university which seemed so much richer, so much more settled, than the University of Iowa. New research opportunities beckoned as well at a much bigger library, and I would have one free, if unpaid, semester's leave every other year in order to facilitate my research and writing. But, above all, I found myself immediately in the midst of a formidable cast of academic characters.

Madison itself, however, was, at the time, not so different from Iowa City. Both towns had only one passable restaurant, which made life difficult for bachelors, who were confined to various "greasy spoons." Most of the better restaurants were outside of town; for example, in the Amana Colonies, pietistic settlements barely an hour away from Iowa City, were various restaurants specializing in excellent Germanic cuisine. From Madison one drove a short distance to the Swiss colony of New Glarus or to the Cornish settlement in Mineral Point. But then eating out was not as common as it is today, and with many good restaurants in town it is not such a special event as it was when one had to make an excursion.

These were small cities, Iowa City much smaller than Madison. I remember when the first travel agency opened in Iowa City at a desk in the middle of the lobby of the main hotel, a lobby which was decorated with friezes showing the conquest of the West. Social life itself took place in the home, and I have the feeling that, among my circle, dinner parties were much more common than they are today.

Academic life was the focus of all of one's activities. The structure of the history department at Wisconsin was not much different from that at Iowa: the key person in charge of day-to-day activities was the departmental secretary rather than the chairman, and I had learned long ago that to be in her good graces made life much easier. Miss Veva Cox at Iowa, who ran the department with an iron hand, had been immensely helpful, and so were the departmental secretaries at Wisconsin. How mistaken some of my colleagues were who treated the Cerberus of the office like a departmental servant.

Among the faculty there was a rich social life which declined in the 1960s with the enormous expansion of the university—a departmental intimacy which would soon vanish forever. Not only among the faculty: who could imagine today the way in which I was promoted from associate to full professor not long after I had arrived. The president of the university, E. B. Fred, used to mix with the students as classes were changing in the main entrances of Bascom Hall, the central building of the university. He listened carefully to what students were saying about the classes they had just left. Apparently they said good things about my teaching, and soon the suggestion came down from on high that it was time for a promotion.

Perhaps this was not so extraordinary; I had, after all, already made a good impression on the university president. When I was interviewed for the position in the history department, the chairman had introduced me to E. B. Fred in order to be looked over. I sat down ready to answer all sorts of weighty questions, but instead the president asked only one question: "Professor Mosse, what do you think of the artificial insemination of horses?" I had been unaware of the president's background as dean of the College of Agriculture, and taken aback I blurted out that I had never given the subject any thought. Honesty paid; that was the right answer, for E. B. Fred, rather than making the usual small talk or addressing subjects of which he knew little, had wanted to test my presence of mind. The manner in which he had judged me for promotion was equally unorthodox. However, this was, after all, not so different from my promotion at Iowa, which had also been unconventional, as Dean McGrath had been frightened by my threat to abandon the Western Civilization course. Both promotions had been due to my teaching rather than my scholarship.

Socializing among the faculty did not mean the absence of tension or controversy; on the contrary, among the American historians in particular, each of whom was a recognized authority in his field, strife was rampant. And all of them were dominating personalities with strong opinions, likes and dislikes. The differences between them not only concerned appointments to new positions, but were based upon different approaches to history. These men cared deeply about the writing of history—it was their lifeblood—and since that time I have rarely witnessed such departmental disputes about fundamentals. My early years in Madison were lived in the shadow of this remarkable group of men, who influenced my own attitude toward my profession and kept an undue presentism at bay. They deserve notice as a group, for their time seems long past.

American history at Wisconsin had an antiestablishment thrust, and I used to characterize it as history from the viewpoint of South Dakota (where Merrill Jensen, the colonial historian, grew up), in contrast to the conventional view from New England. By now I had lived for over a decade in the American Middle West and was familiar with its vast open spaces, which had caused me so much despair when I first arrived in Iowa City. Moreover, I had seen something of its life during my Iowa travels. But now I encountered it intellectually, and as history is usually at the center of regional or national identity, so here the Wisconsin historians developed a distinctly regional point of view.

The patron saint of the department was Frederick Jackson Turner, whose large portrait hung in the departmental office, and whose thesis about the importance of the frontier in American history, written late in the nineteenth century, while he taught in Madison, found its echo among my fellow historians. Their criticism of American expansion was related to his work, and so was their emphasis on the American heartland. Here was an American nationalism which was based on democracy, strength, restlessness, and a virile energy. Nostalgia for a simpler past was part of this, as of most modern nationalisms. The closing of the frontier, an end to the wide-open spaces, which Turner had proclaimed, would lead to the kind of crowded and overdeveloped nation which the American East Coast symbolized. The utopian past was not long gone. I well remember being charmed by Merrill Jensen's description of how a literate farmer in rural South Dakota taught him a love for books.

The criticism of the American establishment and, above all, of American foreign policy by these historians was related to Frederick Jackson Turner's frontier thesis. The expansion from coast to coast had been democratic and had served to define the American character, but further expansion into the outside world, and especially Asia, was imperialist and capitalist, undertaken solely for consideration of economic gain. Their nationalism was isolationist.

The historian Charles Beard had been of almost equal importance in shaping the outlook of this group of historians. I had learned what little American history I knew while a student at Cambridge from his textbook, which was filled with analogies to European history, but for my colleagues, the isolationist Charles Beard (whom I had considered a crank), and the Beard of the economic interpretation of history, was the immediate inspiration. Present-day monopoly capitalism was regarded as a parasitic European import.

I felt closest, in these early years, to William Hesseltine. Like almost all of this group he had once been a socialist (Merrill Jensen, for example, as a young man, had published in the Communist-sponsored journal *Science and Society*). Hesseltine had been a political activist in his early days at Wisconsin in the 1930s, and the left wing of the small Socialist Party had even thought of drafting him for national office in the presidential election of 1948. His socialist activism was in the past when I knew him, but the libertarian streak which had made him call for the abolition of the State Department was still very much present. Moreover, he was a pacifist and had been one of the sponsors of a pacifist journal.

Hesseltine was a very talented and creative historian, even if in his various writings he never quite lived up to his potential. But he was a great teacher, and one of the greatest trainers of graduate students I have ever known. He used a kind of shock therapy, as I would call it: outrageous statements and far-fetched connections (e.g., the Civil War's effect on the insurance industry). He was a small man, somewhat like a pixie, who had constructed his persona as one who loved to shock and to break taboos. He would, for example, make remarks about blacks which to his great delight shocked his liberal colleagues, and yet, at the same time he was one of the handful of white professors at major academic institutions who trained and furthered the careers of black scholars. He was wedded to political history and to archival work, and was outspoken in his attacks against Merle Curti and cultural history, attacks from which I myself as a European cultural historian seemed exempt.

But it was Howard K. Beale, an expert on the age of Theodore Roosevelt, who bore the brunt of his ire, and indeed proved to be the center of most quarrels in the department; he was pugnacious, self-righteous, and inconsistent in his attitudes. In one bizarre incident, he began a quarrel with Merle Curti one day as he was driving him to the airport. Beale stopped the car in the middle of one of Madison's busiest streets, jumped out, detached the handles from the car doors, and left Merle Curti locked up in the car while he walked away. Such outlandish episodes must not distract from the serious work of all of these men. But if I try to visualize one portrait of this group, I see them sitting at a table eating lunch, each one looking in a different direction, avoiding each other's gaze.

The colonial historian, Merrill Jensen, had "discovered" me in Iowa City, through mutual friends, and had been instrumental in my appointment. All of this group, regardless of the tensions among themselves, felt pride in the department and took matters into their own hands in order to improve European history, which lacked the distinction of the American history component.

Merrill Jensen had discovered me, but it was Merle Curti who pressed for my appointment, because he believed that he could not do justice to American intellectual history without the presence of a European cultural historian. Merle Curti, though he was born in Nebraska, on the American frontier, differed from the other noteworthy American historians in the breadth of his outlook and in the fact that he lacked the antiestablishment edge of his colleagues.

My friendship with Merle Curti lasted forty years, from the time he first met me at the railway station, newly arrived and bewildered, until he died at ninety-eight years of age. I suppose that there should be one wise man or wise woman in everyone's life. I was lucky to have had both: the woman, my friend Paula, I will describe in a later chapter, while the man was without doubt Merle Curti. I received no impulses toward new directions from this group of American historians; I was too far removed from any single-minded emphasis upon economics or the workings of power. But they were excellent sparring partners and could in this way serve to sharpen one's own thought, or like Merle Curti, to serve as a wonderful source of advice.

Merle Curti did not look at all like a wise man; he was rather slight and unassuming, but he was a good listener, unfailingly gentle, and sharp until the very last. When I was stuck in my writing I would turn to him, and I remember one piece of seemingly innocuous advice he gave me at a particularly nasty impasse: just sit down in front of your typewriter and start typing. Coming from him it was just what I needed.

Perhaps his wisdom, his patience and understanding, came from his own experience with misfortune. I knew very little about his family life, for he was a very private person; but he had one daughter who was seriously mentally impaired and I am sure he had to support her all her life, while the other daughter, immensely talented, eventually entered a convent. This must have been a blow to Merle Curti, a freethinker and rationalist, a man of the Enlightenment, and yet he respected her decision and was proud of her accomplishments. Only the individual counted.

He was very different in temperament and outlook from the other "greats" I have mentioned, and unlike them he had no firmly held theory of history, though he had been one of Frederick Jackson Turner's last graduate students at a time when Turner had long left Wisconsin for Harvard University. But his very broadness of outlook meant that his books seem to lack firm direction. That is why, though a pioneer in American intellectual history, he influenced me through his personality and not through his writings. This lack of direction, of a theoretical framework, was surely responsible for the lukewarm reception of his last and most cherished book, an analysis of concepts of human nature in American thought. Yet he never complained. As long as Merle Curti was active there was a lively interchange between his graduate students and my own, but under his successors matters reverted to normal: although there was none of the ideologically motivated isolationism I have described, there was still a withdrawal into the self-sufficiency of national history.

Fred Harvey Harrington, the historian of American foreign policy, did fit the intellectual profile of the Americanists. He had founded a school of American foreign policy which centered its analysis upon so-called American imperialism, a view of America's expansionist urge that contradicted the usual benign view of American policy abroad. He himself liked to think big, and he eventually was to be one of the most creative presidents of the university.

These men, with the exception of Merle Curti, were isolationists, focused entirely upon the United States—an attitude I could not share and which I had fought against at Haverford College. Nevertheless, this kind of American populism was also new and refreshing; after all, there was a huge distance between Berlin and South Dakota. Their America seemed to me, at the time, genuine and different from the imitations of Europe which I saw elsewhere. Perhaps I was still nostalgic for the romantic American plains, their Indians and trappers, which I had read about as a child in the novels of Karl May, which were highly popular in Germany.

I was very junior to these men, a listener rather than a partner in dialogue. However, through my friendship with William Appleman Williams, who joined the faculty in 1957, I did enter into an extended conversation which gave me a deeper understanding of the ideology of this group. Williams, a student of Fred Harvey Harrington's, had shared, and indeed had extended, Harrington's view of so-called American imperialism and of the economic basis of American foreign policy. Like his teacher he was interested in the Far East, which seemed to provide proof that economic imperialism had dominated the foreign policy of the United States. I could not help thinking that, just as these men believed that Frederick Jackson Turner's frontier moving across the plains had been necessary for American self-definition, so they also thought expansion beyond the native continent ran counter to American ideals. Williams admired Turner and Beard as well, but he differed from his teachers in the strong moral tone which accompanied his writings, and in his application of concepts derived from European history to his reading of the American past.

We debated many an evening whether terms like mercantilism could simply be transferred from seventeenth-century Europe to nineteenth-century America, and while I learned a lot about American history in the process, I was never able to persuade Williams that historical concepts specific to one period could not just be applied to a different period and continent, or that one could not analyze American imperialism without being familiar with the history of nations like Russia or China against which it was presumably directed. The isolationism of this Wisconsin school of history played a role here, the combination of regionalism and intense patriotism which fed their suspicion of the Eastern Seaboard (which sometimes extended to students from New York). This patriotism also made them highly critical of the United States' role in the world. I

156

believe that a feeling of a lost utopia—disappointment with the lack of effectiveness of their midwestern vision of America—determined to a large extent their outlook upon the past.

Bill Williams stood apart from the student unrest at the time of the Vietnam War because of what he saw as the students' aggressiveness, which ran counter to his ideal of well-thought-out and intellectually prepared change. But the fact that he disliked the student leadership, which was largely eastern and Jewish, played its part. He was not an anti-Semite in the usual meaning of the term, and certainly his teachers would have denied such an imputation. But still, as I used to say, Bill Williams was always looking for the blond and blue-eyed Iowa Socialist, one who shared his own roots, which lay deep in the Iowa prairie.

How did I fit in here, a Jew, a former refugee, whose ties were with Europe and the eastern United States? To be sure, I was always uneasy with the anti-Semitic undercurrent which was part of the nationalism I have mentioned, and which could already be found in Frederick Jackson Turner's fear of the East European Jewish immigration and how it could deform the national character. Here anti-Semitism meant, in reality, opposition to the eastern establishment. I was totally opposed to the isolationism of these historians and said so often enough. Still, I regarded my relationship with them, apart from personal friendship, as a journey of discovery into a different and for me a very "American" world. Moreover, the discussion about history which informed our conversations never touched upon the so-called Jewish Question, and their condemnation of National Socialism and fascism was unequivocal. Perhaps a certain diffidence which I have always shown toward those I consider of a higher status than myself may well have come into play. I blame this diffidence principally on my education in Germany, which made me extremely shy when approaching people in authority. Moreover, I have always assumed half-consciously that a certain level of prejudice is latent in most men and women. And here what may have been latent never confronted me with its actual consequences.

Perhaps another attitude played its role here as well. Jews were used to being diffident about their Jewishness in what had been so often during my life an unfriendly environment. Though my basic attitudes were already changing, I was no exception, and it was only from the mid-sixties onward that I was prominently involved in Jewish concerns on campus. I should add that my other outsiderdom, being gay, presented no such problems. The closet door had to be tightly closed, and was so even with the members of this group whom I knew to have had some gay adventures when younger. Looking back, it is true that despite my friendships with the Wisconsin historians, diffidence was sometimes combined with unease, though the intellectual stimulation I received far outweighed any prejudice or any difference in outlook between them and me.

Bill Williams and I taught a joint seminar on Marxism, which led to Williams' book *The Great Evasion* (1963)—that is, the evasion of Karl Marx's legacy in America. But in reality that book had precious little to do with Marx; it was rather a Christian socialist statement about building a new community suited to the decentralized corporate society which Bill Williams advocated. The strong moral tone here and in all of Williams' writings was due to a spiritual impulse which, during his Madison years, turned into outright religious affiliation. I was largely responsible for his turn to the Episcopal church, for I had told him about my experience with the Oratory of St. Mary and St. Michael as a graduate student at Harvard, and I lent him literature on the church and the working class, as well as on incarnationist theology. I was never to see this material again, but instead heard from completely nonplussed students that Williams, the radical, had been seen passing the collection plate in the Episcopal church. Here was another circumstance which separated him from the 1960s radicals.

I should have been the coauthor of *The Great Evasion,* but I could not believe in this American utopia. Williams' ideal involved a certain retreat into "fortress America," even if it also meant a condemnation of the ruling class and its policies, a stance with which one could sympathize. I remember though attending, at Bill's request, a lunch in Madison with Bill and Adolf Berle, who had been a member of the original Brain Trust of the Roosevelt New Deal, and whom President Kennedy put in charge of the task force that recommended the Alliance for Progress. He was interested in Bill's ideas about corporatism and wanted to recruit him as his assistant and counselor. Bill was flattered, hesitated but then declined. He continued his opposition against the establishment, but he was reformist rather than revolutionary, challenging the mind rather than trumpeting a call to action. And it must be clear from our interchange that unlike the other members of this group he was no intellectual isolationist in spite of his belief in American self-sufficiency.

I still stand by a remark I once made to Bill Williams: If you are right you will be as famous as Beard or Turner; if you are wrong, you will simply be written off as another sign of the times. But for all my criticism, I felt a deep attachment to him and an abiding friendship. Because we disagreed and yet found our quite different viewpoints interesting and worth serious discussion, our relationship was firm, and we learned from each other. I have rarely had such a continuous and exciting discussion about fundamental historical problems since that time, the kind of dialogue which needs a clashing of backgrounds and minds.

I felt once again that I had been lucky; my friendship with Williams and with the other "greats" in the department introduced me to an America most refugees missed, and even though I could not agree with their outlook on history, it did further my understanding of my new nation, just as my stay in Iowa had given a new dimension to my American experience. The iconoclastic ideas of these men also appealed to me as an outsider, but still more as an agent provocateur.

These American historians gave the Wisconsin department its special characteristic, a flavor most other history departments lacked. They were outsiders in the historical profession, and proud of it; only Merle Curti was an honored member of the establishment. With the passage of time, however, their radicalism was apt to become a dogma of its own. This became clear to me in the early 1960s with the establishment of the new field of Third World history, which turned the traditional approach to imperial and colonial history on its head: looking at the subject not from centers like Washington or London outward, as was the custom, but instead from the point of view of the colonized countries, each of which had its own history.

This new history was fiercely resisted by some of the formerly radical American historians, who referred to it derisively as "swamp history," though Fred Harvey Harrington, then the university's president, helped to establish it in the department. Certainly, the strong-arm tactics of the proponents of this new history did not help, though they were necessary to establish a new discipline. The academic establishment, like any establishment, however unconventional its view of history, tends to be conservative, and history is one of the most traditional subjects.

I took part in the debates, or, rather, polemics, which preceded the establishment of the new history. I believed then, and still do now, that Wisconsin got its reputation by pioneering, being outside of the mainstream—and that this was worth keeping—while I also saw the benefits which would come from an expanded horizon. I used to tell my colleagues from time to time that the department would be only as good as the number of screwballs on its faculty. I said this only half in jest; intellectuals should be different from accountants or other professionals: engaged and experimental. Teaching and writing history cannot be a mere profession. Perhaps this was nostalgia for the so-called free-floating Weimar intellectuals, but some of those faculty members I have described, and many younger historians I have known, have not only been committed historians

159

but have refused to be confined by what was accepted as normal by the historical establishment.

The older radicalism had certainly brought a feeling of élan into a usually staid discipline, but it had proved rigid in its America-centeredness, which may have encouraged a certain social conservatism as well. Their patriotism, though anti-imperialist, through its very isolationism had its price to pay.

I have dwelt upon this group of historians at some length because this was my environment, important for my immersion in research and writing, for what I regard in retrospect as the beginning of my most creative period as a historian. But teaching was equally important; after all, as my Americanist colleagues reminded me repeatedly, I had been brought to Wisconsin in order to rejuvenate modern European history. The new appointments in European history soon added excitement to this field as well. The appointment in 1963 of Harvey Goldberg as the French historian deserves special notice.

Harvey Goldberg had done his graduate work at Wisconsin and had impressed my colleagues, especially Harrington and Jensen, who initiated his appointment. To be sure, he was also a radical and had edited a book of intellectual biographies of American radicals together with Williams—a fellow graduate student—when both were teaching at Ohio State University. Yet Goldberg's radicalism was quite different from that of Bill Williams, and the two former friends rapidly drifted apart. Goldberg was an old-fashioned Marxist; this was especially evident in his lectures, while his one published book, a biography of Jean Jaurès, praised a very moderate Socialist hero. Above all, it was his lectures which made his reputation: rousing events, delivered to huge classes. He was a charismatic personality; even so, the highly politicized atmosphere in his lectures certainly helped in creating the enthusiasm which accompanied them. The hour would start, for example, with students announcing meetings, rallies, or demonstrations, and his lectures, always well crafted, were filled with anecdotes which traced the various efforts of "the people" at self-emancipation.

His complex personality, however, often contradicted itself; for example, he lived simply in Madison, in an almost bohemian lifestyle, while his apartment in Paris was more luxurious, bourgeois rather than bohemian. He roused the students to action against the establishment, and at one of his lectures some students shouted "Lead us to revolution," but that was difficult, if only because of his loyalty to Harrington as university president. But in general, rhetoric and reality proved far apart during the period of student unrest in the late 1960s. Harvey Goldberg addressed student meetings, calling for action, but was never present when it came to actions within the faculty in support of the students. I liked him, but not his politics or the history he taught, and he thought me a reactionary who lived in the suburbs. Nevertheless, for many years we were good friends. Harvey Goldberg had an unbounded admiration for Europe (meaning Paris, in this case), rather typical of a boy from the American provinces, and apparently I had a little of the European glamour about me. Looking more like a living corpse than a robust man, to me he was a constant source of wonderment, but also of admiration for his very specialized learning, an integral part of a revolutionary commitment which as a historian I could never share. Practically all his graduate students wrote their theses on left-wing French labor unions. He was certainly a historian with a straightforward and presentist agenda.

Harvey Goldberg, to my mind, even then, was a living example of a political stance whose time had long passed. Yet, in the end, he did more to produce critical minds than most of my mainstream "uncontroversial" colleagues. There were quite a few students who wanted to hear both Mosse and Goldberg, and the clear-cut difference between the two must, I am happy to say, have given them food for thought.

These friendships with fellow historians were intellectual, almost on the model of the Enlightenment; they were not romantic friendships and touched private lives only peripherally. I knew very little about the actual lives of these colleagues. Typically enough, I knew that Harvey Goldberg shared my sexual preference, but we never mentioned such matters. Even though the gay liberation movement had made great strides, the taboo was too strong to be broken, not just on his side but on mine as well. Harvey Goldberg abandoned this anonymity just once, in 1975, when he narrated a film on public television called *The Gay Response,* about Madison gay life. This took more courage than I could have mustered at the time. The age of personal revelations was not yet upon us.

But when it came to renewing modern European history at Wisconsin, for my part teaching was the principal means, and here the ever larger freshman course had to take pride of place. I was already experienced in holding the attention of large classes at Iowa, and it was easy for me to increase the enrollment until the freshman course in European history had grown nearly tenfold. I felt that I had upheld that part of my bargain in coming to Madison. I enjoyed teaching to such a point that when, in 1964, to counter a call from New York University, I was offered one of the most prestigious professorships of the university, I refused because it limited its incumbent to one course a semester.

161

Lecturing to a University of Wisconsin class, 1961

As a result, however, Fred Harvey Harrington let me dictate the terms on which I would stay, and we founded a professorship which included research money but no limitation on teaching—though the salary was by no means equal to that of the chair I rejected. But what was this new professorship to be named? I suggested the Cartwright Chair, which puzzled the university president. He did not know that I was a fan of a television cowboy soap opera called *Bonanza,* and that taking on the name of the Cartwright family (who rode the plains on horseback) might have completed my Americanization. As this name was refused (not without Harrington's saying that the program might have funded the chair), I chose that of a philosopher, John Bascom, after whom the center building of the university was named. If not a cowboy then at least a moral philosopher. Today there is a whole series of Bascom professorships, modeled on what had been my preference well over thirty years ago.

But surely there was a life beyond academe, even if the ins and outs of university life had priority in my own mind. Social and academic life mixed in the university committees of which one was a member, and their meetings, especially if extended, tended to become social occasions which expanded one's friendships beyond the department. This had special meaning for me, as I never joined a synagogue or a civic club, though the local Democratic Party was also a source of new acquaintances.

It would be dreary to say something about all the committees on which I served—almost as boring as sitting through their proceedings. Nevertheless, two deserve mention for their impact and the friends they brought me. Not long after I arrived I was asked to join an informal gathering of scholars to plan a humanities institute for the university. This group was soon officially recognized, though we had scant hope of seeing such an institute created as a counterweight to what seemed to us the undue emphasis placed upon the sciences. Still, we were soon able to obtain the institute, now encouraged by a new president who was a scientist but wanted the support of the humanities. During its first halcyon years the Institute for Research in the Humanities brought to the campus scholars who without its existence would not have joined the faculty, and who became good friends of mine. To spend an evening with Friedrich Solmsen, the classicist and his wife, Lieselotte, or with Germaine Brée, expert in modern French literature, meant being transported into a true realm of *Bildung,* the constant effort to cultivate one's mind.

The committee with the ponderous title of the Ad Hoc Committee on the Role of Students in the Government of the University, which submitted its report in February 1968, was without a doubt the most important committee on which I served. It reordered the entire relationship between the students and the university. This committee was a direct consequence of the student unrest of those years, and it restructured the penal code for students by putting a fair and equitable means of student punishment into place. Before this time the dean of students had almost dictatorial powers; for example, I had to spend an inordinate amount of time defending graduate students threatened with expulsion for some minor sexual offense. Indeed, an almost morbid obsession with illicit sexuality was a hallmark of the office of student affairs at the time. The committee changed all that: proper judicial procedures were instituted and, taking a further step beyond tradition, the committee proposed having mixed-sex dormitories where men and women would live on different floors. This arrangement became a true bone of contention. The university regents balked (during a joint meeting I asked them publicly if they would rather young people used the back seats of cars as shelter). Eventually, however, the innovation was approved.

Through this committee I learned more about student discipline, student activities, and student housing than I ever wanted to know; still, it was with satisfaction that on my beaten-up typewriter I did my bit to abolish the old policy of *in loco parentis* in favor of treating students as adults. Throughout, we had the support of a splendid new dean of students, Martha Peterson, who had begun informal lunches a year earlier during which interested faculty discussed these changes.

Puritanism was not confined to student affairs, but until the 1960s affected the whole university community. To give one striking example, the wives of those in authority thought it their duty to tell junior faculty members how they should dress, behave, and where they should live. At Iowa, the wife of the former president of the university had regularly educated junior faculty in the proper behavior and comportment, and eventually included me in her observations even though she and her husband were retired by that time. The wife of the head of my department at Iowa had similar ambitions, and when she lectured me about the necessary social graces, I had to suppress the urge to tell her about the previous night, when I had had to walk her husband several times around the block so that she would not smell the alcohol on his breath.

Such "mothering" would be inconceivable today, but then this was a time when authority within the university hierarchy had been absolute, from the president to the "head" of the department. I myself lived through the transition to a less autocratic departmental structure at Iowa, and during my service on the Ad Hoc committee at Wisconsin, saw a somewhat more permissive society come into being. In a way, the changing attitudes were apparent to me when, on arrival in Madison, I moved into an apartment in an unfashionable, but cheap and convenient, section of town. The only comment I received was from the wife of a previous head of the department: "But no one has ever lived there before!" Now such a reaction would be ridiculed, and I could easily ignore it even then.

This apartment overlooking one of Madison's lakes had one disadvantage; it was located on an alley which saw a great deal of noisy traffic in the middle of the night. I soon found out that my neighbors were several call girls who were at the service of the personnel at the Air Force base in Madison. We reached an agreement that their suitors should park their cars on the street. Here the wife of the former head of the department may even have had a point.

Soon, however, I moved into the house which I still occupy forty-one years later, certainly on the proper side of town. Merrill Jensen and his wife discovered the small modern house in their neighborhood; the real-estate agent from whom I bought it was Pat Lucey, later, as governor, to play an important part in Wisconsin politics. This coincidence was indeed lucky, for it brought to my notice the engagement of the faculty with state politics, a situation which had made Wisconsin unique and lasted during the first decade or two after I arrived. This interrelationship added a political dimension to university life which was to vanish only in the late 1970s with the growing impersonality of the equally huge state university and state government. The renewed ascendancy of the Republicans in the governor's mansion no doubt played a part, as the vaunted alliance between the university and the state threatened to pass from the scene.

At least that is how it seems to me, looking backward, but at the time I hardly knew any Republicans, as I became friends with those of my colleagues who earlier had helped to transform Wisconsin from a one-party, Republican commonwealth into a two-party state. During the 1960s I experienced the same exhilaration of participating in the local political culture which I had felt when traveling around the state of Iowa, taking part in the Wallace campaign. I regarded myself as being finally in contact with the "real world" of America, and I suppose that I felt the same, though on a more abstract level, through my dialogue with the very American viewpoint of the group of historians I had joined. Moreover, grassroots politics in which anyone could make a difference were unknown in Europe with its rigid party structures and encrusted political hierarchies.

This was brought home to me through watching a fellow refugee, Liesl Tarkow, from Vienna, in action. She became a force in local politics, "dis-

165

covering," for example, a young lawyer, Robert Kastenmeier, who, through her help, became the longtime congressman from my district. I opened my house for a fund-raiser for his campaign in 1958, and I can still see Liesl in a bright red dress sitting in my bedroom collecting the contributions. Surely a picture unimaginable anywhere in Europe. I myself was elected in the late 1960s as a delegate to several conventions of the state Democratic Party and could speak up in favor of and even cosponsor anti–Vietnam War resolutions. This was certainly not a great accomplishment, but it must be seen through the eyes of a onetime stateless refugee who now moved in political circles, however briefly; listening to conversations behind closed doors gave the feeling of finally being an insider.

The outreach from the university to the state was perhaps most effective through the broadcasts of classroom lectures on public radio and television, which fulfilled an educational rather than, as today, a largely public relations function. During the last decades, just as in the relationship with the state, the faculty seem less involved in functioning as the university's conduit to the outside world. But for me, teaching was, after all, my chief means of communication, and with very large classes during all of my career I cannot complain about my reach. While it was impossible to estimate the actual success of these lectures at the time, longevity has given me a better perspective because of the many tributes I have received since I retired. Here indeed one reaps the harvest of one's career—if only one manages to survive into old age.

The impersonality of a large lecture is difficult to break, but small seminars are by their nature personal. I instituted an honors section, my own seminar, in the large freshman course, whose students were selected by the teaching assistants after the first examinations of the semester. I made many friends among these students and was able to follow their careers, even if they did not become historians. Eventually I encouraged the offering of such undergraduate seminars by the whole department. To be sure, one's primary reference group was the graduate students with whom one worked in a more intimate fashion, but undergraduates should not be deprived of the kind of personal interaction which might make their learning experiences more meaningful. I had taken to holding both graduate and undergraduate seminars at home, and that served to produce a spirit of camaraderie not found in impersonal classrooms.

Most academics will live on in memory through their graduate students: their teaching and their writing. I realize that I have been singularly fortunate as I look at the shelves of my students' books and consider the status many have reached in the profession. At Wisconsin we worked hard

Madison, 1979

at placement, with letters, telephone conversations, and personal contact; in fact as long as the "greats" were alive we were known in the profession, in keeping with the university colors, as "the big red machine." We based our success as graduate teachers to a large extent on the placements we made, and indeed helped each other.

Training professional historians was our main task, and I have often been asked why my own method was so successful in getting at least one scholarly book out of most students. Here I tried to copy Bill Hesseltine, who had been a most successful graduate trainer. No permissiveness or attempts to spare feelings were allowed, in my own or in fellow students' criticisms of written papers or of a thesis. Right at the start of my graduate teaching at Wisconsin one student rushed out of the room in despair, and he later became one of the most productive and eminent of all of the future historians I have trained. This sounds brutal, especially in an age of sensitivity training, but it got results, and furthermore did not cost me the friendship of any member of the seminars. Strict standards and scholarly discipline must be taught from the very beginning.

Perhaps this kind of approach was also the result of my own training in self-discipline at school which, as I indicated earlier, had constituted the positive side of my education at the Hermannsberg. However, much depends upon the kind of students who entered graduate school, and here I have usually, but not always, been lucky in my own admission process. The failures mostly left before finishing their doctorates.

When in the 1960s money seemed plentiful, one could also further the students' intellectual experience through inviting visitors from abroad. I had ample opportunity to do so because I was on leave every third semester; unfortunately, by the time I went on half-time in 1978 the money had dried up. Giorgio Spini, from Florence, replaced me in the early 1960s when I still taught early modern as well as modern history. His work on the *Libertini,* the sixteenth-century atheists, had impressed and fascinated me. He too was an outsider, a leader of the Waldensian Church in Catholic Italy. But above all, we also shared a distrust of the Kennedy presidency, about which, while in Madison, he wrote a most prescient book.

Georges Haupt became a kind of permanent replacement until his premature death in 1979. He had been "discovered" by Harvey Goldberg as a historian of the Second International, though he by no means shared Goldberg's old-fashioned Marxist beliefs. Haupt was charming, and though he knew hardly any English when he came, he was an instant hit as a teacher, if mainly for graduate students. He grew up in Romania and had spent some time in a Nazi concentration camp; that weakened his heart and caused his sudden death, which happened as he was about to board an airplane in the Rome airport, on his way home to Paris from a conference. He was handsome, a bon vivant, and at the same time immensely learned. He became a close friend from whom I learned much about international Marxism and the French left-wing academic establishment.

Because of such visitors Madison came to play host to some of the more important historians of Europe. I was able to suggest, for example, that the Humanities Institute invite Roland Mousnier, the historian of early modern France, for a semester, as well as Hubert Jedin, arguably one of the most important German historians of Catholicism of our times. On one occasion, Gershom Scholem, who had given a lecture in Madison, met Hubert Jedin, quite by chance, at Madison's tiny airport. They immediately began to discuss points of theology: the historian of the Council of Trent and papal advisor to the Lateran Council, and the foremost historian of Jewish mysticism. I should have kept a record of that conversation.

Madison never lacked intellectual stimulation as far as I myself was concerned. To the colleagues of the history department who were present at my arrival, I must add some of those in the German department, once it had been awakened from its slumber during the presidency of Fred Harvey Harrington—a sea-change in which I myself played an indirect part. I kept urging Harrington to add new positions to that department, which might lead to the appointment of exciting and productive scholars. My friend Jost Hermand, who was crucial to this revival, had already arrived, and his enormous knowledge and unconventional ideas led to conversations which eventually took the place of those I used to have with Bill Williams. Here much the same magic was at work: an interchange made all the more fruitful through our differences. But unlike Bill Williams, Jost Hermand was an expert in volkish German thought and German Jewish history, which gave our conversations an added depth. I learned much from Jost Hermand about subjects in which I myself was engaged. And the renaissance of the German department attracted others as well, such as Reinhold Grimm, the Brecht scholar, David Bathrick, in film and theater, and Klaus Berghahn, who had interests in a vast span of German literature. They added to an intellectual atmosphere which was difficult to duplicate in my own department once it had attained an unwieldy size and the "greats" had passed from the scene.

The annual German Workshops, which began in 1970, were concrete demonstrations of a renewed energy and became campus-wide events. Each workshop, five of which I participated in, had a separate topic, and for a time the proceedings were published in Germany. These workshops were important intellectual experiences where visitors from Germany often took a leading part. I felt very much at home in this atmosphere. The Wisconsin German department was in reality a department of cultural history, and not the usual department of literature in which text had replaced context. Such departments seemed to float in the air, concentrating solely upon the psychological profile of an author and using language which was incomprehensible outside their own circle. But here the debates were solidly anchored in problems which mattered.

At this time the resistance which I had felt against having my books published in Germany also vanished, especially as a publisher and his wife pursued me to London and even to Jerusalem. I had made no effort to obtain German translations, not because of any enmity against Germans, which I never felt, but because of my own laziness. Being bilingual I thought that I would never be satisfied with a translation and would in the end have to do it myself. When my books, beginning in 1976, were eventually translated, I did have to go over the translations carefully, but only rarely did I have to retranslate parts of a book. Italian translations, which included all my books on modern history, in contrast did not bother me much, for my Italian was not good enough to find fault.

However, it was not solely my fault that my books were kept so long from the German public. The time for their translation was finally ripe, whereas previously there had been no great demand for Nazi topics. I remember vividly what the prominent German historian Hans Rothfels, admittedly a conservative, told me when in 1962 I was about to publish an article on the occult origins of National Socialism: "You had better leave that topic alone" ("Lassen Sie die Hände davon").

Madison was not my only home during those years. Ever since 1950 I had spent several months each year in London, and while these stays had always been research trips, in the end they also had an overriding social and cultural purpose: life in the big city, rather than in what I still regarded as the countryside. But in addition to Madison and London, there was another fixed signpost in my life, for in 1969 I began an intensive seventeen-year association with the Hebrew University in Jerusalem.

I have proceeded chronologically up to this point, imitating in these memoirs the German *Bildungsroman,* which follows an individual's intellectual development in the midst of the ups and downs of his fortune. Neither my intellectual nor my personal development ended with settling down in Madison, but the themes of my life had now been set, the transition from Berlin to the United States successfully accomplished, and my youth as a refugee largely transcended. A certain mind-set which remained European and refugee lasted, however, while my relationship to my Jewishness and homosexuality changed as time went on, with my growing self-confidence. The context had changed as well, making what once had been fraught with risk relatively risk free.

10

Confronting History

T HE HISTORY department at Iowa had been remarkable for its promise; at the University of Wisconsin the department, as I have described it, consisted for the most part of very well established, indeed renowned, historians. It was a rather tight-knit group of scholars
who, whatever their attitude toward each other, were united in their passion for history. As Bill Hesseltine, who exemplified this passion and
whom I respected for it, used to say: We should eat, sleep, and dream
history. This atmosphere proved fruitful for my own work. Though I felt
sure that I had been appointed for my teaching rather than my scholarship,
my colleagues must have believed in my potential, for I had been voted in
by the American historians, who were keen to improve the comparatively
poor state of modern European history at Wisconsin.

At Iowa I had been accustomed to vigorous discussions about history,
and in the charged atmosphere at Wisconsin I felt at home. Ever since I left
Harvard I had lived largely among historians committed to their subject.
While this furthered my own research and writing, it also made me intolerant of those historians for whom writing history seemed to be only a profession like any other. The passion for history seemed to decrease among
my colleagues at Wisconsin as the department became bigger and more
amorphous, and I sometimes said publicly—and certainly unjustly—that
some of my colleagues could just as well have been accountants.

I have repeated in several of my books a phrase taken from W. K. Fergu-
son, an older historian, that "what man is only history tells." That I considered history itself as a faith seems astounding, since I became a historian
almost by accident. If at Cambridge English had been the subject which
those undecided about their future studied, I might well have taken that

subject instead of history. And yet looking at my choice in retrospect, more basic and at the time hardly conscious motives must have pushed me toward the serious study of history.

I had, after all, myself been a plaything of historical forces, forces which drove me into exile and made me confront anti-Semitism as well. As a stateless outsider I could, if I had been religious, have considered myself dominated by fate or by the will of a Higher Being; but in spite of my father's involvement with the Reform Jewish Congregation in Berlin, religion had been a meaningful part of my life only very briefly, and it was not discussed at home or at school. Quaker meetings, mostly involving worship in silence, were for me opportunities for introspection or daydreaming, rather than opportunities for spiritual renewal. Only in graduate school, as I have mentioned, did I join a religious fellowship for a brief time.

Being Jewish dominated my fate, but this did not lead to a preoccupation with Judaism. I had been expelled from the Reform Congregation's Sunday School, it will be remembered, and I was influenced by my father's dismissal of all religion as trickery. Because of my experiences it seemed to me that it was anti-Semitism which defined Jewishness; and the existence and strength of anti-Semitism were obviously determined by the forces of history. Being Jewish meant for me at this stage of my life being a product of historical circumstance, and I kept this belief even when my Jewishness was no longer a burden but had become an opportunity to deepen and propagate the liberal and humanistic values that the German Jewish community to which I belonged upheld in a special manner. But at the same time there remained the feeling that I had a special bond with my fellow Jews through a shared fate assigned to us by history.

History for me took the place of religion, with the advantage that history is open-ended and not exclusive, for one cannot understand one's own history or the history of one's ethnicity without trying to understand the motivations of others, whether they are friendly or hostile. A historian, if he is to get history right, cannot be bigoted or narrow-minded. Empathy is for me still at the core of the historical enterprise, but understanding does not mean withholding judgment. I have myself mainly dealt with people and movements whom I judged harshly, but understanding must precede an informed and effective judgment.

Eventually, at Wisconsin, I was to have a leading role in starting a Jewish Studies Program, having begun in the early 1970s to teach the first course in modern Jewish history ever offered at that university. Teaching modern Jewish history, as far as I was concerned, meant communicating that which has formed the modern Jew; understanding his modern history can give him support and dignity, even while he sees his place and opportunities in society much more clearly.

I emphasize the modern because the last three centuries have been crucial in determining our fate; not just Jewish fate after the age of emancipation, but that of all Europeans. I have often been told that such-and-such ideas and concepts already existed in earlier ages, and indeed every age has contributed to the construction of modernity. Nevertheless, though we must know the history of those ages, what counts is how modern men and women perceived them rather than what actually happened at the time. They looked at them through the prism of their own age. The historian obviously has to know even the faraway past in order to understand this prism and what it means, but I have always opposed drawing a direct line from past to present without taking people's perceptions into account.

Although as I look back, my first book, *The Struggle for Sovereignty in England* (1950), now seems to me very old-fashioned, the way I brought continental European history to bear upon my very English subject did introduce a new note which was due to my peculiar background. That book originated in my doctoral dissertation; I had great difficulty in finding a publisher, but it achieved a modest success and at one point even made the list of recommended books for that Harvard examination in which I had done so poorly.

It was a small book of a little more than a hundred pages, however, that made my name more widely known. One of the publishers' representatives who at that time traveled from one university to another asked me to write a book on the Protestant Reformation for a very popular series of short introductory books. (These men were always welcome for the lavish parties they gave and the gossip they spread; they formed an unofficial line of communication from department to department throughout the region.)

I wrote *The Reformation* (1953) in less than three months in a moment of unprecedented inspiration. As always, I did not revise what I had written a great deal, and, in this case, it just flowed smoothly. Although the reviews were mixed, the sales made it a best-seller within the popular Berkshire Series. It stayed in print for the next thirty years, introducing hundreds of students, and even some of my future colleagues, to the subject. I still cannot explain its success, what it was that I did right. Not even a very foolish idea of the publisher could kill it. He attempted to transform the short book into a newspaper, on the model of the *New York Times,* which could be bought for one dollar. Students preferred the book version, and the project of a newspaper book was a complete failure.

My next book, a study of Puritan casuistry—that is, the determination of right and wrong—was *The Holy Pretence* (1957), with the ponderous subtitle *From William Perkins to the Petition of Right*. In that, I tried to establish the thin borderline between truth and falsehood among the Puritans, but at the same time I was concerned with the reception of Machiavelli in England, thus linking the Renaissance and the Reformation. That book was a great disappointment, for no reviewer understood the larger purpose behind it.

If my real purpose in writing that book did not come out clearly, at least a misunderstanding of it did get me an invitation in 1968 to speak in what was then the German Democratic Republic. As I arrived in Berlin for two lectures (on Thomas Hobbes), I realized to my astonishment that because the book dealt with Protestant casuistry it was read as an attack on Christianity and therefore as support for the Bolshevik view of religion. I was somewhat bemused by that interpretation. I suppose that every writer has one book which he thinks was wrongfully neglected and misinterpreted despite its insights, and this is the relevant book in my case.

The Holy Pretence attempted to solve a historical problem; I have always approached history not as a narrative but as a series of questions and possible answers. Nevertheless, such narrative history as I have written, I have enjoyed, and I believe that historical narrative must provide the framework within which problems of interest can be addressed. I have always been grateful that my teachers in England, and the rigorous examinations I had to pass, gave me such a precise framework. Theory cut loose from its concrete context becomes a mere game, an amusement of no particular relevance.

The discovery of hidden facts about the past is especially satisfying, and I can say that I experienced such satisfaction twice in my career. The first time was entirely by accident. I have mentioned often enough the role sheer luck has played in my life, and it worked again to my benefit as a graduate student at Harvard researching a paper for David Owen's seminar in modern English history. I was not sure what to write about, and so I read through English newspapers of the mid-nineteenth century. Soon I was struck by the mention of an organization I had not heard of before. The Anti-League was a protectionist organization opposed to the repeal of the English Corn Laws. The Anti-Corn-Law League, which championed repeal, was well known as one of the first successful political movements trying to organize mass support in modern English history. The Anti-League, which was led by the landed gentry had, however, been ignored by historians. Yet this was the first time the landed gentry themselves had tried

to organize a mass movement in order to counter that of their opponents—
an important attempt by these conservatives to adjust to one major consequence of the Industrial Revolution. When they failed, Benjamin Disraeli
stepped into the breach to assume the leadership of the landed gentry, a
milestone in his career. As I have already mentioned, this paper was eventually published (in 1947) in the *Economic History Review,* and to my great
pleasure was later used by George Kitson Clark, my much-admired Cambridge teacher, as he continued to research the Anti-League.

My second attempt to resurrect some forgotten history very much later, in 1972, was so successful that several subsequent articles about *Les
Jaunes* conveniently forgot to mention where they first heard about this
large union of French industrial workers. *Les Jaunes*—the Yellow Trade
Union—consisted of industrial workers who adopted an overtly racist
and nationalist program during the decade before the First World War.
The very existence of that union ran counter to socialist belief in the essen-
tially progressive nature of the working class, a belief which I had largely
shared in my Cambridge days. Whether or not this trade union was in
some sense a forerunner of fascism, as has been claimed, is much less
interesting than what it tells us about the volatility of the working class;
indeed, in neighboring Germany, many of those who belonged to the proletariat had voted for Bismarck. I had come across references to *Les
Jaunes*—once more, almost accidentally—while doing research on what
effect the French Right might have had upon Germany.

Such influence as my work may possess, however, does not stem from
concrete discoveries, but rather from the new insights it has managed to
convey, how it may have shifted our vision by giving some new perspectives
and dimensions to aspects of modern history.

My work in early modern history set forth some themes which were
followed up later in my work on fascism and National Socialism and which
have influenced most of my writings on a wide variety of subjects. I am
centering the discussion of my mature work around these themes, for it
would be dreary to recapitulate all that I have written. More important,
this is how I see my work, how it falls into place in my own mind. But
books, once they go out into the world, have their own lives, and my own
view can not determine the ways in which they may strike their readers or
other historians.

The fate of liberalism is one constant theme in my work, tying the earlier period of my interests to my preoccupation with modern history. Reviewers of *The Struggle for Sovereignty in England* mentioned that I had
made its chief character, Lord Chief Justice Coke, into a seventeenth-

century liberal *avant la lettre,* that is, long before liberalism as a creed had come into existence. When, a decade later, I published *The Culture of Western Europe,* several perceptive reviewers discerned as a subtext of this survey, which ended with the outbreak of the Second World War, the triumph of totalitarianism over liberalism in the modern age.

This theme can be perceived in many of my books concerned with the background to fascism, even if their ostensible subject matter is different, as, for example, in *Fallen Soldiers* (1990), which analyzes how people coped with the new experience of mass death in the First World War, or *The Image of Man* (1996), which discusses the historical dimension of the normative male stereotype. That my interest in modern history has centered so strongly upon the failure of liberalism and, I must add, the attempted liquidation of the secular Enlightenment's heritage should not astonish those who have read the earlier chapters of this book. Historians are also creatures of their times, and in spite of my striving for empathy I have never sought to disguise this fact.

If "What man is only history tells" was the motto which dominated my work and teaching, was it equally true that "what you are, your own historical writings will help tell you"? This seems certainly true about my attachment to liberalism, even if it leaned toward social democracy, which, in any case, had occupied the liberal space in German politics. My definition of culture as including perceptions and symbols certainly reflects my own personal inclinations as well as a European tradition in which I felt at home. My preoccupation with the tension between insiders and outsiders within society is obviously related to my homosexuality. Perhaps because, in spite of repressive influences, I managed to find a place for myself in the world, I had a heightened sensitivity toward the position of the excluded, but was at the same time aware of the possibilities inherent in our society.

The attempt to make sense out of the history of my own century, which has seen such an unprecedented and largely self-induced abasement of individualism, was also a means of understanding my own past. The nature of outsiderdom, which has been a constant theme of my work, also related to my identity as a Jew. The modern history of the Jews entered my work first with an emphasis upon the history of anti-Semitism. Even then it was the perception, the image, which interested me rather than the details of persecution, for perceptions seem to motivate people. I had not taken such an approach to the sixteenth and seventeenth centuries; my first footstep in this direction occurred in 1957, ten years after my work on the Anti-League, in an article on the image of the Jew in the novels of two minor but very popular nineteenth-century German writers, Felix Dahn and Gustav

Freytag. This article was for me an almost logical entry into the subject, for I continued to suffer from the shock of having as an adolescent read the unflattering portrait of the "Jew boys," that is to say, of myself, in their novels. At the time when I published that article I was still mainly engaged in pursuing the more conventional methods of constitutional, theological, or political thought, for *The Holy Pretence* was published that same year.

But the course was now set for the method I was to pursue to the end, and while *The Culture of Western Europe,* published in 1961 as a textbook, by and large followed a more traditional course, it still provides a good description of my method of historical analysis: "culture is defined as a state or habit of mind which is apt to become a way of life intimately linked to the challenges and dilemmas of contemporary society." The context within which historical action takes place is essential, but we are dealing here with a matter of precedence: a person's habit of mind is not only dependent on historical reality, but is also formed by aspirations and dreams, a realm which fascism and the Nazis captured only too well. However, even the work which was destined to be one of my most successful books, *The Crisis of German Ideology: Intellectual Origins of the Third Reich* (1965), although it analyzes a nationalist belief system—"The German Revolution," as the Nazis called it—can still be read as part of a traditional history of political thought.

To my mind, the real breakthrough in putting my own stamp upon the analysis of cultural history came with *The Nationalization of the Masses,* published in 1975, which dealt with the sacralization of politics: the Nazi political liturgy and its consequences. The book's success was slow in coming, but eventually the work was regarded as innovative for no longer referring dismissively to Nazi propaganda but instead talking of Nazi self-representation, which interacted with the hopes and dreams of a large section of the population. This was no longer a book in the tradition of the history of political thought as I had been taught it at Harvard by Charles Howard McIlwain; instead it used the definition of culture as the history of perceptions which I had offered in my *Culture of Western Europe. The Nationalization of the Masses* led the way to serious analyses of various aspects of the Nazi cult, as well as to the first book that treated the sacralization of politics in Italian fascism, written by Emilio Gentile.

I began writing *The Nationalization of the Masses* in 1972 while teaching in Jerusalem and living in the apartment of the historian Jacob Talmon, surrounded by the works of Rousseau and of the leaders of the French Revolution. Here the importance of myth, symbol, and the acting out of a political liturgy was brought home to me, especially by Rousseau, who moved from believing that "the people" could govern themselves through town meetings to urging that the government of Poland invent public ceremonies and festivals in order to imbue the people with allegiance to the nation. Though the title of the book was taken directly from Adolf Hitler's *Mein Kampf,* I situated the Nazi political religion of National Socialism within a broader and deeper stream of modern history.

The book had its greatest success in Italy, where fascism was still a matter of lively discussion, and where, fortunately, Renzo de Felice, the biographer of Benito Mussolini and a towering figure among Italian historians, found my work useful. We had first met at a conference on the history of fascism in 1961 at the University of Reading in England and had remained in close touch ever since that time. His wife Livia translated *The Nationalization of the Masses* into Italian. It was presumably as a result of his recommendation that in 1978, like a bolt out of the blue, I suddenly got a telephone call from Italy asking me to write the introduction to the collected essays of Aldo Moro—the kidnapped and murdered former prime minister whose name was, for a moment, well known all over the Western world. Perhaps a neutral figure was wanted, one not embroiled in the partisan warfare of Italy. The introduction took the form of a long interview about the parliamentary crisis of the twentieth century, conducted with the editor of that memorial volume in the New York apartment of a close friend, and it must have helped to make me well known in Italy. (As I have been an almost passionate Italophile ever since I first visited Italy with my mother in 1936, the many invitations to speak and the various prizes I have received there have been among the greatest delights of my life.)

While my historical research has concentrated upon various modern belief systems, it would undoubtedly be correct to see here a continuity between my work on the Reformation and that on more recent history. I was familiar with theological thought as well as religious practices and could bring this knowledge to bear upon the secularization of modern and contemporary politics. It was not such a big step from Christian belief systems, especially in the baroque period, to modern civic religions such as nationalism in its various forms—including fascism—which have occupied me for many decades. Perhaps I have seen the world too much through the eyes of its faiths, but then the times in which I lived have been dominated by belief systems, by an almost fanatical devotion to civic religions, and there are few credible signs that this will change.

Though historical analyses based on these premises dominated the structure of my work, concern with outsiderdom continued to determine much of its content, especially within the last decades. Here the personal enters in a more decisive manner, for while I have addressed outsiderdom in general I have also been concerned with the specific minority groups of which I have been a member. But again I have done so within a more general framework, attempting to show how the fate of outsiders is part of the essential workings of our society, and how, in turn, society itself created the image of the outsider, the shape which he took in people's minds. In *The Crisis of German Ideology* I had already traced how the so-called German Revolution became an anti-Jewish revolution, and I had considered racism as a normative part of the culture of western Europe, along with liberalism, conservatism, and Marxism. I subsequently wrote a history of racism in Europe, called *Toward the Final Solution* (1979), which had considerable success, especially in Germany, where it has gone through several editions. In that book I argued that, though at first European racism was directed against blacks, the eventual focus was upon the Jews, who were considered the most implacable enemies of the superior race in Europe.

The Jews, to be sure, were the most visible outsiders in Europe, but others such as gypsies and homosexuals were also targets of prejudice. I did not become truly aware of the fate of the gypsies until I became a fellow at the Holocaust Memorial Museum in Washington, D.C., in the 1990s, but I did know all along about the persecution of homosexuals. My omission of homosexuals from my early work on National Socialism had deep psychological rather than historical roots. I was by that time fully conscious of my sexuality, but homosexuality could not be mentioned, and certainly not admitted, without paying the steep price of being driven out of one's profession (especially as a teacher) and expelled from normative society. Any success, any attempts at assimilation, at overcoming exile and statelessness, would have been in vain. While it is difficult to explain to today's young Jews the kind of discrimination which I have detailed earlier, it is somewhat easier to explain to young gays the restraints which dominated the lives of homosexuals, who were not even permitted to give a name to their own sexuality, either in public or among most of their friends.

Homosexuals were present indirectly, however, in *The Culture of Western Europe* when I wrote about the German poet Stefan George, whose politics were suffused with his admiration for male beauty as symbolizing the Germanic ideal. I did not articulate the obvious, namely that this icon of the German right wing was certainly gay, with leanings toward pedophilia, even if there is no evidence that he consummated his sexuality. I would be more explicit in 1964 in *The Crisis of German Ideology,* where I was the first, as far as I know, to forge a link between male Eros, the German Youth Movement, and volkish thought. The politics of male beauty grew naturally, as it were, out of the subject matter, and I did not discuss homosexuality for its own sake; at that time it was not considered to have had a history of its own which deserved to become a part of the general history I was addressing.

This attitude changed by the time I wrote *Nationalism and Sexuality: Respectability and Abnormal Sexuality in Modern Europe* (1985), which my friend Jim Steakley, himself a long-time historian of homosexuality, rightly called my coming-out book. There was a chapter on manliness and homosexuality, and homosexuality was a presence throughout the discussion about the role which nationalism played in the preservation of respectability. My preoccupation with the history of respectability, which I had already addressed in various articles, was driven by a sense of discovery and of my own situation as a double outsider. I saw the notion of respectability as an all-important historical factor which historians had somehow taken for granted. It had not been considered respectable to be a Jew in the past, and certainly homosexuality is on the edge of respectability (always ready to fall off) even today.

This book had a very good reception, especially in Germany, which had provided most of the examples in the text, and all reviewers stressed the novelty of the subject matter, even if they did not quite know to what compartment of historical knowledge it should be assigned. Prejudice as a heightened kind of nationalism once again played an important role in this analysis. The repression involved in the maintenance of respectability seemed to strike reviewers, and indeed I might have overstressed this aspect of nationalism and respectability by failing to suppress sufficiently my anger over the fact that the strictures of respectability had made my own life so much more difficult.

But, then, as the historian Steve Aschheim, my friend and former student, wrote, looking at my work as a whole, "George Mosse's Europe has always been peopled by strange and powerful forces threatening to engulf its precious but fragile humanist heritage." These forces did not seem so strange to me: nationalism, which often included racism, has been the chief menace of modern times. And respectability seemed at first glance to belong to these forces. In this case, however, I was of two minds, for while I recognized its repressive aspect, using reason rather than emotion I also realized that respectability—the normative manners and morals— was essential for the cohesion and functioning of society itself. This contradiction between my feeling and my reason once more made me an excellent agent provocateur; I like to provoke, to break taboos, but purely theoretically, as a myth destroyer, to get people to think—not in the practice of daily life. In *Nationalism and Sexuality,* I confined my basic belief in the necessary function of respectability to the very last paragraph of the book; otherwise the criticism of both nationalism and respectability come through loud and clear.

Through this book, I gradually arrived at another realization as well: the dialectic between the quest of society for the maintenance of respectability and the drive of those who hurl themselves against it was not one of absolutes, of revolt and its repression. Rather, normative society always managed to co-opt the core of the revolt; that was its great strength and the main reason why standards of respectability have lasted so long. This realization dawned on me when I dealt with the avant-garde at the end of the last century, for what had become of these iconoclasts? Their once unconventional paintings now fetched millions, and their so-called rediscovery of the naked human body was stripped of eroticism and integrated into society as a mere matter either of art or of health.

The outsiders wanted to become insiders, and many of them succeeded only too well. I did not agree with most of what the philosopher Herbert Marcuse, idolized among many students, had to say about students as the vanguard of revolution (after all, the United States was not a Third World country), but his concept of "repressive tolerance" made sense, for tolerance, as I saw it, always went hand-in-hand with a commitment to respectability, and therefore excluded sexual freedom or the freedom to bring about a fundamental change in manners and morals.

Respectability and nationalism needed discernible and visible foes for their own self-definition. I came to believe that the existence of outsiderdom was built into modern society as a prerequisite for its continued existence and the self-esteem of its insiders. The insider and the outsider are linked; one cannot exist without the other, just as there can be no ideal type without its antitype. The image of the Jew or the homosexual cannot be properly understood without the image of the all-American boy or the blond Nordic man. Type and antitype are a part of the new politics, living and familiar symbols of nationalism and respectability and of their enemies. Because the male image seemed to dominate so much of nationalism—an image which seemed to be taken for granted—I decided to write the history of that particular stereotype in *The Image of Man: The Creation of Modern Masculinity* (1996). To be sure, although I focused on masculinity, women entered at every point of my analysis. Women, for example, were excluded from public life, but as national symbols they played an important and official role; they were often regarded as passive, and yet they were vital as guardians of respectability, and as such policed the boundaries between the respectable classes and the proletariat. Women symbolized the cohesive, structured element in the nation and society.

The themes I have mentioned, such as the "new politics" and the nature of the outsider, were part of the thrust of modern nationalism, a belief system which at various points encompassed racism and defined the appearance and soul of the outsider. I hoped to have advanced the history of nationalism beyond the preoccupation of an older generation with its written sources, and to have demonstrated that fascism must be seen as nationalism reaching its climax. I have been accused, not without reason, of writing teleological history, that is to say, history which always looked to the future, ending up in the fascist or Nazi embrace. However, fascism did provide the climax of many of the trends which have interested me, and if I have shown how what was latent or inherent in nationalism or in the discrimination of the outsider became overt through these movements, then I have filled in a neglected piece of history, one which is also relevant to the present.

My preoccupation with fascism and nationalism needs no explanation for those who have read these pages, and my contribution to an understanding of these movements has given me, as I see it, my greatest influence. The dark side of my writings has dominated this account up to now; the dark and powerful forces which threaten to engulf, and have quite recently engulfed, European humanity. But I have nevertheless been interested in what I consider the points of redemption of the human spirit, even if I did not discuss them in as many articles and books. I have written about Jews in a way that did not undertake to show, for example, that the history of the German Jews led to their inevitable expulsion and destruction. I attempted to recall above all the liberal and Enlightenment spirit which had given German Jewry a positive role within the constantly narrowing nationalistic universe. And I also tried to point out at the same time that European nationalism, at its beginning, had tried to combine patriotism, human rights, cosmopolitanism, and tolerance, before both Germany and France came to believe that they had a national monopoly on virtue.

For this insight I was greatly indebted to a recent school of German historians led by Rudolf Vierhaus, who had researched the beginnings of nationalism in the period before the so-called fathers of the German nation such as Johann Gottlieb Fichte or Ernst Moritz Arndt had been influenced by ideas of superiority and aggression. An aggressive nationalism had indeed informed their old age but not their youth, passed in the shadow of the French Revolution. My examination of the early Zionists in the light of this patriotic tradition also yielded points of hope, although I saw that later, in the state of Israel, an even more conventional type of modern nationalism attempted to supersede what had promised to be an interesting experiment in liberal nationalism. Clearly, such studies tried both to be good history and to relate to contemporary politics.

One could not live in our century and not be interested in Marxism as well as in fascism—in my case not only because of my engagement with the antifascist movement while I was at Cambridge, but also because after the war some of the brightest university students thought of themselves as Marxists. My teaching experience in the Army Specialized Training Program in Iowa had brought me face-to-face with Marxist argumentation. Marxism itself offered much if it was not confused with bolshevism. Apart from the seminar I had taken for a short while with Dirk Struik, I was self-educated in Marxist literature. But my true education in Marxist thought came much later through my long friendship with George Lichtheim, whose book on Marxism is still the best introduction to the subject, though it was published over thirty years ago. I combined some research with my reading, so that I was able to publish several articles which attempted to analyze past efforts to join Marxism to humanism.

This subject looked back to my dream of marrying socialism to liberalism; Marxist humanism substituted the power of reason for the violence of the class struggle, and put the autonomy of man into the center of socialism—man who was the end and must never become a means. Marxist humanism based itself on the Enlightenment, while at the same time considering that the abolition of capitalism was the prerequisite for the creation of a new society. Interest in this type of humanism revived in the 1960s as a result of books by Erich Fromm and the rediscovery of the thought of unconventional Socialists like Gustav Landauer. This was a humanistic instead of a Bolshevik Marx, one that was based on Kant rather than on Hegel.

Students in the 1960s were searching for a third way between Marxist materialism on the one hand and capitalism on the other, and this kind of humanism lay readily at hand. There were by now one or two courses where they could become familiar with the thought of Karl Marx, but these were usually taught from a hostile point of view. I attempted to explain rather than to give judgment in my lectures on European culture, especially in the part of the course which dealt with socialism and in which there seemed to be the greatest interest. It was not easy to turn students from the polemical uses of Marxism back to the thought of Karl Marx, and I often told them, only half in jest, that unless they could read German they could not understand Karl Marx or consider themselves Marxists.

My specific contributions to this revival of socialist humanism, apart from my lectures, were several articles in which I used the phrase "Marxist of the Heart," a phrase that C. Wright Mills, influential among the student Left, popularized as my invention. But I was also critical of this revival, which seemed to ignore reality; this criticism was the same which I had leveled at liberals who failed to understand the new mass movements of our century. I was never able to find in the past an effective bridge between the ideals to which I was committed and the reality of politics as I understood them. Yet, I could not simply walk away from the failure of socialists and liberals to understand National Socialism; this failure in which, as we have seen, my own family's publishing empire had been involved, was constantly before me.

I was never to close the gap between ideal and reality, and I learned myself what I used to tell my students: true maturity is reached only when one realizes that there exist insoluble problems. Nevertheless, late in the day I did find another concept which seems to me still promising, and which, moreover, was part of my own German Jewish heritage, however much it had become deformed with the passage of time. The concept of *Bildung* had meant to me simply the usual humanist education which in Germany conferred social status. But as I studied the origins of this concept I found it was far removed from the rote learning and strict obedience to rules laid down by teachers as I had experienced them during my brief time at a humanist Mommsen Gymnasium in Berlin.

Wilhelm von Humboldt had defined *Bildung* at the beginning of the nineteenth century, putting at the center of the educational process the individual who, through constant self-education, could realize the image of his own perfection, which every person carried within him. Education was to be an open-ended process without set goals, except for each individual striving to perfect himself. I built *German Jews Beyond Judaism* (1985) upon this ideal and attempted to show that in its original, liberal form it took on the appearance of a faith among most German Jews and became a vibrant heritage when most Germans themselves had co-opted *Bildung* to various belief systems, thus precluding an emphasis on individualism and open-endedness.

That book, a collection of lectures given at the Hebrew Union College–Jewish Institute of Religion, is certainly my most personal book, almost a confession of faith. As I traced liberal and humanistic ideals I was dealing, to be sure, with a belief system, but this time with one which denied that it was a system of set beliefs. Nevertheless, from the very beginning this ideal, despite its open-endedness, was restricted by incorporating respectability and citizenship as unquestioned virtues, and thus it contained the seeds of its own foreclosure.

The book was generally very well received, but not among the American Jewish press or those—either religious or right-wing Zionists—for whom the ideals I had set forth seemed subversive of true Judaism. Most people need a firmer and more traditional identity than such an ideal could give them, even if, with its tolerance and open-endedness, it had helped make possible Jewish emancipation. I am sure that *Bildung* as I understood it appealed to the agent provocateur in me, the myth destroyer hostile to conventional belief systems.

And yet here I was far from consistent. My own engagement in Israel told of the need for a more concrete embodiment of my Jewish identity; my accelerated heartbeat when I witnessed the swearing-in of Israeli paratroopers on Masada—Israel's Holy Mountain—reveals the attraction of an emotional commitment even for one who prides himself on the use of his reason. Perhaps such a reaction is based upon the experience and study of anti-Semitism and its constant denial of Jewish manhood—however, once again, ideal and reality differ even within my own person.

Most people, myself included, on the whole do not desire to journey into the blue yonder but would rather look for shelter in a firm belief system or a concrete identity, however much violence or bloodshed may follow. The accusation that liberal and open-ended ideals had been helpless when faced with the German catastrophe was a serious one, and I had myself been critical of my own ideals for precisely that reason. It has been much easier to address the well-organized and powerful dark forces about which I have written most of my life than to analyze the points of hope which have existed and still exist even today.

Culture and Catastrophe do not have to be joined, though they have regularly been partners in modern history. The Holocaust is a constant presence for any Jew writing about European history in modern times, and especially for someone like myself who had barely escaped the prison of the Third Reich with its gas chambers. Though I have written only one book which deals with the Holocaust itself, it is a latent presence in many of my other writings. Such a catastrophe mirrors the chief trends in modern culture; it is like a prism, or, better, a distorted mirror, which reflects in an evil way much that motivates people. The historian Norman Cohn, in reviewing my *Culture of Western Europe,* saw that my discussion of social myths was driven by the decline of liberalism and the memory of the horrors of the Third Reich. He contended that although that book dealt with all the main trends in modern thought, it was in reality chiefly concerned with the growth of totalitarianism. This is a perceptive analysis which I am sure could be applied to some of my other writings as well. As a historian my chief contribution may have been to explore why culture has indeed so often been joined with catastrophe.

I am of course aware of the fact that people very rarely learn from history. One stark example of this fact which haunted me while I wrote *Fallen Soldiers* was that the carnage of the First World War seemed to have led to a process of brutalization rather than to the growth of a pacifist movement. "Never war again" proved to be a fleeting slogan. The transcendence of mass death through mythologizing the war experience after the war, with which that book deals—cleansing war of its horror—certainly helped to produce this effect.

However much my research and writing were driven by my own experiences, by a presentism which I attempted to keep under control, other factors were at work as well. I was propelled by sheer curiosity—why and how it could all have happened—but also by the simple love of history which, as far as I am concerned, does not need any explanation.

This chapter might have been a fitting ending to my autobiography, even though much was yet to come. But there was a further milestone in my personal and intellectual growth which cannot be omitted—my experience in Jerusalem.

11

Journey to Jerusalem

I DO NOT remember many games we played as children, but I can recall one which is called Musical Chairs in the United States, while in Germany we called it Journey to Jerusalem. Children ran around the dining-room table to a tune played on the piano. When this tune stopped abruptly you had to sit down just where you were, and whoever was lucky enough to sit in the chair designated as the throne won the prize. For me the real journey to Jerusalem started in 1951, when, during a stay in London, I decided to travel for a few weeks to the new Jewish state. Such curiosity was not astonishing for a former Jewish refugee. However, I had no relatives in Israel; moreover, during the war I had made some anti-Zionist speeches emphasizing that nothing must be put in the way of Britain's winning the war, not even the quest for a Jewish homeland. I was no Zionist, in any case, but instead thought that planting a Jewish colony in Palestine was asking for trouble. At the request of my sister I even wrote to the *New York Times* supporting the settlement of Jewish displaced persons in Ethiopia.

Now I saw the country as a tourist, to be sure, but almost immediately as more than that, not by design but by coincidence. I had greatly miscalculated my expenses, and after a week of various tours money ran low. The result was that I went to a kibbutz to live for free and help in the cow barn. This was my first contact with the land since I had dug potatoes at my German school, and I enjoyed it just as little. But the communal life, where the only private property was the small houses of the individual members, was impressive.

While this experience lasted only a week or so, as I remember, a startling coincidence led to an interesting end to my first trip. I had almost completely run out of money and decided to spend what was left on a drink at the luxurious King David Hotel. This was a recklessness I would never repeat. Later, I always took ridiculously large sums of money even on short trips, and in general have been as cautious as I was foolhardy in the King David. And yet, this last drink turned out to have been a singularly fortunate decision. I was rescued by my former dean at Iowa, Earl McGrath, who was staying in this hotel and who immediately co-opted me for his mission to Israel as United States Commissioner of Education. For the next few days, until my departure, I visited high schools (Gymnasia), including the Herzlia School in Tel Aviv, whose pioneering headmistress, Toni Halle, made a deep impression because of her personality. But otherwise I remember little from my first encounter with Israel, except for the still rather primitive condition of my boardinghouse in Jerusalem, and the Auschwitz number tattooed on the arms of several of the men that I encountered. I came away impressed, despite my earlier doubts, and happy that such a refuge existed—for who knew what the future might bring? Such thoughts were a sign of a lasting refugee mentality.

Nothing in this first trip foreshadowed what was to come. My true involvement with Israel started slowly, really beginning in 1961, and then being interrupted for several years. My short stay in 1961 was important because it was then that I met members of Jerusalem's German Jewish circle. I had not yet decided to write about German Jewry and German Zionism, but I thought that their knowledge of the German political Right and German nationalism might come in useful for the book on volkish thought I was writing. George Lichtheim, who had become a close friend in London and who had lived in Palestine, furnished the most important introduction, that to Gershom Scholem and his wife, Fania. My boardinghouse was next to their apartment house, and they came over to meet me, an act of courtesy which impressed me greatly.

Why did Scholem from the very start show such particular friendship? With his deep sense of history he found it somewhat of a triumph that a scion of a leading anti-Zionist family had ended up in Jerusalem. Theodor Herzl had previously said unkind words about Rudolf Mosse, my grandfather, and indeed my family remained opposed to Zionism even after I started to teach in Jerusalem. Through the Scholems I made the acquaintance of other members of this group, but at that time my stay was fleeting and I gave little thought to returning again.

My involvement with Israel through the Hebrew University started when I received an invitation to give some lectures at the university and at the Hillel Foundation. There I analyzed Martin Buber's idea of the *Volk* and got into a long public dispute with Gershom Scholem. This centered, if I remember correctly, on the Germanic sources of Buber's thought which, for all his criticism of Buber, Scholem still found difficult to accept. I felt that he was much more dogmatic in 1961 about the supposed lack of integration between Jews and Germans than he became later, though he never abandoned his view that a German Jewish symbiosis had not taken place. Twenty years later, after his death, I entitled an article "Scholem as a German Jew," and I am sure that, could he have known, he would have then been less concerned about Germanic origins—though still skeptical.

It was not Scholem, however, but the historian Yehoshua Arieli, with Jacob Talmon's assent, who had invited me to come in order to lecture to a few classes. During my lectures, I met Zeev Mankowitz, then Talmon's assistant, which led to a lifelong friendship and brought me together with a group of South African Habonim (members of a Zionist youth movement), who became good friends and in turn introduced me to a Zionism whose idealism—still strong and untainted—I found most attractive.

I must have done quite well; I soon returned, this time for a semester, as a visiting professor in the Institute of Contemporary Jewry. Here most fields of study about twentieth-century Jewry had found a home. This insti-

Meeting Schneur Zalman Shazar, president of Israel, 1970;
Gershom Scholem is at the right

189

tute was run on American lines, with secretaries and easy access to various aids such as Xerox machines, which was not usually the case in more traditional departments. Moreover, there was a great deal of collegiality, and I even found some colleagues attending my classes on several occasions. For the next ten years I taught courses on the history of anti-Semitism and racism in the institute, and then, in 1979, I became a member of the history department as holder of the newly established Koebner Chair in German history. I functioned at the Hebrew University at first as an expert on the history of anti-Semitism, and for many years I was one of the principal faculty members teaching courses with such a focus. Subsequently I became the senior expert on German history and regularly brought visiting professors from Germany into the program. Thus I combined two of my main interests which determined the content of so many of my books. For the ten years I was in the Institute of Contemporary Jewry I taught only every other semester. Yehoshua Arieli once said that my comings and goings, my relations with Israel, reminded him of the type of love affair based on mutual independence and freedom: the capacity to love and to be deeply loyal and yet remain master of one's own soul, mind, and fate.

These words are an excellent description of my relationship to Israel, which was not based upon religion, and certainly not upon a mystical love for the land, if only because throughout my life the South German landscape around Salem has remained "my landscape." Rather, a distinctly secular awareness of the Jewish fate in our century determined my basic attitude toward Israel, but beyond that also a love for the "new Jew" and what he had accomplished. This love was stimulated by my awareness of the undesirable Jewish stereotype which has accompanied the Jews in modern times, and which most Jews in the diaspora (including myself) had internalized. This stereotype the Zionists had set out to abolish.

I remember vividly my joy on my first visit when I saw sturdy, self-confident Jews, and though this was, once again, a stereotype, I was only conscious of the contrast between the present and the humiliating past. I knew full well that this "new Jew" represented a normalization, an assimilation to general middle-class ideals and stereotypes which otherwise I professed to dislike. But I could not help myself; faced with this Zionist ideal my reason and historical knowledge were overcome.

When after my first visit to Israel I went to Germany and told of what I had seen, I met general skepticism about the "new Jew," and encountered some sentiment that the Jews must have hired a mercenary army in order to fight their war for independence so successfully. Stereotypes die hard, if at all, even in the face of undoubtable fact.

190

My view that European nationalism had been and was the greatest enemy of the Jews never changed, and yet when I saw the new Israeli Army or attended the swearing-in of the paratroopers on Masada, my heart beat faster. I knew the danger of being captured by images and liturgy and had written often enough about their use in manipulating people, but I myself was far from immune to the irrational forces which as a historian I deplored—especially when it came to that group which I regarded as my own.

Gershom Scholem once berated me for "not loving the Jewish People enough." And indeed as a teacher I continued to be a myth destroyer, which had caused one student to complain to Scholem about my supposed disparagement of Zionist values. I answered Scholem that I did not see how one could love a whole people rather than individuals. About ten years earlier Scholem had accused Hannah Arendt in a letter of the same sin and in the same words. Her answer had been identical to my own, a logical answer for those who located themselves within the spirit of the Enlightenment. Yet, my own answer was disingenuous, for I did feel a sense of belonging, close to love even as I taught the lasting importance of rationality and of the Enlightenment. To be sure, I advocated a Jewishness beyond Judaism (to cite the title of my book of 1984), where I defined nationalism as patriotism, as a sense of solidarity, not as devotion to the land or geographical boundaries. I was somewhat later to write about a binational solution to the Jewish-Arab problem, entering belatedly into a tradition to which so many German Jews—including Scholem—had belonged. And yet, there was always a certain pull toward realism, to the feeling that if one did not belong to a strong nation one could slide back into the statelessness I had experienced. Thus, an emotional engagement always threatened that liberalism to which I tried to remain faithful.

Such personal contradictions proved easier to bridge once I discovered the difference between patriotism and nationalism: patriotism could be cosmopolitan and opposed to aggression and domination, but nationalism usually left death and destruction in its wake.

My deepening commitment to Israel found concrete expression when, at the beginning of the 1970s, I did some marathon lecturing at several of the educational institutions which trained young Zionist leaders, sponsored by organizations like the Habonim, Young Judaea, or the World Union of Jewish Students. Steve Aschheim, a leading Habonim educator, took me with him to these various groups, and I often felt so inspired by the enthusiasm and commitment of these young people that I would speak and discuss nonstop for several hours. It must not be forgotten that I actually

191

loved teaching, and here this love was given full rein. This was not actual Zionist propaganda—these people were already committed Zionists—but these lectures were intended to give some historical depth to this commitment. I should add that I was engaged with anti-Semitism, racism, and National Socialism in my research during those years, and this undoubtedly helped to keep me so strongly involved.

Teaching at the Hebrew University had its own rewards; it provided a complete change from Wisconsin, much appreciated by someone as restless as myself. But it also conferred prestige, and I have never been indifferent to my own reputation. I suppose that is part of ambition, but also of an academic environment where, as we used to say sarcastically, everyone prayed to the east—meaning Harvard—every morning. That time is thankfully long past, but for those of my generation—including myself—a certain snobbery remained in place for a long time.

The Hebrew University offered a kind of intellectual excitement not readily available at Wisconsin: a heterogeneous and more mature student body and, still more important, among the German Jewish faculty, a replay of some of the intellectual ferment of the Weimar Republic which I had missed because of my youth.

The students came from many nations, but on the whole they were much better prepared than those who had received their education in the United States. They knew how to write, for one thing, and knew some history besides. Their motivation was a given, for many had come to Jerusalem as self-conscious Jews, and the interest of all the students in the history of anti-Semitism and racism (which many had experienced) could be taken for granted. Later, the German history I taught attracted a self-selected student body at this university where, in many departments, the German intellectual atmosphere of its founders was still alive. To be sure, teaching in Jerusalem had its negative side as well, as among the students some were always *Besserwisser,* those who knew everything better than anyone else, including the teacher. Because they lived in a politically charged atmosphere and one in which a continual debate seemed to be taking place, they were more sophisticated than most Wisconsin undergraduates, but at the same time lacked their refreshing curiosity and openness. My colleagues at the Hebrew University warned me correctly not to overestimate the students, because mine were among the best, a self-selected group as a result of my teaching in English rather than Hebrew.

Certainly, my ignorance of Hebrew was a handicap which I never overcame. Not learning the language was one way to keep from being swallowed up by my new environment, to keep a distance between myself and

Zionism—to preserve the rational against the strong pull of emotions. I was one of the very few faculty members who were allowed to teach in English for so many years, because for ten years I was considered a permanent visiting professor (it sounds better in Hebrew). But this changed in 1979 when I was appointed to the chair in German history, named after Richard Koebner, the founder of the department. My letter of appointment stated that I would eventually make aliyah, that is immigrate, an eventually which never occurred. Nothing was said about language, and so I taught in English until my retirement.

"Weimar in Jerusalem" continued to fascinate me, though I had many friends outside the circle of elderly German Jewish intellectuals. My first contact, as I mentioned, came in 1961, specifically with Gershom Scholem, but also with other important members of this intellectual circle. Thus I interviewed Martin Buber several times in 1961 for my book *The Crisis of German Ideology*, which I was then researching. He was certainly an impressive figure with his white beard, which he stroked often, and his resonant voice. But he kept talking in generalities about Jerusalem and Mount Zion when I wanted to hear details about the influence of German volkish nationalism on his own thought and about its theoreticians, some of whom he had known in the past.

When I told Scholem of my frustration, he explained that Buber was now visited mainly by Christian theologians and that I should make clear that I was a Jew. This advice worked like a charm, and Buber did tell me much of what I wanted to know. I must admit that I was very critical of him at the time because of his pose and his flights of irrationality; moreover, he seemed to have little to say to present-day Israeli youth, while I was mentally and emotionally engaged in a dialogue with some of them. This skepticism vanished when, some time later, I investigated Buber's Zionism in greater depth and acknowledged him as a pioneer in the attempt to humanize nationalism. His speeches on Judaism given in Prague in 1911, which called for the complete inner renewal of the Jew, were for many later pioneers the most convincing and at the same time most humane Zionist manifesto. Though Martin Buber died shortly after my interviews with him, the archives in the Jewish National and University Library provided a fruitful source of research for many years to come.

As far as I was concerned, Gershom Scholem and his wife were at the center of German Jewish intellectual life. On their "Saturdays" and at their dinner parties, one met many other members of this circle: not refugees from Hitler's Germany, but usually committed Zionists who had come to Palestine in the 1920s. This circle was like a floating discussion group, always in deadly earnest about intellectual questions, while maintaining the lifestyle these people had known in Germany. I was fascinated by this aspect of that circle as well, since both at boarding school and in my fragmented yet luxurious family life I had largely missed the *gemütlich* side of the cultivated German bourgeoisie. The birthday celebrations, with their poetry readings, are particularly vivid in my memory, but also the love of recitation in general, combined with a devotion to the German classics. Here one met a veritable hunger for culture so largely absent in outside society.

If I contrast this group of academics with those I had joined when I entered Wisconsin, the difference is distinct and can tell us something about the process of *Bildung,* of self-cultivation, so deeply ingrained among German intellectuals. The "greats" at Wisconsin concentrated upon their profession as historians. Apart from Merle Curti, they did not have wide intellectual interests. In Jerusalem, the conversation would include history, literature, and theology within broad cultural themes. Politically, these men at the Hebrew University were liberals, without the radical past or unorthodox involvement in social concerns of so many of the Wisconsin historians. And yet, they inclined toward a left liberalism which, for example, made Scholem—the one time I accompanied him when he voted in an election—support a dissident and pro-Israel Communist faction. But this was an exception, perhaps an extension of the earlier support of a binational Palestine which had been typical, as far as I know, for almost all the members of this circle.

Their attitude to Germany itself varied: some remained hostile, while others tried to reconcile themselves. Scholem's position was firm; for many years he visited Germany only reluctantly to acquire books for the Hebrew University library. He proclaimed constantly that the German Jewish symbiosis had never taken place at all. I was struck at the time by the contradiction which existed between the German lifestyle and German culture of the Scholems, as well as many of their friends, and their rejection of Germany, and, in Scholem's case, of the whole German Jewish experience. In this instance German culture and much of the German intellectual tradition was separated from German life as a whole. German scholarship and its methods were considered indispensable, and Weimar thought, as long as it was not directly anti-Zionist, was admired. For example, I met Herbert Marcuse at the Scholems' house, and Scholem's regard for Adorno is well documented.

But then, there was no culture to which these intellectuals could have assimilated themselves in Palestine; that of the Orthodox Jews was foreign to them, and Zionism itself had not produced a culture of its own. No real, dominant Zionist lifestyle existed which could have been substituted for that which they had known in Germany.

I disagreed strongly with Scholem's view of past relationships between Germans and Jews, but I kept this disagreement to myself, partly because I was always overawed by Scholem's strong personality and an erudition which frightened me. He was an almost maniacal scholar who brought to mind the German tradition of learning in the past century, which a modern generation could not match. Such learning was often accompanied by a self-assurance and a single-minded focus which seems to have been lost among the many temptations of modernity. Scholem's unwavering belief in the Zionist cause, in the Jewish peoplehood, gave his thought and personality a solid, ironclad foundation. He could be charming and kind, but there was no bending when it came to what he called the love of the Jewish people.

He must have sensed my innate skepticism and my disagreement with his publicly expressed view of the failed German Jewish symbiosis. Thus his courteous but rather heated comments after my talk on the influence of German volkish thought on Buber, to which I have referred already. When I got to know Scholem better I found that he did not really deny the influence of German culture as such on German Jews, but sought to transcend it through an emphasis upon an all-encompassing Zionism, blaming the German Jewish symbiosis, which for him had no specific Jewish content, for blinding German Jews to their true status in Germany. I did not necessarily disagree with his analysis, but saw in that symbiosis, which took place on the bedrock of liberalism and the Enlightenment (which Scholem abhorred), a missed opportunity, and an example of hope for the future. Yet German culture claimed Scholem in spite of himself. Today he is almost as much a German cultural figure as Martin Buber, but through his scholarship, unlike Buber, he also played an important cultural role in Israel.

At times, however, this German culture proved too much for my taste, especially when it contained a heavy lacing of German romanticism. I was intolerant of a German heritage which in this case was opposed, I thought, to rigorous scholarship, playing upon feelings and lacking precision. I would criticize Martin Buber for having accepted such a heritage, but it was Ernst Simon, a towering figure among the German Jewish refugees, who seemed most to exemplify this particular aspect of German culture. Today I am sorry that I never really came to know him better; he was, after all, a leading proponent of Arab-Jewish reconciliation and a philosopher of merit, but his pronounced neoromanticism kept me at a distance.

Members of this German Jewish group were, of course, not the only friends I made among my colleagues. Jacob Talmon, for example, stood outside this circle. He was the most prominent modern historian at the university. His books, even his most famous on the origins of totalitarian democracy, do not seem to have withstood the test of time successfully. That is a pity, for there is much truth in his tracing of the origins of totalitarian, populist democracy to the French Revolution; and what he wrote about figures like Rosa Luxemburg in his subsequent volumes on political messianism is still worth reading. He was a lively, fidgety, small man, and was a superb lecturer. Talmon was born in Poland but pursued higher education in England, and therefore his turn of mind and his writing were quite different from those of the German Jews.

He was a great talker, but, unlike Scholem, not such a good listener. We used to go for walks during which he talked about his research and sometimes about his great fear of a coming Arab invasion. His expressions were vivid, and I could almost see an Arab army coming up Chernokowsky Street. But Jacob Talmon, despite his great reputation, was still insecure and in need of frequent reassurance. He provided a good counterpoint to the sharply focused discussions in the Scholem Circle; his approach to intellectual history was based not so much upon an examination of texts as upon a synthesis relying on personal insights—the kind of intellectual history close to my own view of cultural history.

Yehoshua Arieli had been instrumental in bringing me to the Hebrew University; he was the deciding voice in the history department as far as modern history was concerned. The role which he played was entirely due to the strength of his personality—not to be confused in this case with undue forcefulness or involvement with one's own ego. He was immensely learned, and at the same time a really kind and good man. Arieli's proper field of study was American history, but he had taught early modern European history as well. Knowing him made my integration into Israeli academic life much easier. Tall and gaunt, he was always a calming influence, though he did not conceal his own viewpoint, which, like Talmon's, was that of an avid proponent of peace between Arabs and Jews.

Yehoshua Arieli was decidedly on the left of the Israeli political spectrum. Looking back, it seems positively bizarre that in all my years in Jerusalem I hardly had any friends who were close to the right-wing Likud party. But then, how many Republicans did I know in Wisconsin? As a student of right-wing movements I did perforce come to know those who were racists as a result of my research, so to speak, and much later I had good friends who were neoconservatives. But though I regard myself as a left-liberal, still the relative isolation of my academic life from those political and social forces which proved to be important in Israeli and American national life was astounding.

Though students, with some justice, called the Hebrew University the last German university, with time it became ever more Americanized. The German tradition of academic authoritarianism was eroded, though when I first arrived the professor, like a German *Ordinarius,* was an absolute ruler in his own sphere. I was taken aback when the dean told me that, as occupant of the Koebner Chair in German History, I alone could determine the fate of a junior lecturer in German history, and could start or stymie the process of his promotion.

I chose the subjects for my classes carefully in order to arouse interest. Among the attractions which the Hebrew University held for me, not the least was a newfound relevance that was much more difficult to attain at Wisconsin, especially since the return to "normalcy" after the intellectual excitement and student unrest of the 1960s. Such political immediacy is often rightly deplored among historians as presentism, but I felt that while this stimulated me, it had only an indirect effect on my actual teaching, for I used the same approach to my teaching as in Madison, where such immediacy did not exist. But then I have always felt that history, in order to be absorbed, must be shown to have relevance to the students' lives, that it is more than just a good story of wars, adventures, and kings.

During this time in Israel, my personal life was on an upswing. There existed not only a circle which in its intellectual stimulation and its lifestyle seemed to duplicate a desirable past which I had missed, but also a group of young friends deeply involved in the Zionist enterprise, who with some sense of amusement tolerated my more ambivalent relationship to the Jewish state. They helped me cope with mundane chores, such as finding a new apartment every time I came to Jerusalem. The result was that I have lived all over town. The lack of Hebrew was no real handicap in daily life; not only did most of the tradesmen I dealt with speak a little English, but for many years I made good use of my French in talking to those who had arrived from French-speaking North Africa not very long ago.

My experience in Jerusalem was relevant to my outsiderdom as Jew in Western society. But what of my homosexuality? That I have not mentioned it often up to this point corresponds to the necessary suppression of that part of my personality, or rather its sublimation into work and a fantasy life. I had finally come out to myself in Paris, but in Jerusalem, of all places, I was out not only to myself but, so it seems, also to a small circle of Israeli friends because of a relationship which began in the early seventies and was to last for some twenty years. We never actually lived together, but when I was in Jerusalem we were often together, and we managed to meet abroad several times a year. David was a little over thirty years younger than me; my intense personal relationships have most often occurred with those who were very much younger. I was lucky here, for this helped to keep me young as well—perhaps this was a dividend of living in a society so largely dominated by youth. David and I knew each other from a class he had taken, but we were really introduced to each other as partners by a young graduate student at the Hebrew University who was "out" for all intents and purposes and who worked partly under my direction.

At a time when the old stereotype of the gay teacher seducing his students still has currency, it is important to clarify that this was from the start a relationship based upon mutual affection. David was the first gay man to whom I dared to declare my affection and who returned it in full measure, and that after I had passed middle age. Even so, we had to be discreet—and yet I was not as closeted as I had imagined, for twenty years later over lunch in New York, the graduate student I mentioned told me that I had been all along a role model for Jerusalem gays. By then I had long been out of the closet and I was elated by that confession, something that would have distressed me very much at the time. Since then I have learned that however much I might have wanted to hide my double outsiderdom, a surprising number of people seem to have been aware of it. In Jerusalem I regularly frequented the only Turkish bath and sauna on the Jewish side of town, the Ha'Am, built at the beginning of the century when Palestine was under Ottoman occupation. The regulars who visited the baths knew my disposition. I encountered a variety of interesting people there, but nothing untoward ever happened. As time went by, the so-called Bukharin quarter which surrounded the baths became a stronghold of Jewish Orthodoxy, and by the 1980s the baths had been forced to shut down. The hypocrisy involved was clear to me, as I had seen many Orthodox Jews frequent the baths.

David had been brought to Israel from England as a child and was a patriotic Israeli, while at the same time committed to the peace movement. His patriotism sometimes clashed with what he saw rightly as my own ambivalent Zionism. And yet, here too my Jewishness played an important role. I have just written of how outsiders internalized hostile stereotypes of themselves, and said that I was no exception. I must regard this as one of the legacies of my youth in Germany, surrounded by people, including my own family, who for all their Jewishness had also internalized the image of

198

the puny, weak, and ugly Jew. I myself look very "Jewish," and, as I have recounted, my mother had indeed been shouted at as "an old Jew-bitch" as she was walking in a neighboring city on one of her visits to Salem.

This atmosphere, which was present also in the United States until well after the Second World War, led me to admire the "new Jew" whom I found in Israel as well as in the United States, especially in my friend Allan at Harvard. And now I saw David as an example of such a Jew. These were well-built young Jews who carried their ethnicity openly and proudly without any of the mental contortions to which I was accustomed. Their looks and their normality seemed stunning in contrast to what I considered European Jewry. I am sure that this perception is related to my own scholarly work, in which much later I wrote about the "new Jew" in historical context. I was not without some ambivalence, however, for intelligence was for me a crucial attribute; it had not been an integral part of the Zionist image of the "new Jew," a reaction against the image of the intellectual ghetto Jew. To be a tough Jew was impressive, but not good enough for me.

In addition to being together in Israel, David and I often met on travels, which stretched from London and Berlin to a cruise on the Nile. We shared a love of travel, though in David's case it was not reinforced by innate restlessness. He seemed stable and secure, at least compared to myself, though when I met him he was still trying to find himself and was only starting to focus on a career and profession. Security within a general insecurity was a paradox, but perhaps an endemic national insecurity produces a sharp personal reaction, just as many people (myself included), though nervous in daily life, feel calm when faced with a crisis.

Unlike many Israelis, David had English manners and tact. Personal relationships with Israelis often tended to be painfully honest and immediate, lacking many of the graces which assure a smooth functioning of social life. This, as I experienced it in daily life, was still in many ways a frontier society. The contrast with the German Jewish intellectuals and with David's English-inspired attitudes and manners was striking.

And yet when I first knew Jerusalem, there was a refreshing simplicity about life; ostentation was still thought bad form. This was brought home to me in 1972 when I visited President Shazar a few times in his official residence, which, situated on an obscure side street of Jerusalem, looked more like a barracks than a palace. His office had something provisional about it, and the president himself was like family, simple and warm, not surrounded by the usual trappings of office. As Israel grew, became more modern and prosperous, this lack of ostentation could not last, but even today some of it remains, especially among Israel's political elite. It was the surroundings of the president and his person which impressed me, and I do not remember what we actually talked about.

Even after my formal teaching ended in 1986, I still returned to Israel each year, partly to give some special lectures, but mostly to see my friends. Within such a close-knit society where friendship meant so much, I eventually had as many close friends as in Madison. Life in Jerusalem was incredibly rich because of the wide variety of people who formed its context. These were mostly academics, but from different German, English, or French backgrounds. But I also got to know many nonacademics, from the painters Anna Ticho and Lillian Klapich to the photographer Tim Gidal. Among these people conversations were usually intense and intellectual; there was relatively little of the small talk of the American cocktail circuit. To be sure, occasionally such earnest conversations could be wearisome, but I generally found them refreshing, for I have always had intellectual curiosity, even as an "ungovernable child" in Berlin. Indeed, I have made it a principle always, where possible, to guide the conversation to the interests and life of my interlocutor in order to learn something about his or her ideology. It is possible that I have inherited from my father the admonition never to talk about oneself (the rest, never to talk about other people or one's illnesses, I ignored). I have, in fact, always felt uncomfortable doing so, just as I feel restless during the often fulsome introductions when I am giving a talk or being awarded an honor. I am very pleased to warrant such praise, but I am uneasy and embarrassed at the same time.

My journey to Jerusalem began in slow motion, picked up steam, and soon became one of the most meaningful involvements of my life. This did not mean that I approved of the Israeli government and its policies; I was a supporter of "peace now" from the very beginning. But when the state was in mortal danger I rallied to its defense. Former students at Wisconsin have told me of their astonishment when, although known as a "peacenik," I gave a fervently patriotic speech at the beginning of the Six-Day War to a crowd outside the Hillel House on the campus. A wartime situation produced a different response than did the nation at peace.

Thinking about the "Israel problem" in terms of nationalism came naturally to one who had spent the early part of his life as a victim of nationalism and then had later spent a great deal of time researching and writing about it. As a result, I was eventually able to reconcile my own attraction to and, at the same time, fear of Israeli nationalism by recognizing the distinction which early Zionists, including Theodor Herzl and Martin Buber, had drawn between a good and a bad nationalism. They must also have felt something of the paradox: those who had been prime victims of nationalism then had to construct a nationalism of their own. When Herzl in his novel *Altneuland*—the new yet ancient land—imagined what the future Jewish state should look like, nationalist chauvinism was the designated archenemy. I do not think that nationalism as a belief system will soon vanish; today it still seems more powerful than most traditional religions, and indeed at its extreme it has all the attributes of religious belief. "Can Nationalism Be Saved? Zionism, Good and Bad Nationalism" was the title of a lecture I gave in Tel Aviv a few years ago, and it expressed my own credo, a guarded optimism about nationalism, which many of my friends, even those who may have sympathized with the sentiment, found out of place.

Jerusalem, in a manner which I had not experienced earlier, fused my research interests with my environment. This could not have happened earlier when I was concerned with early modern Europe, English constitutional history, and Christian theology, though the latter, together with my experience at the Oratory of St. Mary and St. Michael while I was studying at Harvard, did eventually serve an unforeseen purpose. During my first stay in Jerusalem as a visiting professor I was asked to teach the Reformation, and I soon found out that my students knew nothing of the Christian

On the terrace at Maiersdorf, Hebrew University, Jerusalem, 1989

201

liturgy. I took them to the church of a religious order where one of the members had been an English friend of mine, and showed them how a Catholic mass actually worked.

But it was, of course, my work in modern cultural history which was most relevant to my life in Israel. Jerusalem served as a *Praktikum,* as an example of a present and immediate application of the problems inherent in nationalism and Jewish identity. For me, truth has always been what history tells us, and so whatever the contemporary state of affairs, I gave it at once a historical dimension. Nevertheless, it was certainly a sign of my commitment, in spite of myself, that I cared so deeply and, like the early Zionists, wanted to hold the Jewish state to a higher standard of conduct than other nations.

I could afford to divide my time between Madison and Jerusalem because I was by then a bachelor of some means and did not have to worry much about salary or pension. If I had been a parent, combining two academic positions on two different continents would not have been quite so easy: as it was, I could actually have lived on a Jerusalem salary, if not a Hebrew University pension. That I could fulfill my dream and have the best of two worlds, in which I found great intellectual stimulation, still gives me great satisfaction. Indeed, I have been extraordinarily lucky throughout my life and this autobiography, as I write it, seems to contain much more light than shadow, which may detract from its interest, but not from my happiness.

12

Excursus

London as Home

O F ALL THE many cities I have mentioned and experiences I have thus far recalled, London is missing simply because it is so familiar to me and has been ever since my Bootham days. Except for wartime, no year has passed that I did not stay for some time in that city. Moreover, the basic research for most of my books was done there, at first in the British Museum, watched over by the ghosts of Karl Marx and Charles Darwin, and then in the Wiener Library, which specialized in the history of National Socialism.

This library deserves a special mention because it became for all intents and purposes the center of my London experience, an extension of my own private library, so much so that I dedicated my book on the cultural origins of National Socialism not to a friend but to the library and to Ilse Wolff, its longtime librarian. The Wiener Library was a private library founded by Alfred Wiener, a former official of the Central Association of German Citizens of the Jewish Faith, the most important association of German Jews. During his exile he began gathering Nazi materials, much of them ephemeral, which previously had been trashed as mere propaganda. I had begun working in its always expanding holdings in the 1950s, and eventually sat on its governing board for eighteen years. The library's colorful and eccentric staff of Central European refugees, all marvelously helpful librarians, could have provided the stuff for a novel.

Libraries are the center of any scholar's life, and for me, memories of a foreign city are mostly memories of the libraries where I would spend much of my time. Though I had known Paris extremely well ever since my visits in the 1930s, the Bibliothèque Nationale with its convoluted catalogue, dangerous steps in the reading room, and graceful interior, was Paris at its most familiar—while the walk to the library through the gardens of the Palais Royal seemed to sum up all the charm of that city.

But during the early 1960s I also frequented another, smaller library, the Bibliothèque du Centre de Documentation Juive Contemporaine, which specialized in recent Jewish history. This was the time of the Algerian war, and the elderly lady who supervised the library was given a decidedly odd commission, as extraordinary as it was imaginative: to collect the graffiti on the walls of the toilets in several Paris metro stations—*vox populi*—as the voice of the people. I helped her a little, and these splashes, filled with political prejudice, are now, if I remember correctly, recorded in the library at the University of Paris-Vincennes, raw material for works on racism. But perhaps the most scary venue for my research was the library of the Paris Prefecture of Police, the police headquarters, where on the top floor I sat surrounded by instruments of torture and other tools of the trade which in the past had been used by the Paris police to spy and to intimidate. Perhaps not such a bad venue for a work on *Les Jaunes,* the nineteenth-century right-wing and racist French labor union about which I was writing.

For oral history there was the Librairie Hébert, a right-wing bookstore where, sitting with its patrons around the potbellied stove, one could in the 1960s still pick up lore about French fascism. Its entrance was shared oddly enough with the Jewish Hillel Foundation, surely a rather bizarre coincidence. But then my pursuit of the history of fascism and National Socialism did lead me into byways, such as research in Paris subway stations or meeting as many Nazis and fascists as I could find. I frequented bookshops like the Librairie Hébert which were the favorite places of retired fascist intellectuals, and which allowed them to continue their propaganda whether in Rome or in Paris. The bookstore which succeeded the Librairie Hébert as specializing in fascist and royalist literature was run by a former fascist man of letters, Maurice Bardèche, and it put out an advisory letter about "books to be read and books not to be read," which I still treasure. The bookstores I knew are all closed now, after the deaths of their usually aged owners. I was just in time.

The time I spent in these bookstores fitted in with my efforts to supplement my documentary research by probing the minds of former Nazis or fascists, in order to make it easier for me to understand their aims. I did so quite extensively when researching my *Crisis of German Ideology* from 1960 to 1963; at that time I also attended a meeting of former Nazi writers led by the onetime cultural administrator of the SA. In order to avoid suspicion I even took on the name of a friend who belonged to the aristocracy.

Excursus: London as Home

When working on *The Nationalization of the Masses* in the 1970s, I became acquainted with Albert Speer, one of the main architects not only of Nazi buildings but also of the Nazi political liturgy. As a historian I was lucky enough to get to know such committed National Socialists; my quest for understanding what they were about by far outweighed the unease I felt in their company.

I was mostly in search of concrete information, and, for example, told Albert Speer straightaway that I was not trying to confront him with his past, but instead wanted to grasp National Socialism in as many dimensions as possible. I hoped that the books which resulted would contribute to an understanding of National Socialism and fascism; books, in my view, are the true voice of antifascism today, when the immediate menace which had stimulated my earlier antifascist involvement is long past. I was often confronted by friends who could not understand how I could enter into personal relations with former Nazis, many of whom were still committed to the failed regime. But it was precisely this commitment which made them valuable witnesses. You could even learn something from noticing that Albert Speer's eyes, in the midst of his latter-day rejection of National Socialism, always lit up when Adolf Hitler was mentioned.

My research on the various different topics which engaged my attention carried me far afield. Thus I spent time in 1959 in the Vatican Library, which was then a very private place, a good environment for my work on seventeenth-century religious thought. I also worked for some months in the excellent library of the Australian War Memorial, this time surrounded by some of the engines of war. Then, later in the 1970s, the Staatsbibliothek, the Federal Library in Munich, became for many years a home away from home, for it contained the best collection of German written material that had escaped the Allied bombs. "Destroyed by bombs" nevertheless served as a convenient excuse for failing to fetch some requested books. And when I researched my book on *Nationalism and Sexuality,* I had to get permission for each individual book dealing with sexuality that I wanted to see; respectability, even here.

Eventually, in the 1970s, I began to make good friends in Munich; one of them, Thomas Nipperdey, the German historian whose work I most admired, would invite me in 1983 to inaugurate the new chair in modern Jewish history at the university. I became so familiar with Munich that at one time I seriously considered retiring there. Munich was a large city with superb cultural institutions, and yet it was easy to live in. Still later, in the 1980s, I added Amsterdam to Munich as a city where I thought of settling down after I had finished teaching: it lacked a good library for my purposes

205

With friends in Amsterdam, 1980s

but on the other hand was host to a lively gay intellectual scene with the sort of lectures, discussion, and large conferences which I had never experienced before, and in which I joined enthusiastically when I was there.

But it was London which was a constant presence, not just through its libraries but also through close personal relationships. My closest and defining friendship had its roots in Germany but flourished in England. Paula

was the daughter of August Weber, the former leader of the liberal Staatspartei to which my family belonged, and whose own estate was near Schenkendorf. But at that time I was barely acquainted with Paula, and instead
had formed a close relationship with her twin sisters, who had been my
classmates at the Hermannsberg. However, once in London, I became a
steady guest at the home of Paula and her husband, Roger Quirk, a senior
English civil servant who died much too young, and from that time onward
Paula and I became close companions. I stayed with her whenever I was in
London, she visited me in Madison, and we often went on vacations together. Paula, tall and full of vitality, was a little older than myself; she had
also been at Salem, but not in the junior school during my time there.
Paula's twin sisters had also immigrated to the United States, but we gradually lost touch with one another—they moved to parts of the country
which I hardly visited, while I was a constant visitor to London.

Paula had become thoroughly acclimatized to England, though this
was never easy. It is doubtful whether anyone not born in England could
ever become an Englishman, or -woman; for all its liberal policies English
society was in reality a closed society with its own longstanding customs
and rituals, and it was difficult for any foreigner to learn to play by its rules.
Language was also involved, down to the specific upper-class pitch and
accent. What I wrote earlier about the set rituals in Cambridge colleges
held in a different form for all of England's upper middle class.

Paula and her three daughters became family who also met and became
friends with my male companions. She was an independent woman with
her own ideas and could be a rather strong presence, but then, I have always been attracted to powerful and independent-minded women. They
provided the kind of sharp and critical dialogue that I have always valued.
Ever since I can remember, I have disliked anything mushy, from personal
attitudes, to human bodies, to ripe fruit. This preference did not mean
opposition to compromise and accommodation—after all, I consider myself a liberal—but rather, a demand for strong personalities who could
hold their own, however much their firmly held opinions might grate upon
me. I suppose that I myself am rather overwhelming and opinionated, and
yet I have always gotten along best with those rather like myself, people
with whom I could empathize and whose company I could enjoy.

As Merle Curti served as a special kind of wise friend in my academic
life in Madison, Paula played a similar role on a more intimate, personal
level. Our friendship was a constant presence—its beginnings almost coin-
ciding with my settling in at Wisconsin—an accompaniment to much that I
have written in the last chapters.

England, 1950s

Europeans regularly take vacations at Christmas, at Easter, and in the summer; they serve to define the rhythm of their year. Americans rarely seem to take regular vacations, time free from work and in new, fresh surroundings. I was brought up within a regular rhythm of vacations: Christmas meant skiing at St. Moritz or Davos in Switzerland and summer meant mountain climbing in the Alps, in Chamonix at the foot of Mont Blanc.

But in America such vacations ended for me, not because of a conscious decision, but almost imperceptibly. What used to be vacation time was taken up with research trips. That such frantic activity—as it seems in retrospect—was unnecessary for scholarly productivity should have been

208

clear to me from the example of my friend and distant relative Francis
Carstens, who lived in London; he regularly took long vacations with his
family, and his productivity as a historian exceeded my own.

I was not consistent in my new vacationless lifestyle, however. By the
middle of the 1960s I reinstated at least an abbreviated summer vacation,
sometimes in the company of my stepmother, but usually Paula. I preferred
Italy even then, long before my close academic and scholarly association
with that nation. We explored Sardinia, for example, in the mid-1960s, but
I usually preferred the Dolomites, a combination, as I saw it, of beautiful
mountains and Italian food. But such vacations were merely an episode,
and eventually I reverted to an unbroken year of study, where the venue
might change to London, Rome, or Paris, but always with libraries in
mind. When I became better known my travels were often determined by
speaking engagements. Travel for its own sake, for enjoyment alone,
dropped out of sight.

Here also I was becoming Americanized (although lately many of my
American friends have started taking short seaside or mountain vacations).
Was this absence of a regular cycle of vacations due to an exaggerated work
ethic, or to a heightened competitiveness to get ahead in a fearfully competi-
tive society? Was this a good example of capitalism almost out of control? I
was myself a witness to what my late colleague Bill Hesseltine called the
need to eat, sleep, and dream history. I confronted history not only through
my experiences in Germany, England, and the United States, but through
my constant preoccupation with the past; it became an integral part of my
life's pattern. Life has always been for me a learning and educational experience, a part of my unrestrained curiosity.

Although I never actually became part of the London intellectual
scene, I acquired a group of close friends, for the most part historians.
Logically, this group could have been connected to my English past, but, as
I have mentioned, the war had provided a clear break. Even when this
circle came to include Cambridge and not just London, these were with a
few exceptions colleagues whom I had met either in the 1960s or, more
recently, in the 1990s when I taught at Cambridge for a few terms.

Helli Konigsberger, whom I knew when both of us were Cambridge
undergraduates, was such an exception, and when in 1965, nearly ten
years after I had closed the books on early modern history, I was asked to
write a book on Europe in the sixteenth century, to be published in England
in the prestigious Longman's History of Europe series, I asked him to join
me as coauthor. This came about when another friend, Jack Hexter, apparently lay dying in Edinburgh and asked me to take over his contract. (Hap-

pily, Jack Hexter lived on for many more years.) Helli Konigsberger took over the economic sections and I wrote the theological and religious part of the book, but we also contributed to each other's chapters. We never quarreled or even argued much, which must be some sort of a record for an academic collaboration.

The writing of that book I found easy, smooth, and immediately satisfying, in contrast to my books in modern history, which were hard work. Is this because I had begun writing about religion and theology when I started out as a historian? I have had a similar feeling of inspiration only with my little book on the Protestant Reformation, which I wrote in publishable form in 1952 in only a couple of months. Both those books have been great successes, and surely this must have some relationship to the easy and fluid manner in which I wrote them.

In London my friends Francis Carstens and his wife, Ruth, ran a hospitable house. He was tall and earnest, while his wife, from South Germany, was lively and equally knowledgeable. Both in their own ways were important and committed historians, Francis writing seminal books spanning the time from the sixteenth century to the modern age. With his mastery of the sources, Francis was a different kind of historian than I was, with my bent for theory and analysis, and he was justifiably often critical of my work. If he were to write the kind of memoir I have attempted, however, it would be filled with the drama of politics, for in his early days he was for a time an active Socialist and involved with a German underground antifascist movement. In his house I met George Lichtheim and the sociologist Norbert Elias (who played Santa Claus at the Carstens' Christmas parties).

Elias was then quite unknown, though his famous book about the civilizing process had already appeared in 1939, published by an obscure Swiss publishing house. He later obtained positions in Kenya and the University of Leicester before retiring in Holland and enjoying his very belated fame. (I thought that gave hope to all the rest of us.) But the many times I stayed in Amsterdam I never visited him, for I had caused him great offense because of the arguments we had when we met, and because I had written a not too favorable review when his book was republished without taking modern scholarship into account.

Norbert Elias was without doubt difficult to get along with, touchy and opinionated. At the time when I wrote *The Crisis of German Ideology* we quarreled, especially about the nature of the German National Party, which he defended against the charge of racism, in spite of its undoubtedly racist and anti-Jewish propaganda. I would not give in either, full of my discovery of the Janus-like face of these German conservatives: respectable

210

in public but racist on the street. Unfortunately this disagreement never became the kind of dialogue built upon different points of view from which I have benefited so much. Later, however, it was some of my students who quite rightly helped organize a New York symposium to honor him when his seminal book was republished in English. Elias was a lonely pioneer in the history of respectability, a history in which I myself became interested in the 1980s. If I had been involved in it earlier, I might have had a better appreciation of Elias himself, and we might have had a fruitful relationship. The civilizing process which he had analyzed was crucial in establishing the manners which became normative in our society, and these in turn became an integral part of the behavior patterns which constituted respectability. And respectability, in turn, became the cement holding society together, as important for this purpose as any economic activity.

A passion for history was important in all these friendships and in the meaning which London—my second home—and, much later, Munich and Amsterdam held for me. I rarely came up for air, forgetting even for a short time the project upon which I was engaged. This was no mere academic interest, for I believe that history can hold no lessons if first the measure of the past has not been taken by means of scholarship.

13

The Past as Present

M Y LIFE *would* have been different had circumstances allowed me to remain in Germany and live a life of abundance. Almost certainly I would not have developed a passion for the study of history. But the world of my childhood was not to last. All that my grandfather had founded and accumulated seemed forever lost. And indeed, his newspapers did not appear again after the war, although my father told me, before his death in 1944, that he planned to reestablish them, and even had an editor in mind for a new *Berliner Tageblatt*. It would not have worked, not only because of his own lack of realism, but also because no one who came back from exile and reclaimed a pre-Nazi newspaper was destined to succeed.

And yet, as I write these lines, thousands of miles from Berlin, my grandfather has managed, in spite of the Nazis and the Second World War, to make us wealthy once again. The postwar government initiated a process through which the properties confiscated by the Third Reich were returned to their former owners. The West German federal government started this process soon after the war, and East Germany followed only after its Communist government had collapsed. Such a restoration of the past seems miraculous, a totally unforeseen irony of history. No other such restoration has taken place in the last two centuries after any other upheaval and revolution. The Russians who fled from the Bolshevik revolution, for example, were apt to remain poor for the rest of their lives, and this was also the case for those who had fled from the rest of fascist Europe. But our property returned bit by bit, not the moveable goods but the real estate which my Mosse grandfather had accumulated. Once Communist Germany collapsed I could again have resided in Schenkendorf, or, even before then, in the house in the Maassenstrasse where I was born.

But I never once contemplated such a return, and, as I have mentioned, experienced no nostalgia when I saw the places where I had spent much of my childhood. I was now a different person, and moreover felt defensive about my heritage. I wanted to be measured solely by my own accomplishments, which were the fruits of exile, and not by what my name might represent. I am still not comfortable when in Berlin I am presented to audiences as the grandson of Rudolf Mosse.

The claims of restitution for our family were very large, but initially involved only West Germany and West Berlin; most of our former properties remained hidden behind the Berlin Wall. At first these claims were handled by a former lawyer of the firm, who, as I have already mentioned, cheated us out of some properties. But through friends of my stepmother's, this time in Berkeley, we obtained the services of a first-rate German lawyer, Carl Hermann, who succeeded in having our Berlin villa restituted, and, more important, the large complex of upscale apartments, theater, and shops in the heart of West Berlin, which had been designed by Erich Mendelsohn. This project had been regarded as one of my father's financial mistakes; like so many others in Berlin at the time it was built with short-term loans from the United States, and repaying these was difficult during the depression. The risks had seemed too great, and no one could foresee that eventually it would support my mother for the rest of her life. Today this complex is a jewel in the architectural desert of rebuilt Berlin.

After my brother's death in 1958, I became involved in the restitution effort, stopping several times a year in Cologne where our lawyer lived, and visiting Berlin at the same time. Yet, I can claim no credit whatsoever for the success of this or later restitutions. I did learn something about German land laws and, when the theater in the complex lost its tenants, about what one could or could not tolerate as a place of public entertainment adjoining luxury apartments. And I did play a small part in placing this project in the hands of the German conservation authority, thus narrowly defeating the scheme of a real-estate speculator who wanted to build a skyscraper over its tennis courts.

If we were fortunate in our Cologne lawyer, we were doubly fortunate in our West Berlin lawyer, who dealt with the return of our East German properties after the fall of the German Democratic Republic. Indeed, we were, as far as I know, the only refugees to have the restitution of their holdings (in our case, rather large, including the former publishing house

The reconstructed Mendelsohn facade of the Mosse Haus, Berlin, 1995;
the building is now called Mosse-Zentrum.

and the mansion of my grandparents) concluded so smoothly and in such short order. The properties outside of Berlin were in the hands of another able lawyer who had a singularly difficult task on his hands. My grandfather had bought several large estates in Brandenburg, the province surrounding Berlin. But they had been broken up into many small holdings under Communist rule and sold separately. Moreover, there was no proper record to show where these estates were located.

Here, in one of the most important cases, my own memory proved decisive. Half awake one morning, I suddenly recalled that when I was a small child my parents had shown me an estate, telling me that in addition to Schenkendorf this also belonged to us, together with the surrounding farms. Then I remembered the name, Dyrotz, in itself a miracle, given my usually faulty memory. But such trivia often come to mind more easily than that which has to be remembered, and this time to good effect. The lawyer and I drove out to the village, and I asked a young girl to lead us to the house of one of the oldest inhabitants. We were in luck, for the loquacious elderly lady told us naively that Mosses owned this and that parcel of land as well as the manor house. The conversation ended when the husband returned, furious at his wife, fearful that we wanted to take back his own

214

house. But now our lawyer, with the help of local land deeds, could reconstitute and reclaim our long-lost properties.

Eventually we sold all these properties. Schenkendorf proved most difficult to sell, because there were now many such empty country residences in the province; moreover, having served as a barracks for the officer corps of the German Democratic Republic, it was in a run-down condition. Finally, it was bought by a charming German who had been adopted by a Romanian prince with the ancient title of Count Dracula, a title which had existed long before it became associated with a blood-sucking nobleman. He restored the house splendidly, and I was impressed as he led me through the halls and the rooms I remembered so well. And I had no objection to the beer garden he installed in what was left of the park, or to the fact that the place where I had grown up was to become a Dracula theme park. This purchase created more of a sensation in the press than in my own mind. The only scene of my pre-exile existence which can today arouse true emotion is the Swabian landscape associated with Salem and the Hermannsberg.

Life seemed to have come full circle, but the restitution, though it was a unique and spectacular experience, had no great effect on the course of my life. The money was welcome and so were the renewed ties to Berlin,

Outside the gate to Schenkendorf, in the early 1990s

Visiting the family mausoleum at Weissensee Cemetery, Berlin, 1995 (the burial place of
Rudolf and Emilie Mosse and Wolfgang and Ulrike Mosse)

though I allowed myself to hope that these were due to my own accomplishments (after all, my books had been translated into German and I now lectured often in that city)—and not to the fact that the past was once again present.

The gulf which divided me from my own past was created by my assimilation into a new world, but almost in equal measure by the new way I looked at the world and my place in it, by my immersion in the study of history. This change is difficult to put into words—briefly, it meant seeing everything in perspective, ordering all phenomena according to their past and present effects. This manner of thought does make a difference; it gives the mind a certain stability, and it determined the nature of my confrontation with the present according to the experiences of the past.

As I look back on my life, I feel that although the past has certainly formed me and provided me with many opportunities, it has also presented me with many obstacles to overcome. The naughty child out of control, locked in the broom closet for punishment, managed over time to transform himself into a respectable citizen. That was no easy transformation, and I had significant help in accomplishing it. The discipline of boarding school and, once I got interested, the discipline of scholarship were essential, but so was my ambition to make a mark and to assimilate in the new worlds which had opened up for me. And I engaged with these new worlds, not just academically, but, as in Iowa, in public affairs as well. I served mainly as a public lecturer, but in Wisconsin I was also active as a delegate to Democratic Party state conventions and got to know the leadership. To be sure, I was concerned with the opposition to the Vietnam War, but above all I wanted to experience how American politics really worked at the grassroots level. I might have continued in local politics, but my teaching in Jerusalem soon made this impossible, as I had to be away from Madison over long periods of time. From being a stateless immigrant I had managed to become a responsible citizen. And yet, this statement does not quite ring true.

I remained filled with a restlessness, a "travel fever" which was never to leave me. While its roots lay no doubt in the experience of statelessness during my formative years, the continuing fascination with the "free-floating intellectual" of the Weimar years played its part. I too wanted to be an intellectual not tied down to time and place, solely guided by his analytical mind—something of an eternal traveler, analyzing, observing, suspended above events. My view of history encouraged such an attitude, since it recognized the need for empathy even with those considered evil and dangerous. But, of course, such an ideal did not work in practice, as my various commitments plainly showed, for example, in my adherence to New Deal politics in the United States and in my complex attitude toward Zionism. Still, in the midst of a respectable career there remained this restlessness and eventually in my writings there emerged a criticism of the respectability which I had apparently so wholeheartedly embraced.

But what of my double outsiderdom? I had faced and come to terms with my Jewishness. This was not so difficult, given the change from the anti-Semitism I first encountered to the complete acceptance of Jews by the end of the 1960s. Then I could take a leading role in establishing a program in Jewish studies at my university, something that would have seemed rather daring earlier in my academic career.

Keeping one's homosexuality hidden, leading a secret (and hardly respectable) sexual life, was also no longer strictly necessary, though coming out was still fraught with risks, especially for those not firmly established in academia. I had fully experienced closeted gay life in Europe, but from

217

With John Tortorice at home in Madison, 1996

the 1970s onward I had slowly edged out of the closet. I was now an established and tenured professor, and as long as I did not make a show of my gayness, I was pretty secure. But old habits die hard, and while I came to accept my outsiderdom here as well, this was vastly more difficult in an atmosphere still filled with hate and prejudice. Even so, I eventually lived in an open union accepted by all my academic friends.

Once again, scholarship helped as I continued my research on the relationship between insiders and outsiders in our society, and indeed wrote on the history of homosexuality. Only two decades earlier I had asked a doctoral student of mine to eliminate sexually explicit expressions in his thesis, as using them might hurt his career. The acceptance of my double outsiderdom was made possible by the advances of society rather than by my own inner strength. Here too I had no need to regret the world I had lost.

But my acceptance of myself was set within the constant awareness of a past which refused to go away, and indeed I did not try to transform or overcome the vivid feeling that I was a survivor. The Holocaust was never very far from my mind; I could easily have perished with my fellow Jews. I suppose that I am a member of the Holocaust generation and have constantly tried to understand an event too monstrous to contemplate. All my studies in the history of racism and volkish thought, and also those dealing with outsiderdom and stereotypes, though sometimes not directly related to the Holocaust, have tried to find the answer to how it could have happened; finding an explanation has been vital not only for the understanding of modern history, but also for my own peace of mind. This is a question my generation had to face, and eventually I felt that I had come closer to an understanding of the Holocaust as a historical phenomenon. We have to live with an undertone of horror in spite of the sort of advances that made it so much easier for me to accept my own nature.

Though in a sense the return of our former possessions might suggest that life had come full circle, at the heart of the matter that was irrelevant. The crimes of the Third Reich were writ large in my consciousness, a part of my personal transformation from the irresponsibility of youth, a past which had to be faced. I had rejected the worlds of my past and had sought to transform myself, but in my anxieties, fears, and restlessness I was still a child of my century.